QUR'AN DISCOURSES

A COLLECTION OF TALKS

Shaykh Fadhlalla Haeri

QUR'AN DISCOURSES

A COLLECTION OF TALKS

Shaykh Fadhlalla Haeri

Zahra Publications

ISBN: 9781776490158

Published by Zahra Publications

Distributed and Published by Zahra Publications

PO Box 50764

Wierda Park 0149 Centurion

South Africa

www.shaykhfadhlallahaeri.com

www.zahrapublications.pub

Designed and Typeset by Quintessence Publishing

Set in 11 points on 15 points, [Palatino Linotype]

Printed and bound by [Lightning Source]

TABLE OF CONTENTS

CONCLUSION

ACKNOWLEDGEMENTS

Over a number of years, several people have assisted in bringing this compilation together.

Sincere thanks to all who contributed to the compilation and editing of this publication.

PUBLISHER'S NOTE

References in this text to *Allah Azza wa Jal* mean an honorific for Allah, referring to His Might and Majesty; references to Prophet (S) mean 'May Blessing and Peace be upon him' an honorific to the Prophet Muhammed and references to '(A.S)' mean 'Alayhi al-Salām (upon him be peace) an honorific to the Prophets.

INTRODUCTION

There is a purpose to this life. There is a beginning, and an end, and within it lies a light that has no beginning and no end. We are most fortunate to have been given the total package of truth, of *haqq*. We have come to this world in order to discover the qualities and attributes of the Creator of it, the Maintainer of it, the Sustainer of it; He who is within it, He who is before it, He who is after it. We have been bestowed with the ultimate purpose and meaning of our existence, along with the direction and way we must conduct ourselves to become in tune with the ever-present light of Allah. The *Qur'an* affirms that there cannot be two unless I am with you, there cannot be three unless I am the fourth (58:7); and I am closer to you than your jugular vein (50:16) And certainly We created man, and We know what his mind suggests to him, and We are nearer to him than his life-vein. Where is it that His *nūr* (light), or its trace and pattern, is not already there?

We are most fortunate to have embraced the divine light of the Prophet Muhammad (S). We are truly blessed to have trust and love for the *Qur'an* and to have profound admiration for the conduct and all that which has to do with the perfect being of Prophet Muhammad (S).

Why is it then, that this miraculous guide, this revealed knowledge, has not been in every way adored, used and internalised? The answer is simple. You may have the recipe for a meal, but if you don't put the ingredients together to cook it and eat it, you will not get nourishment from it. Similarly, simply possessing knowledge without implementing it will not illuminate your mind. And at a higher level, it will not enlighten your heart.

A child must be treated as a child for them to experience physical harmony. As the child progresses in age and grows in wisdom, mental harmony is essential and is developed through experiences. A mature adult needs spiritual wisdom. All of these levels of development achieve a state of completeness which has been activated by something spiritual. If our *dīn* (life transaction; way of life) does not lead to spiritual awakening and a subtle awareness of the light within us, then we practice the rituals without achieving their true essence. That is what *rahmatal lil'aalameen* (mercy for all the worlds) signifies. In other words, we need to absorb our life transaction; our way of life, understand it at its various levels and be energised and nourished by it in every way.

The *Qur'an* does that for us. There are four levels at which the *Qur'an* may be read and understood. The first is the pronunciation and grammar, and there are intricate ways of understanding it. In Arabic, one word may have many different meanings. The second level, *ishāra*, involves understanding the signs in the *Qur'an* and their meaning. The third is *latifa*, which refers to a more subtle and higher level of understanding the *Qur'an*. Finally, the highest level is *haqīqa*, which is the realisation of the light of Allah within the text. If you approach the *Qur'an* with courtesy, you will discover these multiple levels, and ultimately you will discover the *nūr* (light) of Allah within it.

The Quran is a remarkable gift for us to use to change our attitude. The information contained within it has the power to lead to our transformation. The voice of truth from beyond time and space can be applied in our lives within time and space.

In the following pages, we will dive into the *Qur'an* and its multi-layers of wisdom, knowledge and light. There are no ends to these horizons. As far as the *Qur'an* is concerned, it is the book of existence; it is the manual that any true believer in the One will find of immediate help in any situation and for any circumstance. One of the meanings of the *Qur'an* is that which gathers and has within it everything. The *Qur'an* has come with a language that surpasses the limitations of an ordinary terrestrial language. It contains terms that refer to the physical and material world, yet they also carry celestial connotations, evoking higher and subtler meanings. The *Qur'an* was revealed in the Arabic language, which originates from Aramaic and possibly Phoenician or an even older language. When it discusses a particular thing and connects it with its roots, it unveils deeper meanings related to that thing. Therefore, those who read the *Qur'an* and have the opportunity to study it in Arabic will find themselves constantly challenged yet refreshed. At all times they find themselves gaining new insights that inspire a love for the *Qur'an* and it gives them the energy they need for the journey of life.

In that light, what follows is a brief introduction to the *Qur'an* and other sacred revelations and unveilings. The past 10,000 years have witnessed many developments in the story of Homo sapiens. This includes the beginning of settlements, social interaction, agriculture, and the serious use of tools and metals. This culminated in tremendous effulgence in human history: the age of prophets. Prophethood was already in the gene of the first human being Adam (AS), who was also the first prophet.

A prophet was an earthly being who had a strong and direct heavenly connection. In modern terms, we could say that prophets were men of limited or conditioned earthly consciousness, who yearned for that which lasts forever, namely, limitless and sacred heavenly consciousness. Prophets were beings on this earth who were not content or satisfied with the world alone. When prophethood began to flourish, there were thousands upon thousands of prophets and messengers. This yearning for the divine is inherent not only in the prophets, but in all of us too.

Throughout history there have been events related to the nature of the earth, such as the Great Flood, which may have been caused by a meteor falling near Madagascar, creating massive flood waves. Many cultures have their own accounts of a Great Flood, with the earliest recorded account found in Gilgamesh, Iraq. The capital of Iraq at that time was called Uruq which means "root" in one of the ancient languages. As these events unfolded, humans began to ask fundamental questions about their existence: "Who am I? What is life about? What is death? Who is God? Is there a God? How can I have access to that which I constantly yearn for?" These questions were explored by cultures and tribes and in the communities of the Middle East, Central Asia and the Mediterranean. These groups interacted with each other while still maintaining different languages and cultures. These were nomadic tent dwellers and agriculture and the idea of settlement were new. With this way of life came new problems and issues such as intermarriage, inheritance, rights and wrongs, and duties and responsibilities. Around 15,000 years ago, nomads would migrate if the land they occupied became depleted of its agricultural value, or if they were affected with calamities such as famine or flooding. It was a precarious existence. Until about 5,000 years ago, people living then had reliance and trust in Allah. There was nothing other than *tawakkul* (reliance on Allah). They had few possessions, clothes or insurance policies so it came naturally for them to trust that something will come their way. Carry on. Don't worry! So indeed, they did carry on!

Humankind seems to have abandoned that *tawakkul*. We possess and grab and take because over the last 2,000 years we have become insensitive. Consequently there have been more prophetic unveilings that attempt to shake us out of this lethargy of associating with matter, energy, money or status. Humans would benefit from seeing things in perspective. We are a product of a life that began some 500 million to 600 million years ago on earth. The earth, as far as we know, is about 4,5 billion years old and life on it began about 400 million to 500 million years ago. If we put that on a time scale of one day equalling 24 hours, then 5,000 years is equivalent to one second. The reason we misunderstand our life transactions; our way of life to a great extent is because we do not have the right perspective, the right context.

In the same manner, we have abandoned context in our regard for the Prophet Muhammed (S) and his sayings. It is pertinent to ask – when we contemplate a particular *hadeeth* –when did the Prophet Muhammad (S) say it? To whom did he say it? For how long did he intend that order or request to apply? If we take a Prophetic saying out of context, we will fall into what the *Qur'an* also describes as taking only a portion of a revelation to justify our actions. We cannot do that! Life is whole. If we want to live wholesomely then we must accept all aspects of life.

As humans, we are composed of matter and minerals. We are also vegetative beings. We tend to be consumed with seen, visible, tangible and discernible things. Yet what drives us and gives us life, but more than that, what leads us, our battery, our source of life, is intangible: the *rūh* (spirit). Has anybody seen it? Touched it? Weighed it? There is no existence, whether it is tangible, material, discernible, or in meaning unless it is one of two. There cannot be matter as we know it, without having dark matter as we do not know it. In the cosmos, 9.9% of everything is called dark matter. There is no possibility for pleasure without displeasure. There is no security without insecurity. This is the law of Allah.

The only being that is unique and that transcends all dualities is *Al-Wāhid, Al-Ahad* (the One, the Absolute One). Everything else is one of two; it is endless and the pluralities are endless. Physics has similar laws which relate to symmetries or mirror images, where the left becomes the right and so on. Our present-day technologies are based on how these molecules fit with each other as a mirror image. Some turn this way, and some turn that way, according to the movement of the electrons within the atom.

A seeker must have this perspective before they can truly appreciate the *Qur'an*, and its depths. The *Qur'an* is the Book of books, which describes to us how things work, how they don't work, how things relate and why they don't relate, both in the seen and the unseen. The Prophet (S) said the *Qur'an* has numerous levels and layers. It commands us to read, apply and begin to understand that which is easy for us. Do not be fancy about it. We must have courtesy towards the *Qur'an*. We must come to the *Qur'an*, approach the gate of infinite knowledge, with humility and an acknowledgement that we don't know. Allah knows all and He will give us what we need to know – in the right way and according to our state.

Chapter 1

AYAT AL-KURSI

Quranic Verses

The Arabic text and the English translation of *Ayat al-Kursī*, verse 255 of *Sūrat al-Baqarah* follow immediately below. Thereafter, I will focus my commentary on selected phrases and words.

اللَّهُ لَا إِلَٰهَ إِلَّا هُوَ الْحَيُّ الْقَيُّومُ لَا تَأْخُذُهُ سِنَةٌ وَلَا نَوْمٌ لَّهُ مَا فِي السَّمَٰوَٰتِ وَمَا فِي الْأَرْضِ مَن ذَا الَّذِي يَشْفَعُ عِندَهُ إِلَّا بِإِذْنِهِ يَعْلَمُ مَا بَيْنَ أَيْدِيهِمْ وَمَا خَلْفَهُمْ وَلَا يُحِيطُونَ بِشَيْءٍ مِّنْ عِلْمِهِ إِلَّا بِمَا شَاءَ وَسِعَ كُرْسِيُّهُ السَّمَٰوَٰتِ وَالْأَرْضَ وَلَا يَئُودُهُ حِفْظُهُمَا وَهُوَ الْعَلِيُّ الْعَظِيمُ ﴿٢٥٥﴾

Allah – there is no deity save Him, the Ever-Living, the Self-Subsistent Fount of All Being. Neither slumber overtakes Him, nor sleep. His is all that is in the heavens and all that is on earth. Who is there that could intercede with Him, unless it be by His leave? He knows all that lies open before men and all that is hidden from them, whereas they cannot attain to aught of His knowledge save that which He wills. His eternal power overspreads the heavens and the earth, and their upholding wearies Him not. And he alone is truly exalted, tremendous. (2:255)

1

Commentary on Selected Verses

We who have faith, who believe and trust in Allah's mercy and His great revelation as the culmination of the story of the heavens and earth, of this life and the hereafter, we must internalise the transmission that emanates from the *Qur'an*. This will revive and rejuvenate us, enabling us to resonate with permanent life and live fully. As an example, the Prophet (S) has said that *Sūrat al-Ikhlās* comprises one-third of the *Qur'an*. By this, he meant that if we grasp its inner and outer meanings, we have comprehended a considerable portion of the unveiling that came upon Muhammad (S). Similarly, there are many other chapters in the *Qur'an* that are described as significant. *Sūrat al-Yā Sin* is described as 'the heart of the *Qur'an*', while *Sūrat al-Wāqi'ah, Sūrat al-Mulk* and up to 20 other chapters are noted for their greatness. If we consider and internalise the message of these chapters, we begin to move away from the myth and the illusion that we are separate from Allah. We begin discovering that Allah is with us. But are we listening? Are we hearing? If we are fully occupied with our own noise, with our minds, it is difficult to listen to that which is more subtle.

Ayat al-Kursī is one of the most renowned verses of the *Qur'an*. Translation of this verse into English or any other language is difficult. At best, it offers only a partial understanding of its meaning. During the time of the Prophet (S), *kursī* referred to the dominion of a king and was known as *Kursī ul- Mālik,* which emphasised the extent of the king's power. For instance, the phrase "his Kursī was only up to Northern Turkey", meant that the dominion of the kings' governance or of his influence only extended to that point. Therefore, *Ayat al-Kursī* can be translated as 'The Verse of the Dominion' or 'The Seat of Divine Power,' which means 'Where is it that the Divine Power is not operative, is not effective, is not totally in it, above it, before it, after it?'

This verse is also described by the Prophet (S) as *'Sayyidatu Ayat ul Qur'an'* which means the Queen, or the foremost Lady of all the verses of the *Qur'an*. When Abu Dharr Al-Gifari asked the Prophet (S) to identify the greatest verse ever, he replied that it was *Ayat al-Kursī*. The Prophet (S) provided an elaborate explanation of the meaning of *kursī* and *'arsh* to Abu Dharr, saying the verse was the greatest of all and was given to him from the greatest of all treasures, from beneath the *'arsh*. This once again links the verse to the throne, which is the translation of both *'arsh* and *kursī*. The Prophet (S) said the *kursī*, in comparison to the *'arsh*, is like a ring flung at the edge of a vast desert.

The Prophet (S) also said that *Ayat al-Kursī* contains everything imaginable. It is the 255th verse of *Sūrat al-Baqarah*, and the verses preceding it discuss Allah's signs and messengers, and how these lights emanate from the same source. *Ayat al-Kursī* is the culmination of this section. It has also been given other descriptions, such as the 'Ultimate pinnacle verse of the *Qur'an*.' Like *Sūrat al-Ikhlās*, this verse refers only to the Ultimate Source, the Essence. As such, it is the connector, the collector and the compounder of all aspects of *tawhīd* (Oneness). Meaning that, in truth, before manifestation, before many different lights, rainbows or shadows, there existed pure sacred light.

Ayat al-Kursī begins by saying 'Allah, there is no god but He,' meaning, 'None other than He.' Allah, the ultimate, is the God of gods, or Deity of deities. The early Arabs knew that name. In other words, a few hundred years before the advent of the Prophet(S), it was known that Allah was the God of gods. At that time, they still held the belief that gods ruled over our affairs. For instance, they believed in the God of harvest, the God of wealth, the God of plenty, the God of power or the God of winning a war. Before the advent of *Islām* (submission), corruption and confusion had set in. The Prophetic message was clear, there is only One God, and the other so-called gods are actually qualities and attributes that emanate from the One God.

Later on, a tradition emerged that if we know or acknowledge any of the 99 attributes we will be on our way to the discovery of the Garden. This would mean we are escaping our own darkness and confusion. Consider, for example, how Allah is *Al-Qawī*, (The Most Powerful), and we all want to be powerful. Yet, every intelligent person knows that he or she will never be powerful for any length of time. We spend a portion of each 24-hour cycle asleep. During this time, we have no power. What we love is sustained power, yet this is a description that belongs to Allah alone.

$$ \text{ٱللَّهُ لَآ إِلَٰهَ إِلَّا هُوَ ٱلْحَىُّ ٱلْقَيُّومُ} $$

Allah – there is no deity save Him, the Ever-Living, the Self-Subsistent Fount of All Being.

Many early commentators refer to *al-Hayyu al-Qayyūm* as the greatest of all names. *Hayy* means ever-living. *Qayyūm* means 'in charge of, responsible for.' You, I and most others occasionally have some responsibility towards something. When we are driving, or when we are cooking, eating, or praying, we are responsible for our attention, our behaviour, and our outer conduct.

Allah is *al-Hayyu al-Qayyūm*. He is ever-living, meaning that He is not subject to time and space. It means 'forever' and we love that which is forever. If something is good we want to have it forever. This is because the *nūr* (light) of Allah, known as the *rūh* (spirit), resides in our hearts forever. However, the ego-self, represented by the *nafs*, also craves the permanence of goodness. This shadow of the *rūh* is personified as you, me, he, or she. As one of the greatest attributes of Allah, *al-Hayyu al-Qayyūm* is considered one of the seven mother attributes and from it derive many names of actions such as *Al-Khāliq* (The Creator), *Al-Musawwir* (The Fashioner), *Al-Bā'ith* (The Resurrector), *Al-Mumīt* (The Death Giver), *Al-Jamīl* (The Beautiful, The Graceful), *Al-Jalīl* (The Majestic), *Al-'Adhīm* (The Magnificent), and *Al-Qawī* (The Most Strong). All these attributes relate to *Al-Qayyūm*.

Al-Hayyu al-Qayyūm encompasses almost all of the Divine names and attributes except for those of essence, like Al-Quddūs (the Most Pure, the Holy), which is even higher. *Al-Hayyu al-Qayyūm* is what we need all the time. An authentic tradition recounts that the Prophet's (S) daughter Fatima (RA) asked him: "Tell me what I can hold on to in my mind and heart during times of difficulty." He responded: "Every morning, noon and afternoon, recite *'Ya Hayyu Ya Qayyūm'* and then say 'Let me not ever rely on any entity or myself. Let me rely only on *Al-Hayyu al-Qayyūm*.'" This does not deny the need for means. On the contrary, we acknowledge the source of it. We do not deny that goodness comes to us from people, from nature, or other ways, but ultimately, all of it emanates from *al-Hayyu al-Qayyūm*.

The *ayat* continues with this description of the manifestation of the divine light, as close as possible to the source and essence of the sacredness.

$$\text{لَا تَأْخُذُهُ سِنَةٌ وَلَا نَوْمٌ}$$

Neither slumber overtakes Him, nor sleep.

This blessed sacred reality, *Al-Hayyu al-Qayyūm*, is never at rest or in slumber.

The *Qur'an* tells us in *Surat al-Furqān* (25:58): And rely on the Ever-Living Who dies not, and magnify His praise; and Sufficient is He as being aware of the faults of His servants. In *Sūrat al-Hadid* (57:4) it tells us that 'He is with you wherever you are,' which means that Power is what empowers you. The verses imply that He is never distracted nor is He absent. This relates to at least a dozen Divine names, including *Al-Raqīb* (The All Vigilant), *Al-Hasīb* (The Reckoner), and *Al-Muqīt* (The Sustainer).

The entire *Qur'an* can be divided into that which is similar and that which is unique. Allah is incomparable. We can participate a little bit in some of Allah's attributes, for example, with 'The Ever Generous.' Every one of us likes to be seen to be generous because generosity also takes us away from the selfish nature of the ego and opens up the ever generous within our hearts. We like to be generous, as much as we like to please others. These are little attempts along the ladder of returning to the Garden from where Adam (AS) was sent down to see the dualities. Each of us possesses a small measure of some of the attributes that we regard as the great virtues or the great names of Allah (*Asmā' al-husnā*).

The verse continues and gives us the story of this being, this reality, who is not seeable, not touchable, and not discernible when He says, 'whatever is in the heavens and on earth belongs to Him.'

لَّهُۥ مَا فِى ٱلسَّمَٰوَٰتِ وَمَا فِى ٱلْأَرْضِ

His is all that is in the heavens and all that is on earth.

It is recommended to recite this verse many times during the day. The Prophet (S) says that he who truly recites this verse after every prayer, no *shaytān* (satan; ego-self) can ever enter his house. He will always have harmony because when you say everything belongs to Allah, you belong to Allah.

Since everything we do belongs to Allah, why do we bother with fussing, quarrelling, accusation, greed, and anger? We all belong to Allah. When I recite this verse I am asking Allah to forgive me, excuse me and remind me. It has been related that anyone who reads this verse at *fajr* (dawn prayer) and also attends to the cleanliness of the entrance to their room or home for 40 continuous days will not be overwhelmed with need or serious desires.

I recall an experience from my childhood when I wanted to excel in my exams, so I recited the verse for 40 days. I passed the exam but pondered the significance of it. My wonderful nanny said: "But look, your room has never been as clean as this before, isn't that a good thing? And you were up earlier than any other day and full of energy, isn't that a better thing? If you had not done all that, you would have not done as well." One step towards wellness leads to another step. When we truly admit that all of it belongs to Allah, we see that our mistakes, while still our own, are allowed by Allah so that we could be more vigilant and diligent in the future. I pray and hope that I will remember to be more vigilant in my *dhikr* (remembrance of Allah) and more diligent in my *wudhū'* (ritual ablution) so that I do not repeat the same mistakes in the future.

This vigilance extends to all our conduct. Allah says, 'He possesses what is in the heavens' which means we are Allah's guests and as a guest we have to abide by boundaries of good conduct. We do not behave discourteously in someone else's home. Think of yourself as Allah's guest and witness what this Magnificent Host is showing you. As unveiling increases, you know you are in Divine presence. It is for this reason the Prophet (S) reminded his friends on many occasions that the most important qualification in *salāt* (prayers), after all the other conditions are met, is the presence of the heart. What this means is that you have no anxiety, fear, jealousy, anger, or rancour.

Then it is declared:

$$ مَن ذَا ٱلَّذِى يَشْفَعُ عِندَهُۥ إِلَّا بِإِذْنِهِ $$

Who is there that could intercede with Him, unless it be by His leave?

Shaf'i is derived from the root word *sha-fa-'a*, which means 'to double.' The verb *shafa'a* means 'to mediate, use one's good offices, put in a good word, to intercede.' If I want to raise a loan, for example, I may ask someone who knows me to put in a good word for me with the lender. There are up to 30 verses in the *Qur'an* that describe this concept of interceding. Allah is described as *Witr* (One), incomparable, and everything else is *Shaf'i* (in pairs). Allah says, 'I created everything in pairs.'

The concept of *shaf'i* can also refer to a friend or a teacher, designated by Allah, who will guide you to the path. The *shaf'i* is that teacher who will give you an easier ascent back to the state of bliss of being in the Garden. However, Allah reminds us in *Surat al-Yunus* (10:3), 'There is no intercessor except by His leave.' This means that all affairs are organised perfectly, and nobody can ever be a teacher or help you along the path of enlightenment except with Allah's permission. If I am in a mess, if my mind is confused and my body is sick, how can I ask anybody to show me how to enter into the delights of the Garden? This is not possible. If there is no *idhn* (permission), then it is out of line. It has to connect. That is why the Prophet (S) said: 'Even if you are hard-hearted, give a bit, cry a bit, soften your heart.' The head is easy: we exercise discipline in the world we are living in. But what about the heart? It is not possible to ascend higher unless the path taken is that of the perfect pattern, which has all of the requisite connectors. Without a proper connection, nothing will happen.

$$يَعْلَمُ مَا بَيْنَ أَيْدِيهِمْ وَمَا خَلْفَهُمْ$$

He knows all that lies open before men and all that is hidden from them.

Allah knows whatever you are doing and whatever you have done. Some commentators say that this verse refers to this life and the hereafter. In other words, that which you are attending to now and that which will come later.

$$وَلَا يُحِيطُونَ بِشَيْءٍ مِنْ عِلْمِهِ إِلَّا بِمَا شَاءَ$$

whereas they cannot attain to aught of His knowledge save that which He wills.

This means you and I can never attain any aspect of the vast knowledge of *Al-'Alīm* (The All-Knowing) except, again, where it connects: where Allah wills it. We are inspired most when we have no thought. Creative people or scientists, for example, are inspired when their mind is not cluttered with too many thoughts, objectives or concerns. Allah gives us what is appropriate for us according to our makeup and not what you and I hope and wish for. It is good for us to always hope for better, but what we hope for may not be better for us. I may fail at something, but those difficulties may open other doors.

We are preoccupied with our own silly little worldly project, but are we limited only to the physical world? Where do we go after we die? As human beings, we must acknowledge that we are essentially *arwāh* (souls or spirits) caught in bodies that are influenced by our genetic background, environment, and interactions. What we think will give us higher consciousness is not necessarily what we truly need. It is like a child who discovers a stash of chocolate and gorges on it until they become ill. In this case, stopping the child from consuming too much chocolate is an act of kindness.

At times, you and I may feel we are stopped in our tracks, and we may blame Allah, saying: 'Allah has given me difficulties. Is He punishing me?' However, Allah reminds us: 'You are only punishing yourself.' He is here acting, operating, and transmitting only in order for all of creation to know Him! That is the objective. Were we truly on the path of knowing Allah, or was it merely a project to accumulate more houses, cars or other world things. Life can be divided in two parts. One part is worldly, where more is considered better. But is that enough? When is enough? Then there is the other part, which is in all of us, where more is actually less. We perform the ritual ablution, then we open our arms, open our palms, and say *Allahu Akbar* (Allah is Great) with nothing in them, and we disappear into our *sajdah* (devotional prostration in prayer). We are both heavenly and worldly. With our heart and our mind, we must not deny either part of ourselves. Consider the following additional verses from the **Quran** in this context:

> *Sūrat ad-Duhā (93:11): 'and talk about the blessings of your Lord.'*
> Surat al-Isra (17:72): *'Whoso is blind in this world, in the hereafter he shall be even more blind and more astray from the path.'*
> *Sūrat al-Qasas (28:77): 'and forget not your portion of the present world.'*

You cannot deny any of this. It is a stepping stone back to the ever-present eternal garden.

$$وَسِعَ كُرْسِيُّهُ السَّمَوَاتِ وَالْأَرْضَ$$

His eternal power overspreads the heavens and the earth.

It is from this part of the verse that *Ayat al-Kursī* gets its name. It means that the power of Allah, that Sovereignty and Supreme Lordship, encompasses the Heavens and the Earth. Whatsoever there is, Allah is before it, within it, and after it. There is a sacredness in all, and we are sensitive to that. From the verse above, *kursī* means that the Lordship is beyond limitations. That is why the Prophet (S) says: 'the dominion and the throne are ever connected.' He adds: 'the *kursī* is the evident door and the *'arsh* is the subtle door.' They are ever together. The Prophet (S) says: 'If the Heavens and the Earth are represented as a ring and that ring is at the edge of an infinitely vast desert, the ring is like the *kursī* and the vast infinite space within it is like the *'arsh.'* The soul belongs to the higher, subtler realms. The body is earthly; it is made originally from material: earth, water, air and fire. This is the cosmology of the human being and Allah holds it all in a way which is beyond our ability to fathom. It is perfection.

$$وَلَا يَئُودُهُ حِفْظُهُمَا وَهُوَ الْعَلِيُّ الْعَظِيمُ$$

and their upholding wearies Him not. And he alone is truly exalted, tremendous.

The verse concludes that Allah is never exhausted in keeping this incredible Universe in a state of perfection. When we are occupied, we forget about some things. We will find that the water has run over, or the fire is suddenly burning out of control. We become focused on one task only to forget another. Allah is never preoccupied with just one thing. He never forgets and leaves something unattended to. He is an entity that is altogether incomparable. He is beyond

10

definitions, and this verse captures His immensity. For this reason, it is said, 'By remembering Allah, all things become insignificant' and we are taught, when we are confronted with a major issue, again, to completely leave it in Allah's hand. Trust in Allah and we will see wonders. There is no such thing as a big issue or a big problem, it is all in our minds. We built up our issues because we try to exert power over our home or business. It is a minor play. For this reason, in *Sūrat al-An'ām* (6:32) Allah describes this life as 'And nothing is the life of this world but a play and a passing delight.' We are actors in the theatre. We are acting because soon after it will no longer be there, so it was not the truth. The real truth is the eternal *nūr* (light) which by Allah's *Rahma* (mercy) is a flash in our hearts.

Allah declared in a *Hadeeth Qudsi*: 'Neither my Earth nor my Heavens can contain Me, but the heart of a *mū'min* (believer) can contain Me.' Bistami explained that this means that even if the seven earths and a thousand more, and the seven heavens and a thousand more were to fall into the heart of a believer, they would not ever feel it because it is a sacred entity. For this reason, if we do not recognise the sacred light within other human beings, we cannot be truly respectful towards them. That is why all talk about humanity and human rights without acknowledging this sacred relationship is superficial and an exercise in public relations. However, if we constantly remember that at any minute we may die, we can reflect on whether we have fulfilled our duty towards Allah or are still preoccupied with our own desires. Through this process, we begin to liberate ourselves from ourselves. The more we recite this great verse, the more we discover deeper layers of meaning in it and everything around us. We become reflective of the highest light, the Divine Light, which resides in our souls; and then we can truly begin to see the glory of *Islām* (submission) and the wonderment of *Imān* (certainty and security that Allah knows, and Allah sees) and the amazing bliss of *Ihsān* (inner and outer excellence in thought and conduct).

Chapter 2

SURAT AL-INSHIRAH /
SURAT AS-SHARH

Quranic Verses

The Arabic text and the English translation of *Sūrat al-Inshirah(94)* follow immediately below. Thereafter, I will focus my commentary on selected verses and words.

بِسۡمِ ٱللَّهِ ٱلرَّحۡمَٰنِ ٱلرَّحِيمِ

In the name of Allah, the Merciful to all, the Compassionate to each!

أَلَمۡ نَشۡرَحۡ لَكَ صَدۡرَكَ ﴿١﴾

1. *Have We not expanded for you your breast.*

وَوَضَعۡنَا عَنكَ وِزۡرَكَ ﴿٢﴾

2. *And taken off from you your burden.*

ٱلَّذِىٓ أَنقَضَ ظَهْرَكَ ۝

3. *That weighed so heavily on your back,*

وَرَفَعْنَا لَكَ ذِكْرَكَ ۝

4. *and raise your reputation high?*

فَإِنَّ مَعَ ٱلْعُسْرِ يُسْرًا ۝

5. *So truly where there is hardship there is also ease.*

إِنَّ مَعَ ٱلْعُسْرِ يُسْرًا ۝

6. *Truly where there is hardship there is also ease.*

فَإِذَا فَرَغْتَ فَٱنصَبْ ۝

7. *When your work is done, turn to devotion,*

وَإِلَىٰ رَبِّكَ فَٱرْغَب ۝

8. *and turn to your Lord for everything.*

Commentary on Selected Verses

A considerable portion of the *Qur'an*, approximately 40% of all its verses, was revealed to Prophet Muhammad (S) in Makkah. At that time, the emphasis was on remembrance of the next life and on answering questions like: Who are you? Why are you here? What is death? The purpose was to awaken people from their lethargy and break free from the darkness of culture which existed at that time, and which continues to exist in varying degrees at all times. For this reason, the Makkan verses and chapters primarily address the theme of submission to Allah. Trusting that Allah's ways are perfect and recognising that Allah's *nūr* (light) is the source of existence and of the cosmos, reminds us of our own weakness. We are dependent on that light. Indeed, that light is within us in a form called *rūh* (soul). The verses remind us that we are the creators of our hell and heaven, through the ignorance and the layers of the *nafs* (ego-self) that cover the light of the soul. The majority of the Makkan verses and chapters give the immediate responsibility to the individual; to wake up to one's duties, to know the Creator, and the direction to accept and follow Allah's way and Allah's will.

After the revelation of *Sūrat al-Fajr* verse (89:1 to 89:2), there was a gap in revelation which led to questions about whether Allah had forsaken his Prophet (S). To address these concerns *Sūrat ad-Duhā* was revealed, followed by *Sūrat al-Inshirah*.

Before we begin with *Sūrat al-Inshirah*, it is worth setting up the context with a few verses from *Sūrat ad-Duhā*. Allah reminds His noble and perfect representative, Prophet Mohammed (S), that:

$$\text{وَٱلَّيْلِ إِذَا سَجَىٰ ﴿٢﴾ \quad وَٱلضُّحَىٰ ﴿١﴾}$$

By the morning brightness. (93:1) and the night when it settles. (93:2)

By the Effulgent Day, by the height of midday's light and consciousness after the darkness has gone: darkness implies not knowing what your duty is, how to avoid the troubles that come to you or the path, boundaries, or knowledge of nature and *sharī'a* (revealed law or code of conduct).

He says, 'By the effulgent light,' now that you have discovered that you are *'Abd Allah* (a servant of Allah), you have discovered that you are only here to perfect your worship. Allah says elsewhere in the *Qur'an*, 'And I did not create *jinn* (invisible beings) and *insān* (humankind) except to worship me.' How can you worship something you don't love? How can you worship something you don't adore? How can you worship something that you are not completely passionate about? That is the *mihrāb* (sanctuary, prayer niche), where you wage war against your ignorance and stupidity so that you worship He whose qualities can be worshipped.

We all love the effulgence, the everlasting, the *Al-Awwal* (The First), and *Al-Ākhir* (The Last). He is the source of all power. He has no beginning and no end. He is the source of *shifā'* (healing). He is *Al-Kabir* (The Incomprehensibly Great, The All-Cognisant). He is *Al-Rahīm* (The Compassionate), and *Al-Rahmān* (The Merciful). We adore these qualities. Allah says, 'By what is already in your heart, as a soul, by the design of the Creator, the Perfect Creator, you as a created being, by my command, you have never been left alone.' How can you ever be alone in this World? Where did you get this energy? How do you know that you are now tired? How do you know you are now awakened? How do you know that you are now dying? By He who never dies! By He who has given in you a spark of His Divine Reality, which is called the soul. The ego-self is only there as a shadow for you to realise that it is not it. Your ego-self is moody. One minute you are happy, the next you are not. One minute you accuse, the next minute you do not. How can you know these moods unless there is in you a mood that is constant? Allah says: 'By the comings and the goings of light and darkness, there is in you something constant and that is the presence of your Lord.'

مَا وَدَّعَكَ رَبُّكَ وَمَا قَلَىٰ ٣

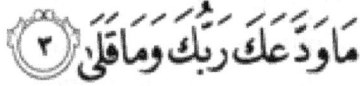

your Lord has not forsaken you nor disdains. (93:3)

Rabb is Lord, Supreme Being. Everything has a Lord, and everybody has a Lord. We believe that the ultimate Lord exists within each person's soul. If one fails to recognise their inner Lord, they may experience confusion. Know your real Lord, the ultimate Lord, the Lord of lords, through that which is in you. Once you do, you can discover that that which is in you is truly obedient. Allah says in the *Qur'an* that all the *arwāh* (souls) have been exposed to the Lord and bear the imprint of 'Am I not your Lord?' But we as human beings are like a veil or shadow that covers this connection to the divine. By connecting with our true Lord, we can discover a deep sense of obedience – and ultimately, our life's purpose.

Your Lord never takes time off. He never rests. He never sleeps. He is forever present. You need both rest and sleep, and you make mistakes. But your Lord does not make mistakes.

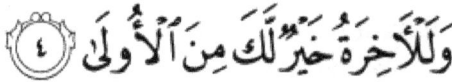

وَلَلْآخِرَةُ خَيْرٌ لَّكَ مِنَ ٱلْأُولَىٰ ٤

And surely what comes after is better for you than that which has gone before. (93:4)

The timeless nature of what existed before time and space makes it inherently superior. Whatever we do, whatever we like, we want it forever. We want to prolong it. Is it going to last? Even a child hides some of their sweets, hoping to savour and prolong the joy it brings. But is fleeting pleasure worth the long-term cost? We want joy. Yet true joy comes from a spontaneous connection with Allah. These moments are like divine breadcrumbs, leading us back to our source.

Our glorious father Adam (AS) resided in the eternal garden, yet he was unaware of its eternal nature. From this we can learn that we must come to the ephemeral to realise that we love the eternal. This is the essence of our journey. Allah has completed His work, and now it up to us to follow, imbibe it, and be transformed by it.

Now we can turn to the glorious chapter *Sūrat al-Inshirah*. I would like to journey with you through some of the Arabic terminology.

We access our soul with a clear heart, which is why we emphasise the importance of having a healthy body. If my body is sick, I cannot have a clear mind. If my mind is sick and too disturbed, I cannot talk about my heart. Verse 93:7 is a reminder to begin with our basic duties. Begin with what demands your attention. For example, you cannot sit in glorious reflection of the *Qur'an* if five or six children are bickering in the room. Take care of that disturbance first. Similarly, hunger and sickness are material concerns that must be addressed before we can focus on our spiritual growth. Consider this a "hierarchy" for your attention.

Care for your body. Make sure it is in reasonable order. Do not be abusive. Do not overindulge or under nourish. Similarly, it is equally important to clear your mind. Be willing to let go of your thoughts and start afresh, like a rebooting computer. Otherwise, it will affect you negatively: your health; your inner qualities, and your discipline will suffer.

We strive to have a healthy body that is in unison and balance because we worship at the altar of constancy. Allah is ever-constant; but we are not. That is why it is called *Haqq*, the truth. The truth never changes, but realities change. A reality is nearest to the truth if it does not change (for example, the goodness of generosity). The more constant you are in your generosity, the more you can connect with *Al-Jawād* (The Generous).

When you call upon Allah, you are refining your own self, which is already there in a latent fashion. It is in your soul, in a pattern that now must be brought to life. It must become your operating system. However, you may not have switched it on because you were immature in body and mind in childhood. Once you attain spiritual intelligence (not IQ or EQ, but SQ), you realise truly and fully that you are made of two entities: a soul that reflects eternal truth and a personality that is a unique individual, shaped by genetic, cultural, and environmental factors. These are the lenses through which the so-called you—the soul, the ever-charging battery—see the world.

And you will find that the world you experience is a reflection of your inner state. What you and I experience of the outer world reflects the inner world. The same event can have different meanings for different people. How come? The soul is the same, but the lenses are different; One person may perceive something as a bad event while another may perceive it as a good event. I recall a story about a fellow whose dog died one night on his farm. His neighbours visited and inquired: 'How do you live, because we are all under threat every night?' He replied: '*Al-hamduli'Llah*, I did my best, but the dog died.' The next day his donkey died. Again he said: '*Al-hamduli'Llah*'. On the third day his family left him and he responded with: '*Al-hamduli'Llah*.' Days later thieves raided his village, and they were guided to homes by the bray of a donkey or the bark of a dog. However, his house was silent so everybody, with the exception of this fellow, was slaughtered.

Do your best, have faith and live. But faith must be transformative. See the world as a reflection of your inner state. The man understood that whatever Allah has done to him, despite his best efforts, was best for him. To achieve this we must accept the will of Allah and unify our will with His. If we fail to do that we are fighting with a being against whom we can never win. Allah is forever the winner. This is the submission that we must give in to. It is up to us to rise to the occasion, be courageous, and say: 'I tried my best, Allah is the winner always. May He make me realise what He wants so that it makes me want that because I want to be happy.' Happiness and unity imply synchronicity.

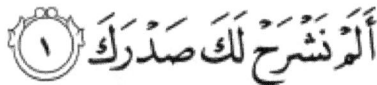

$$\textarabic{أَلَمْ نَشْرَحْ لَكَ صَدْرَكَ ﴿١﴾}$$

Have We not expanded for you your breast. (94:1)

وَوَضَعْنَا عَنكَ وِزْرَكَ ﴿٢﴾

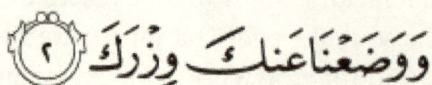

And taken off from you your burden. (94:2)

You come to the realisation that Allah is the doer, working through you and by you, whether through your judgement or misjudgement. All the weight that you have been carrying – the anxiety, concern, or sorrow about the past or fear about the future – vanishes. Allah is addressing the Prophet Muhammad (S), and therefore, Allah is addressing each of us who follow in the Prophetic footsteps.

Look back at your past, and the stumbling blocks you've encountered along the way. If I asked you what happened on this day one year ago, would you remember? Those memories are gone. It is worth remembering: if there is anything you can do about it, do it. If not, then leave it in Allah's hand. He has brought the situation upon you to challenge you, to make you more submissive, to soften your heart, or to humiliate you because you have been arrogant. There is no room in this realm for arrogance. Allah is *Ya Dhū-l-Jalāli wa-l-Ikrām* (The Master of Majesty and Nobility) (see *Sūrat ar-Rahmān* verse (55:27). Humans cannot have *jalāl* (majesty) or `*izzat* (honour, prestige). Consider the leaders of Arab states. They crave honour and prestige, but they don't deserve it. Allah will give honour and prestige to whomever he wills and loves. Our Prophet Muhammed (S) had honour and prestige, yet he maintained his humility. There are well-known stories of humble men like Hazrat Abu Bakr (RA) and Hazrat Omar (RA). Allah gave them honour and prestige because they comprehended their nothingness and Allah's everythingness.

وَوَضَعْنَا عَنكَ وِزْرَكَ ﴿٢﴾

And taken off from you your burden. (94:2)

$$ \text{(٣)} \ \tilde{ك} \text{الَّذِىٓ أَنقَضَ ظَهْرَكَ} $$

That weighed so heavily on your back. (94:3)

These verses describe the weight of how the Prophet Muhammad (S) is going to dispense with the message. Is he going to bring people to realise that they are all `Abd Allah (servants of Allah), even if most of them deny it? What a responsibility upon the Prophet (S), when he suddenly realised the immensity of the *nūr* (light) that had descended upon him, that pulverised him, so that he could not take it anymore.

$$ \text{(٧)} \ \text{فَإِذَا فَرَغْتَ فَٱنصَبْ} $$

When your work is done, turn to devotion, (94:7)

When you have done away with your immediate responsibility (which is to do only that which you can) leave the rest to Him. You are Allah's instrument. Be His *'abd*, His agent, and wake up to immense possibility and potential, rather than focus on titles: 'I am this man and this husband'. These things are never going to give you the nourishment and the connectedness to He who is forever connected, to you. Allah reminds us, repeatedly in the *Qur'an*: 'You cannot lie. Do not be a hypocrite. Do what you can, what is appropriate and if you cannot do something then apologise and be intact. Do not be shattered and all over the place, everywhere and nowhere.'

Once we are freed from our physical and material obligations, we are ready to stand in front of the One who has always been there.

$$ \text{(٨)} \ \text{وَإِلَىٰ رَبِّكَ فَٱرْغَب} $$

and turn to your Lord for everything. (94:8)

Ultimately, there is nothing left to do but turn to your Lord, who is with you. Allah tells us: 'Do not deny the other responsibility.' All the things that mattered so much some time ago don't matter anymore. Use those experiential happenings, memories, and events to your advantage so that you are available and present. One of the prerequisites of *salāt* (prayer)—apart from the *sharī'a* (revealed law or code of conduct) such as *wudhū'* (ritual ablution) and *ghusl* (ritual bath)—is presence of heart. If your heart is somewhere else, if it is shattered, then what you are doing is just a bit of standing and sitting. This kind of *salāt* is not going to transform and recharge you. This is why the Prophet (S) says (in a *hadeeth* reported by Abu Huraira): 'Perhaps a fasting person will gain nothing from his fast but hunger and perhaps the one who stands up at night for prayer will gain nothing but tiredness.'

Chapter 3

SURAT AL-RAHMAN

Quranic Verses

The Arabic text and the English translation of *Sūrat al-Rahmān* follows immediately below. Thereafter I will focus my commentary on selected verses and words.

بِسْمِ ٱللَّهِ ٱلرَّحْمَٰنِ ٱلرَّحِيمِ

In the name of Allah, the Merciful to all, the Compassionate to each!

ٱلرَّحْمَٰنُ ﴿١﴾

1. The All-Merciful!

عَلَّمَ ٱلْقُرْءَانَ ﴿٢﴾

2. Taught the Qur'an.

خَلَقَ ٱلْإِنسَـٰنَ ﴿٣﴾

3. *He created man.*

عَلَّمَهُ ٱلْبَيَانَ ﴿٤﴾

4. *He taught him eloquence.*

ٱلشَّمْسُ وَٱلْقَمَرُ بِحُسْبَانٍ ﴿٥﴾

5. *The sun and the moon follow their calculated courses.*

وَٱلنَّجْمُ وَٱلشَّجَرُ يَسْجُدَانِ ﴿٦﴾

6. *Prostrate themselves the stars and the trees.*

وَٱلسَّمَآءَ رَفَعَهَا وَوَضَعَ ٱلْمِيزَانَ ﴿٧﴾

7. *He has raised up the sky. He has set the balance.*

أَلَّا تَطْغَوْا فِى ٱلْمِيزَانِ ﴿٨﴾

8. *Transgress not in the Balance.*

وَأَقِيمُوا۟ ٱلْوَزْنَ بِٱلْقِسْطِ وَلَا تُخْسِرُوا۟ ٱلْمِيزَانَ ﴿٩﴾

9. *weigh with justice and do not fall short in the balance.*

وَٱلْأَرْضَ وَضَعَهَا لِلْأَنَامِ ﴿١٠﴾

10. *And earth – He set it down for all beings,*

فِيهَا فَٰكِهَةٌ وَٱلنَّخْلُ ذَاتُ ٱلْأَكْمَامِ ﴿١١﴾

11. *with its fruits, its palm trees with sheathed clusters,*

وَٱلْحَبُّ ذُو ٱلْعَصْفِ وَٱلرَّيْحَانُ ﴿١٢﴾

12. *its husked grain, its fragrant plants.*

فَبِأَىِّ ءَالَآءِ رَبِّكُمَا تُكَذِّبَانِ ﴿١٣﴾

13. *Which, then, of your Lord's blessings do you both deny?*

خَلَقَ ٱلْإِنسَٰنَ مِن صَلْصَٰلٍ كَٱلْفَخَّارِ ﴿١٤﴾

14. *He created mankind out of dried clay, like pottery;*

وَخَلَقَ ٱلْجَآنَّ مِن مَّارِجٍ مِّن نَّارٍ ﴿١٥﴾

15. *and He created the jinn of a smokeless fire.*

فَبِأَيِّ ءَالَاءِ رَبِّكُمَا تُكَذِّبَانِ ﴿١٦﴾

16. *Which, then, of your Lord's blessings do you both deny?*

رَبُّ ٱلْمَشْرِقَيْنِ وَرَبُّ ٱلْمَغْرِبَيْنِ ﴿١٧﴾

17. *He is Lord of the two risings and Lord of the two settings.*

فَبِأَيِّ ءَالَاءِ رَبِّكُمَا تُكَذِّبَانِ ﴿١٨﴾

18. *Which, then, of your Lord's blessings do you both deny?*

مَرَجَ ٱلْبَحْرَيْنِ يَلْتَقِيَانِ ﴿١٩﴾

19. *He brought the two seas together.*

بَيْنَهُمَا بَرْزَخٌ لَّا يَبْغِيَانِ ﴿٢٠﴾

20. *yet there is a barrier between them they do not transgress.*

فَبِأَىِّ ءَالَاءِ رَبِّكُمَا تُكَذِّبَانِ ﴿٢١﴾

21. *Which, then, of your Lord's blessings do you both deny?*

يَخْرُجُ مِنْهُمَا اللُّؤْلُؤُ وَالْمَرْجَانُ ﴿٢٢﴾

22. *From both come forth pearl and coral.*

فَبِأَىِّ ءَالَاءِ رَبِّكُمَا تُكَذِّبَانِ ﴿٢٣﴾

23. *Which, then, of your Lord's blessings do you both deny?*

وَلَهُ الْجَوَارِ الْمُنشَئَاتُ فِى الْبَحْرِ كَالْأَعْلَامِ ﴿٢٤﴾

24. *His too are the ships that run, raised up in the sea like landmarks.*

فَبِأَىِّ ءَالَاءِ رَبِّكُمَا تُكَذِّبَانِ ﴿٢٥﴾

25. *Which, then, of your Lord's blessings do you both deny?*

كُلُّ مَنْ عَلَيْهَا فَانٍ ﴿٢٦﴾

26. *All who are upon it shall perish.*

وَيَبْقَىٰ وَجْهُ رَبِّكَ ذُو ٱلْجَلَٰلِ وَٱلْإِكْرَامِ ﴿٢٧﴾

27. *And there remains the face of your Lord, Majestic and Noble.*

فَبِأَيِّ ءَالَآءِ رَبِّكُمَا تُكَذِّبَانِ ﴿٢٨﴾

28. *Which, then, of your Lord's blessings do you both deny?*

يَسْـَٔلُهُۥ مَن فِي ٱلسَّمَٰوَٰتِ وَٱلْأَرْضِ كُلَّ يَوْمٍ هُوَ فِي شَأْنٍ ﴿٢٩﴾

29. *All in the heavens and earth beseech Him; He is ever engaged upon some matter.*

فَبِأَيِّ ءَالَآءِ رَبِّكُمَا تُكَذِّبَانِ ﴿٣٠﴾

30. *Which, then, of your Lord's blessings do you both deny?*

سَنَفْرُغُ لَكُمْ أَيُّهَ ٱلثَّقَلَانِ ﴿٣١﴾

31. *We shall apply Ourselves to you, you two great masses of creation!*

فَبِأَيِّ ءَالَآءِ رَبِّكُمَا تُكَذِّبَانِ ﴿٣٢﴾

32. *Which, then, of your Lord's blessings do you both deny?*

يَـٰمَعْشَرَ ٱلْجِنِّ وَٱلْإِنسِ إِنِ ٱسْتَطَعْتُمْ أَن تَنفُذُواْ مِنْ أَقْطَارِ ٱلسَّمَـٰوَٰتِ وَٱلْأَرْضِ فَٱنفُذُواْ ۚ لَا تَنفُذُونَ إِلَّا بِسُلْطَـٰنٍ ﴿٣٣﴾

33. *Species of Jinn and humans, if you can make your escape from the regions of the heavens and earth, escape! You shall not escape except by divine authority.*

فَبِأَىِّ ءَالَاءِ رَبِّكُمَا تُكَذِّبَانِ ﴿٣٤﴾

34. *Which, then, of your Lord's blessings do you both deny?*

يُرْسَلُ عَلَيْكُمَا شُوَاظٌ مِّن نَّارٍ وَنُحَاسٌ فَلَا تَنتَصِرَانِ ﴿٣٥﴾

35. *A flash of fire and smoke will be released upon you and no one will come to your aid.*

فَبِأَىِّ ءَالَاءِ رَبِّكُمَا تُكَذِّبَانِ ﴿٣٦﴾

36. *Which, then, of your Lord's blessings do you both deny?*

فَإِذَا ٱنشَقَّتِ ٱلسَّمَاءُ فَكَانَتْ وَرْدَةً كَٱلدِّهَانِ ﴿٣٧﴾

37. *And when the heaven is rent asunder, and then becomes red like red hide.*

فَبِأَىِّ ءَالَاءِ رَبِّكُمَا تُكَذِّبَانِ ﴿٣٨﴾

38. *Which, then, of your Lord's blessings do you both deny?*

فَيَوْمَئِذٍ لَّا يُسْئَلُ عَن ذَنبِهِۦ إِنسٌ وَلَا جَآنٌّ ﴿٣٩﴾

39. So, on that day neither man nor jinni shall be asked about his misdeeds.

فَبِأَيِّ ءَالَآءِ رَبِّكُمَا تُكَذِّبَانِ ﴿٤٠﴾

40. Which, then, of your Lord's blessings do you both deny?

يُعْرَفُ ٱلْمُجْرِمُونَ بِسِيمَٰهُمْ فَيُؤْخَذُ بِٱلنَّوَٰصِى وَٱلْأَقْدَامِ ﴿٤١﴾

41. The criminals shall be known by their outward visage, and they shall be seized by forelocks and feet.

فَبِأَيِّ ءَالَآءِ رَبِّكُمَا تُكَذِّبَانِ ﴿٤٢﴾

42. Which, then, of your Lord's blessings do you both deny?

هَٰذِهِۦ جَهَنَّمُ ٱلَّتِى يُكَذِّبُ بِهَا ٱلْمُجْرِمُونَ ﴿٤٣﴾

43. This is the Hell the guilty deny.

يَطُوفُونَ بَيْنَهَا وَبَيْنَ حَمِيمٍ ءَانٍ ﴿٤٤﴾

44. They shall wander between it and water, fiercely boiling.

فَبِأَيِّ ءَالَآءِ رَبِّكُمَا تُكَذِّبَانِ ﴿٤٥﴾

45. *Which, then, of your Lord's blessings do you both deny?*

وَلِمَنْ خَافَ مَقَامَ رَبِّهِ جَنَّتَانِ ﴿٤٦﴾

46. *And for him who fears to stand before his Lord are two gardens.*

فَبِأَيِّ ءَالَآءِ رَبِّكُمَا تُكَذِّبَانِ ﴿١٨﴾

47. *Which, then, of your Lord's blessings do you both deny?*

ذَوَاتَآ أَفْنَانٍ ﴿٤٨﴾

48. *Both covered with foliage.*

فَبِأَيِّ ءَالَآءِ رَبِّكُمَا تُكَذِّبَانِ ﴿١٨﴾

49. *Which, then, of your Lord's blessings do you both deny?*

فِيهِمَا عَيْنَانِ تَجْرِيَانِ ﴿٥٠﴾

50. *In it are two running springs.*

فَبِأَيِّ ءَالَاءِ رَبِّكُمَا تُكَذِّبَانِ ﴿٥١﴾

51. *Which, then, of your Lord's blessings do you both deny?*

فِيهِمَا مِن كُلِّ فَٰكِهَةٍ زَوْجَانِ ﴿٥٢﴾

52. *In it are, of every fruit, two kinds.*

فَبِأَيِّ ءَالَاءِ رَبِّكُمَا تُكَذِّبَانِ ﴿٥٣﴾

53. *Which, then, of your Lord's blessings do you both deny?*

مُتَّكِئِينَ عَلَىٰ فُرُشٍ بَطَآئِنُهَا مِنْ إِسْتَبْرَقٍ وَجَنَى ٱلْجَنَّتَيْنِ دَانٍ ﴿٥٤﴾

54. *They will sit on couches upholstered with brocade, the fruit of both gardens within easy reach.*

فَبِأَيِّ ءَالَاءِ رَبِّكُمَا تُكَذِّبَانِ ﴿٥٥﴾

55. *Which, then, of your Lord's blessings do you both deny?*

فِيهِنَّ قَٰصِرَٰتُ ٱلطَّرْفِ لَمْ يَطْمِثْهُنَّ إِنسٌ قَبْلَهُمْ وَلَا جَآنٌّ ﴿٥٦﴾

56. *There will be maidens restraining their glances, untouched beforehand by man or jinn.*

فَبِأَىِّ ءَالَآءِ رَبِّكُمَا تُكَذِّبَانِ ۝٥٧

57. *Which, then, of your Lord's blessings do you both deny?*

كَأَنَّهُنَّ ٱلْيَاقُوتُ وَٱلْمَرْجَانُ ۝٥٨

58. *Like rubies and brilliant pearls.*

فَبِأَىِّ ءَالَآءِ رَبِّكُمَا تُكَذِّبَانِ ۝٥٩

59. *Which, then, of your Lord's blessings do you both deny?*

هَلْ جَزَآءُ ٱلْإِحْسَٰنِ إِلَّا ٱلْإِحْسَٰنُ ۝٦٠

60. *Shall the reward of good be anything but good?*

فَبِأَىِّ ءَالَآءِ رَبِّكُمَا تُكَذِّبَانِ ۝٦١

61. *Which, then, of your Lord's blessings do you both deny?*

وَمِن دُونِهِمَا جَنَّتَانِ ۝٦٢

62. *There are two other gardens below these two.*

فَبِأَىِّ ءَالَآءِ رَبِّكُمَا تُكَذِّبَانِ ۝٦٣

63. *Which, then, of your Lord's blessings do you both deny?*

مُدْهَآمَّتَانِ ﴿٦٤﴾

64. *Over shadowing*

فَبِأَيِّ ءَالَآءِ رَبِّكُمَا تُكَذِّبَانِ ﴿٦٥﴾

65. *Which, then, of your Lord's blessings do you both deny?*

فِيهِمَا عَيْنَانِ نَضَّاخَتَانِ ﴿٦٦﴾

66. *Therein two fountains of gushing water.*

فَبِأَيِّ ءَالَآءِ رَبِّكُمَا تُكَذِّبَانِ ﴿٦٧﴾

67. *Which, then, of your Lord's blessings do you both deny?*

فِيهِمَا فَٰكِهَةٌ وَنَخْلٌ وَرُمَّانٌ ﴿٦٨﴾

68. *In both are fruits and palms and pomegranates.*

فَبِأَيِّ ءَالَآءِ رَبِّكُمَا تُكَذِّبَانِ ﴿٦٩﴾

69. *Which, then, of your Lord's blessings do you both deny?*

فِيهِنَّ خَيْرَٰتٌ حِسَانٌ ﴿٧٠﴾

70. *In them are maidens, virtuous and beautiful.*

فَبِأَيِّ ءَالَآءِ رَبِّكُمَا تُكَذِّبَانِ ﴿٧١﴾

71. *Which, then, of your Lord's blessings do you both deny?*

حُورٌ مَّقْصُورَٰتٌ فِى ٱلْخِيَامِ ﴿٧٢﴾

72. *Dark-eyed, sheltered in pavilions.*

فَبِأَيِّ ءَالَآءِ رَبِّكُمَا تُكَذِّبَانِ ﴿٧٣﴾

73. *Which, then, of your Lord's blessings do you both deny?*

لَمْ يَطْمِثْهُنَّ إِنسٌ قَبْلَهُمْ وَلَا جَآنٌّ ﴿٧٤﴾

74. *Man has not touched them before them nor Jinni.*

فَبِأَيِّ ءَالَآءِ رَبِّكُمَا تُكَذِّبَانِ ﴿٧٥﴾

75. *Which, then, of your Lord's blessings do you both deny?*

مُتَّكِئِينَ عَلَىٰ رَفْرَفٍ خُضْرٍ وَعَبْقَرِيٍّ حِسَانٍ ﴿٧٦﴾

76. *They will all sit on green cushions and fine carpets.*

فَبِأَيِّ ءَالَآءِ رَبِّكُمَا تُكَذِّبَانِ ﴿٧٧﴾

77. *Which, then, of your Lord's blessings do you both deny?*

$$\text{تَبَارَكَ اسْمُ رَبِّكَ ذِى الْجَلَالِ وَالْإِكْرَامِ} \quad \text{۷۸}$$

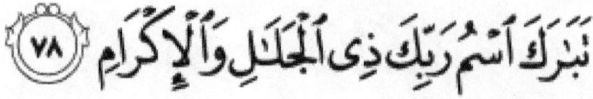

78. Blessed be the name of your Lord, Majestic and Noble!

Commentary on Selected Verses

Each chapter in the *Qur'an* has a special flavour. This is partly because of how the verses were revealed to the Prophet (S), the context and the extent to which the verses address matters of *Haqq* (eternal truth) as opposed to matters which deal with community and rules for a society to flourish and grow.

Most of the chapters revealed in Makkah deal with the hereafter, the ways of Allah, our realisation of our inadequacies, reminders of death, as well as remembrance of the ultimate, so that our worldly projects do not become overwhelming and we interact with the world to see the light of our Maker through His divine attributes.

Most of the great chapters in the *Qur'an* remind us that our purpose for coming into this world is to realise the All-Powerful and Mighty Creator who is sustaining it and permeating it so that we come to know Him or know His qualities in order for us to perfect our worship. You can only worship an entity or a reality if you know more about it. You love a house because you have already seen that it is secure and comfortable. You adore something by knowing it.

Sūrat al-Rahmān is one of those great chapters described by the Prophet (S) as the bride of the *Qur'an*. A bride complements the household and brings to it an additional quality of goodness and wellness. Similarly, *Sūrat al-Rahmān* complements and completes or echoes that which is the *Qur'an*.

The chapter can be divided into three sections. The first section describes Allah's greatness, grace, and mercies. It is the only chapter that begins with a Divine Name, *Al-Rahmān* (The Merciful), to highlight it universally. Existence has come about out of Allah's mercy and His love of *shar*ing His Magnificence, Might, Beauty, and Majesty, and to *share* the fact that He knows all, hears all, and sees all. He has given us a little bit of sight so that we may appreciate what Allah sees. He has given us a little bit of knowledge so that we may appreciate what Allah knows and be in awe of the power of Allah. This first section of about 25 verses describes Allah's bounty and grace upon us.

The next 25 verses describe the duality in this world, the flimsiness of this world, and that worldly matters are based on opposites. There is constant dark and light, up and down.

The third section describes the *ākhira* (the Next Life) and the reward for those of us who have done our duties, and our jobs in this world. The next life is a garden that has no beginning and no end. In this world we all seek gardens, good relationships, good health, harmony, comfort, ease, and security. However, we can never attain any of these for any length of time. Allah promises us that this is all a practice for the Next Life. This world is like the gymnasium or the school for us to return to where we originated from. The first of creation and the first rise of Prophethood was designed in the garden. Adam (AS) only knew the garden, and so Allah in His mercy showed him that there is a dark side to the garden, that is filled with discord, disturbance, insecurities, and shadows. Our purpose in this world is to deal with the ups and downs. Equally, we have within us our *rūh* (soul), which knows its creator directly. It is from the command of Allah that we all have souls. These verses imply that from the beginning we shall see how Allah reminds us that he has created us and has given us the soul so that we are in total gratitude rather than being constantly concerned with outer projects without realising inner pleasure.

There are at least seven well-known commentaries on these *Qur'anic* verses. Your task is to absorb its inner meaning and take from it that which makes sense to you at the time. When you come back to it, you may find that something else makes more sense to you.

بِسْمِ اللهِ الرَّحْمَنِ الرَّحِيمِ

In the name of Allah, the Beneficent, the Merciful.

الرَّحْمَنُ ﴿١﴾

The All-Merciful! (55:1)

عَلَّمَ الْقُرْءَانَ ﴿٢﴾

Taught the Qur'an. (55:2)

خَلَقَ الْإِنسَـٰنَ ﴿٣﴾

He created man. (55:3)

Many of the early commentaries on the *Qur'anic* verses define *Rahmān* as He who has given the soul because it is from *Rahma* (mercy), which means graciousness, mercy, and the ultimate beneficence. It is by creation that mercy comes into view. If there is no creation, no existence, you would not know about mercy or its opposite, *niqmah* (indignation, resentment, affliction).

When Allah created Adam (AS), the angels believed that this entity, which had some limited freedom, would cause chaos in this world. But Allah said this Adamic creation, through his soul, has knowledge of the attributes and qualities of Allah. The chapter opens with the assertion that mercy is based on *'Ilm* (knowledge). Every entity within this creation has within it a programme of what to do and what not to do. Seasons change, the temperature changes and the leaves fall. When rain falls on the earth the seed becomes wet and begins to grow.

This is knowledge. The electron that whizzes around the nucleus of the atom does not act in that way consciously. It does it because it has been programmed that way. Allah has created it that way, and that is its *fitra* (original nature). Our *fitra* is, by nature, inquisitive. That is why when someone wants to tell you something but doesn't, he has you on tenterhooks. You want to know. We all want to know because we love wellness, inner tranquillity, and happiness, which all come as a result of inner contentment. We want knowledge, and one of the definitions of the *Qur'an* is that which contains all that is known and unknown of the heavens and the earth. Through that eternal, divine, boundless knowledge Allah created humankind.

$$عَلَّمَهُ ٱلْبَيَانَ ۝$$

He taught him eloquence. (55:4)

$$ٱلشَّمْسُ وَٱلْقَمَرُ بِحُسْبَانٍ ۝$$

The sun and the moon follow their calculated courses. (55:5)

Bayān means clear evidence, articulation, and an ability to express. It is an aspect of *furqān* (discrimination, or that which differentiates): this is worldly and that is heavenly, or this is communal and that is personal, and so on, so that you can distinguish between different facets.

Allah immediately plunges into a magnificent exposure of the sun and the moon existing according to *hisāb* (measure), meaning it is not haphazard. The cycles, the gyration, and the turning are all according to a measure. There is nothing in existence unless it is based on a measure, and a measure only changes if another measure has superseded it. The fact that we can see the moon sometimes and it is masked at other times is according to the measure for which it has been programmed.

$$\text{وَٱلنَّجْمُ وَٱلشَّجَرُ يَسْجُدَانِ ﴿٦﴾}$$

Prostrate themselves the stars and the trees. (55:6)

$$\text{وَٱلسَّمَآءَ رَفَعَهَا وَوَضَعَ ٱلْمِيزَانَ ﴿٧﴾}$$

He has raised up the sky. He has set the balance. (55:7)

Allah shows us that what we have been made for is programmed within us. This knowledge is for us to understand how to differentiate between things on this earth. There are the heavens and then there is all that goes on in the earth and the heavens relating to each other. Verse 55:6 refers to herbs and plants and how they respond to the sun and the inter-relationship between the heavens and the earth. It reveals this treasure of Allah's bounties and gifts. If we take time to reflect upon them, then we may see the meaning behind the forms.

$$\text{أَلَّا تَطْغَوْا فِي ٱلْمِيزَانِ ﴿٨﴾}$$

Transgress not in the Balance (55:8)

$$\text{وَأَقِيمُوا ٱلْوَزْنَ بِٱلْقِسْطِ وَلَا تُخْسِرُوا ٱلْمِيزَانَ ﴿٩﴾}$$

weigh with justice and do not fall short in the balance. (55:9)

Mīzān is balance. How can you have good health if you do not balance what you eat, what you drink and the extent to which you rest? It is not possible to have good health if you do not work towards and achieve such balance. Everything is according to balance. It is for that reason that principles of justice include the concept of achieving a balance between the parties. When someone is ill we say they are in an unstable condition, meaning they are not in balance. It has to be according to discrimination, balance, and clear evidence. If I don't know it then how can I have discrimination? How can I exercise justice and correctness? Every occasion and every aspect of our lives demands us to do it justice so that we have no regrets. Justice means doing the right thing, in the right place, at the right time.

$$وَٱلۡأَرۡضَ وَضَعَهَا لِلۡأَنَامِ ١٠$$

And earth – He set it down for all beings, (55:10)

$$فِيهَا فَٰكِهَةٌ وَٱلنَّخۡلُ ذَاتُ ٱلۡأَكۡمَامِ ١١$$

with its fruits, its palm trees with sheathed clusters, (55:11)

$$وَٱلۡحَبُّ ذُو ٱلۡعَصۡفِ وَٱلرَّيۡحَانُ ١٢$$

its husked grain, its fragrant plants. (55:12)

$$فَبِأَيِّ ءَالَآءِ رَبِّكُمَا تُكَذِّبَانِ ١٣$$

Which, then, of your Lord's blessings do you both deny? (55:13)

Allah challenges us. *Alāi* means bounties. In verse 55:13 this word is used in plural form, so Allah is addressing two entities. Some people of knowledge say this could be a reference to men and women because we are complementary. Without a union, we would not have perpetuity in this life. It could also refer to *ins* (human) and *jinn* (invisible beings). These are all *qudrah's* (powers) of Allah. The best translation of *alāi* is that which has to do with Allah's abilities,

41

capabilities, and creational commands. How can you deny all of these diverse issues? Some of them are short-lived and some of them are long-lived. Some relate to attributes, or actions, or even intentions. Some of them relate to the subtle, while others relate to manifested gross. All of these are the bounties of Allah. He is challenging us. How can you deny the magnificent presence, bounty, and generosity of your Lord? Look at all of these things and ponder upon them.

$$خَلَقَ ٱلْإِنسَـٰنَ مِن صَلْصَـٰلٍ كَٱلْفَخَّارِ ﴿١٤﴾$$

He created mankind out of dried clay, like pottery; (55:14)

$$وَخَلَقَ ٱلْجَآنَّ مِن مَّارِجٍ مِّن نَّارٍ ﴿١٥﴾$$

and He created the jinn of a smokeless fire. (55:15)

These are the two creations on this earth, *ins* and *jinn*. *Ins* are made from solid matter, earthly matter. The word *Adam* relates to dust; dust on earth is called *Adīm*. The *jinn* are made from fire and smoke, which is why they cannot be seen. They are another entity on this earth, and they dwell in different areas, especially open spaces, deserts and elsewhere. They are a bit like us in that they procreate, marry, and have quarrels. If you want to know more, read some of the other verses and chapters, especially *Sūrat al-Jinn* (chapter 72). These invisible beings do exist, but we establish a boundary with them. We say 'That is not my affair. It is a *jinn*-related matter.' Leave it and do not be tempted.

$$فَبِأَيِّ ءَالَآءِ رَبِّكُمَا تُكَذِّبَانِ ﴿١٦﴾$$

Which, then, of your Lord's blessings do you both deny? (55:16)

$$\text{(١٧)} \quad رَبُّ ٱلْمَشْرِقَيْنِ وَرَبُّ ٱلْمَغْرِبَيْنِ$$

He is Lord of the two risings and Lord of the two settings. (55:17)

Rabb is translated as Lord but in Arabic, it also relates to *tarbiyah*, which means 'brought up properly', to the ultimate level to which that system can rise. *Tarbiyah* of a human being is that which is correct. It is for us to realise we have only come here to adore and to know the qualities of Allah and to constantly be ready to leave. The concept of *tarbiyah* is much like parents who instil in their children a love for knowledge, courtesy, obedience, and discharging one's responsibilities to humanity and creation.

Much is written about this verse (55:17) because of its reference to two sunrises and the two sunsets. Elsewhere in the *Qur'an*, there are similar references. There are numerous possible explanations. One possible reference is to our soul, which has come as though it has been revealed from the unseen and when it leaves this world, it departs. It can also be *'aql* (knowledge), *nafs* (ego-self) or anything that comes and goes, it comes as light, and it disappears. Imam Ali (AS) suggests it is a reference to the extreme positions of the sunrise and sunset in summer and winter. The summer rise of the sun is different from the winter rise and so too do many things within us rise in use then they depart from us. Allah reminds us when he says, 'Look and consider so many things, so many *masharik* (sunrise) come, so many *maghrib* (sunset) come, and the two *mashariks* essentially is that of realising.' First, you think you are separate, and then you realise that you are dependent on Allah. This is also a reference to two rises and abandoning back into him is another sunset.

$$\text{(١٩)} \quad مَرَجَ ٱلْبَحْرَيْنِ يَلْتَقِيَانِ$$

He brought the two seas together. (55:19)

بَيْنَهُمَا بَرْزَخٌ لَّا يَبْغِيَانِ ﴿٢٠﴾

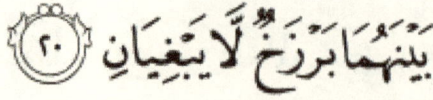

yet there is a barrier between them they do not transgress. (55:20)

The most likely explanation is of two bodies of water (salty sea and inland freshwater) and land is the barrier to keep them separate. Everything in existence is based on two. You cannot have a bad experience without a possibility of goodness and vice versa. You cannot have knowledge without an aspect of ignorance, or ignorance that does not lead you into a zone of knowledge. Inseparable are these meetings of two opposites. They are complementary opposites, and so Allah says in verse 55:19: 'The two seas flow,' which means the ocean of light and the ocean of ignorance or darkness, or the oceans of this unseen world and the seen world are bound together. How can this world of the seen not be related to the unseen? How can your intention, which is unseen, not relate to your action? They meet in you but there is a separation between them. One of them is the sea of pure water and the other one is the sea of salty water. In other words, I have within me potential access to purity, but equally, I have access to a lot of rubbish (that which will not nourish me).

The two oceans, the higher and the lower, are also the oceans of perpetuity. My soul is forever but my body is not forever. They have met, they are together here on the earthly plain, but one does not overcome the other. If I have pain in my body, it asserts itself so I must attend to it, and if my soul is hungry for knowledge and calls me then I have to attend to it. I have two entities or two cosmologies — one is boundless, and one is bounded, but one does not overcome the other. You cannot deny your earthliness if you do so you will be denied your heavenliness. In the world we live in today, the priority is this world, and all that rational, workable, and pragmatic. What about the other world which is forever? We are suffering because we are out of balance. The suggestion is not that we should turn away from this world. Instead, we should tackle this world but be open, and reflective upon the other world that is forever.

Chapter 4

SURAT AL-FATIHA

Quranic Verses

The Arabic text and the English translation of *Sūrat al-Fātihah* follows immediately below. Thereafter I will focus my commentary on selected verses and words.

$$\text{بِسْمِ ٱللَّهِ ٱلرَّحْمَٰنِ ٱلرَّحِيمِ ﴿١﴾}$$

1. *In the name of Allah, the Merciful to all, the Compassionate to each!*

$$\text{ٱلْحَمْدُ لِلَّهِ رَبِّ ٱلْعَٰلَمِينَ ﴿٢﴾}$$

2. *Praise be to Allah, Lord of the Worlds.*

$$\text{ٱلرَّحْمَٰنِ ٱلرَّحِيمِ ﴿٣﴾}$$

3. *Merciful to all, the Compassionate to each!*

مَٰلِكِ يَوۡمِ ٱلدِّينِ ٤

4. *Sovereign of the Day of Recompense.*

إِيَّاكَ نَعۡبُدُ وَإِيَّاكَ نَسۡتَعِينُ ٥

5. *It is You we worship, and upon You we call for help.*

ٱهۡدِنَا ٱلصِّرَٰطَ ٱلۡمُسۡتَقِيمَ ٦

6. *Guide us to the straight path.*

صِرَٰطَ ٱلَّذِينَ أَنۡعَمۡتَ عَلَيۡهِمۡ غَيۡرِ ٱلۡمَغۡضُوبِ عَلَيۡهِمۡ وَلَا ٱلضَّآلِّينَ ٧

7. *The path of those You have blessed, those who incur no anger and who have not gone astray.*

Commentary on Selected Verses

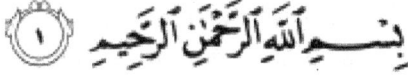

بِسْمِ اللَّهِ الرَّحْمَٰنِ الرَّحِيمِ ﴿١﴾

In the name of Allah, the Merciful to all, the Compassionate to each! (1:1)

The *Qur'an* contains the same number of *Bismillahs* as there are chapters, 114. All the chapters begin with this verse except for *Sūrat al-Tawbah*. Each *Bismillah* is different from the others. The *Bismillah* of *Surat al-Zilzāl* is, 'By the command of He who is the destroyer of it all, the returner of it all.' Similarly, one could replace the Divine names (*Asmā' al-husnā*) used here with any others and you will find it will apply. Given the content of that chapter, the *Bismillah* for *Surat al-Zilzāl* could be rendered as: 'In the Name of He who resurrected you and will guide you, and to Him you will return.' In contrast, the *Bismillah* of *Sūrat al-Fātihah* could be rendered as: 'By the name and command of He who has created the seen and the unseen.' For this reason, it is called *al-Fātihah*, the 'opener.' It is the opener to all these multiple layers of knowledge. You have knowledge that, you know you exist, but your existence is secondary to the *nūr* (light) that created everything in creation and overflowed into it, and that a spark from that Original *Nūr* (Original Light) is in you – your *rūh* (soul)! That is why each one of us is carrying a sacred spark, and that is also why, as many of the commentators say, especially if you go to *Sūrat al-Nūr*, it is a Light of the Origin before creation. In other words, Allah existed, nothing was with Him, and He is the same now. Allah is before any overflow into creation. That is why nothing of this creation will satisfy us on this earth because the earth has come only to go; it is part of a cycle, part of a return.

We yearn for something that is beyond the occurrence of earthly matter. The Prophet (S) said, 'If Adam's son had a valley full of gold, he would like to have two valleys, for nothing fills his mouth except dust.' The soul has been exposed to wealth beyond measure: you have within you knowledge in your soul that has been exposed to *Alastu bi Rabbikum,* when the souls were asked: 'Am I not your Lord?' Wealth beyond measure does not belong to the earth, so you can never be satisfied. If part of you knows wealth beyond measure, then how can you, as a combination of soul and *nafs* (ego-self), ever be satisfied with a measure? It's not possible. Know for sure that you will never be secure with this life on earth, no matter how much power, wealth, or achievement you might acquire, you can never be satisfied. This means you must give up searching in the realm of reason, mind, or ego-self. You then begin to learn the art of stopping or abandoning.

What is that art? It is the art of being in the *mihrāb* (sanctuary; prayer niche), 'fighting' against the lower self. *Mihrāb* comes from the root *harb* (war). Thus, the prayer niche is also referred to allegorically as the place of war because it is where one does battle with the lower self. Maryam (AS) was in her prayer niche when her guardian Zakariya (AS) found strange food around her. He asked: 'What is this?'. He was asking from a place of measure and reason, because before him he found foods that were not in season and some were unknown to him – this is where the seen and the unseen meet. The power of an open heart is that it won't be shocked by the appearance of something unexpected. That is why the closer you get to higher knowledge, the less surprised you are by what others call miracles. People of knowledge, seers, or those with insight do not read the future. For them, or anybody with an open heart, there is no future and no past, there is only Eternal Presence. They read the signs and see what is happening now and they say, of course, if this continues, say, for example, tension and mistrust amongst people, it will lead neighbours to kill each other. It is quite clear. It is not a magical interpretation.

If everybody clamours for more and is obsessed with acquiring possessions whilst giving less, it will end in a rampage, as we already experience in parts of the world. Allah reminds us in the *Qur'an* to watch out for trouble that will not only afflict the perpetrators but would affect everybody. Do not ever think you will be spared! Whatever happens in one part of the world will also have its effect somewhere else. There is unity on the outer, but we don't see it because it is vast, and we are limited. We cannot see what is going on in areas that are light years away. It is impossible to see or measure it. We can barely measure the temperature within our own environment.

This *Qur'an* unveils infinite layers and varieties of interconnected nets and networks. That is why it is awesome! We approach the *Qur'an* with humility and in *tahāra* (a state of ritual purity), which is not only *wudhū'* (ritual ablution) and not only mental purity but, more importantly, with purity of heart. To know that you are nothing – not even a speck – and yet, here is the unveiling of that which is beyond anything that we can fathom. It is endless! That is why there is no such thing as a physical building block, which we loosely call the atom. The deeper you go into the atom, the vaster it is. The same applies to the universe, the spheres of galaxies and the endlessness of the outer world. We must keep that as our perspective. That endlessness is also, in a way, enfolded into our hearts and into our souls.

We have amazing, deep and rich heritages of *tajrīd* (absolute) and *tashbīh* (affirming similarities). *Tajrīd* is that Allah is beyond anything you and I can imagine. To reach closer to that unimaginable precinct, we need similarities or likenesses of His qualities, which is *tashbīh*. Allah's generosity, for example, is beyond measure. But your generosity, my generosity, or that of the most generous person is within measure because it will stop in the case of death or when circumstances change. The similarity is nearness. It is how Allah wants us to grow up. All of the affirming similarities relate to growth and refinement to bring us up. Bring us up to what? To the realisation that we are both limited and also beyond measure.

Human nature is a composition of that which is beyond measure, which is the *nūr* (light) of Allah in your heart, and that which is measurable. In other words, we are *haqīqah* (heavenly) and *sharī'a* (earthly). If you deny the one, you will deny the other. It is like Makkah and Madinah. Makkah is *haqīqah*, where anything goes. With Allah, anything is possible! But in Madinah, you must have *adab* (courtesy) and apply the *sharī'a* (revealed law or code of conduct). It is for that reason that civilisation grew when human beings gathered. It could not happen until the invention of agriculture. With settlements came thievery – before that there was nothing to steal. The nomadic way

49

of life was a band of a few hundred people with camels walking across the desert with nothing much on them. They hoped to find berries or animals. Once there is a bit of spare food those who are more mobile will attempt to take advantage. The biggest raids and invasions occurred with the rise of horseback riding. The horse was already tamed over 6,000 years ago, but it was mostly used to drive chariots, especially among the Persians. Once the Central Asians began to realise how this amazing animal could be an extension of themselves, then riding on a horse presented amazing power and advantage hence the beginning of villages being raided and ultimately the invasion of other countries.

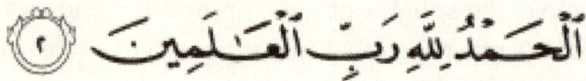

٢ الْحَمْدُ لِلَّهِ رَبِّ الْعَـٰلَمِينَ

Praise be to Allah, Lord of the Worlds. (1:2)

You can visualise this verse as written in the upper heavens. It is declaring itself, like anything praiseworthy such as goodness, friendship, *mahabba* (love), and knowledge. All these praiseworthy attributes belong to Allah.

There is nothing in existence unless there is a counter side. What is the counter side of *Ar-Rahmān* (The All-Merciful)? It is *shaytān* (satan; ego-self). What is the counter side of knowledge? It is ignorance. Ignorance is what you and I suffer from, and we hope to emerge from it into knowledge. That is why the Prophetic teaching says that if there is anything good, it belongs to Allah. Allah has given it to you. If anything is wrong that you are unhappy with and that is detrimental, it is from you.

There are two sides. One is humanly, for example, unkind behaviour, and it comes from and belongs to us. Allah's generosity is beyond our measure and so it is only His generosity that we aspire to, and that is part of *Al-Hamīd* (The Praiseworthy). You praise 'The Praiseworthy,' you do not praise meanness. We all try to justify our behaviour and give excuses: 'I am not mean, I only took this and that.'

Our justification for our behaviour comes from our *nafs al-ammārah* (the tyrannical self). This is where grooming and upbringing come in. The *Rabb* (Lordship) is to bring yourself up from the lower *nafs* (ego-self) to the higher soul, to the *nūr* (light) in you. Do not deny the shadow because as long as you are alive you have a shadow. But to what extent is that shadow being contained? When the Prophet (S) was asked about this *shaytān* (satan; ego-self), he said, 'Satan is in submission, in accordance.' Do not ever think that you do not have a zoo in you, but how well managed is that zoo? Watch out for all the humans in you!

So '*Al Hamdu*' is a declaration of truth. Praise anything praiseworthy amongst you. *Rabb* is *tarbiyah*, to bring out. '*Ālamīn* is that which is known, from the same root as '*ilm* (knowledge). How many '*alams*' (worlds) are there? Infinite! What about those worlds that we can't discern? Multitudes! What about the different worlds of the *jinn* (invisible beings) and the worlds of the *malā'ika* (angels)? What about our inner worlds? What about the worlds of all the other creatures within us? There are more living entities in us – such as microbes and viruses – than there are cells, which number 100 trillion! These are worlds within worlds within worlds, and they all have boundaries, comings and goings and cultures.

'*Lillā*' is from *ila-Allah*, and Allah is from *al-illāh*, meaning 'the god,' where once any number of deities was an *illāh*. It comes from the Aramaic language but is also in Hebrew and Arabic. The spoken pronunciation made *Al- illāh* into Allah.

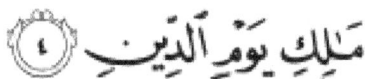

مَٰلِكِ يَوْمِ ٱلدِّينِ ٤

Sovereign of the Day of Recompense. (1:4)

Yawm is a period, day, or occasion. *Dīn* is from the root word for debt. Translated very cumbersomely as religion, we can also render it as a way of life, a life transaction. It is a higher transaction than give and take. The *Qur'an* tells us, 'Say, I do it for Allah's sake.' Do a bit of business with Allah! There's nothing wrong with that. But move on to the ultimate business that there is only that eternal light. Start from where you are. Do not deny that you are calculating and hoping to add zeros, but make sure you also reach the point that is beyond numbers to a quality zone that is not quantifiable. Then you are at the edge of *tawakkul* (reliance on Allah). You are at the edge of being able to say, "Only Allah exists."

إِيَّاكَ نَعْبُدُ وَإِيَّاكَ نَسْتَعِينُ ﴿٥﴾

It is You we worship, and upon You we call for help. (1:5)

Having discerned that anything praiseworthy belongs to this Reality, which is beyond our ability to measure and fathom, you then say: 'I want to rely on that – `Na'budu.' Now, *'ibādah* (worship) operates on different levels. Worship, as we have been taught in the Prophetic teaching and expounded upon by others, has three categories, and within them, there are further sub-categories. One is the worship of the traders, which is the way of people in business. How much is it? Can I get more? Is there a sale? If I give that for Allah's sake will I get more? I will do more *nawafil salāt* (supererogatory prayers), and more worship, in the hope that I will get more. That is one way and there is nothing wrong with it, to start with.

Then there is the worship of the *'abd* (servants of Allah). Many people, because of poverty or uncertainty, superstition, or fear, are afraid of being punished. With fear, you are a bit more proactive and even aggressive. If I give God this mosque, will I get into the Garden? The second *'ibādah* is from *tama`* (greed). If I do this, will He give me another house or another car? Or if I give this, do you think I will suffer less? This is worship out of fear and worship out of greed.

Thirdly, we have the worship of the free, those who love Allah for His qualities alone. He is *Al-Hamd*, which is Praise because He is Praiseworthy. We love Allah because what else can you love?

All love emanates from Allah and keeps diluting. In Arabic, we have at least 11 categories of love. It begins with *'Ishq* (yearning, love for the Divine) and ends with simply liking someone. One of our great Sufi teachers, Jami, tells of a beautiful thing, the station of *Al-Insān al Kāmil,* the completed being. The ultimate category is this station. It is so passionate that the lover and what he loves, and the process of loving have all merged. The seer, the seeing, and what he has seen have unified. In other words, you cannot discern one from the other, which is why Majnoon in Nizami's tale was in such passion that when he does eventually find Layla, he asks, 'Who are you?' She replies, 'I am Layla,' and he says, 'It cannot be!' meaning that there was such a merging that the 'other' could not be physicalised.

Beauty has the habit of also appearing as objects. If you love beautiful objects, watch out, because objects come and go but it is beauty itself that you love. Accept the beautiful object as yet another landmark in your journey towards realising the essence of beauty, which is also in your heart, and which is a Divine name. Love takes us from physical things into their essence, and that again, is His mercy.

Do not deny objects, and do not deny the form or the earth because then you will be denied the heavens. If the earth does not lead you to the heavens, you will have misled yourself. For this reason, the *Qur'an* says: 'He who is blind in this world will be blind in the next, and worse.' Accept reason and rationality. In addition to that, we want the intuition that was killed once we stopped roaming and settled down. Once you have a fixed abode, a cave, or a house, your intuitive side is blunted. You do not hear it anymore and you do not sense it anymore. The frogs do. They smell the rain, and they start croaking in anticipation.

Similarly, once you write something down, transmission is also lost. The Arabs and early Muslims had the advantage of strong oral communication, and until now, if you want to learn the *Qur'an*, you should sit next to someone who can pass on what they know. Nobody knows everything but take what you can and move on until you absorb it. How can you absorb it if you are not a sponge? It is said to those who seek knowledge to, 'Come with an open heart.' The *Qur'an* tells us, 'It is the hearts that become hardened. Even stone sometimes yields water, but hearts can become worse than stone.' Most people are hardened already because their hearts have been deadened. Why? It is because of the excessive use of reason, fears, anxieties, and hoarding. You are dead because of whatever you have chosen to associate yourself with—numbers and electronic blips.

A few thousand years ago, metals were mediums of exchange. The most useless metal of all is gold. It has become something of value because it shines and has lustre and you want to show it off. Earlier on, gold was only used for a deity, it was never bought or sold. A gold mask or armour was for the gods. The first time that gold became a medium of exchange was in Lydia (present-day Turkey), where it was coined and thus became accessible. Once coins were used as a medium of exchange, we tried to hold on to them. Then we made the gold standard, and we held onto that for 70 years. In the current financial system, money is a reference on a computer screen! The value of money has decreased significantly with the passing of time and yet we refer to it as wealth! The more zeroes we add, the more anxieties we have.

In Baghdad, people would buy the *wilāyat* (government). That is why for 500 years Iraq was destitute and in the worst possible situation in the history of that land. In the 400 to 500 years that the *walis* (heads of government) were in charge, they would buy the government, so they had to earn money quickly. The previous heads of government would always be dragged through the streets when the new head of government arrived, or they would attempt to escape. There is a fable of a man who presented the newly crowned head of government with a big bundle of gold. When he was asked: 'why are you giving me this?' the man said that his father died and left him the gold, but had told him to give it to the most miserable man on earth. He then said: 'I think it is you because you saw what they did to the previous head of government before you, and still you sit here, so you must deserve this. I have been walking around for seven years with this bag of gold and I haven't found anybody as miserable and destitute as you!' We are miserable people because of this attachment to the fantasy that our security lies in a relationship, status, house, car, or position.

54

'Die before you die,' we say, but how many of us do it? Do we remember that the air that goes in might not come out? At any minute, we could have a heart attack and die. We are flimsy! How many of us use the opportunities we get, day after day, to stop the mind in our *sajdahs* (devotional prostration in prayer) or our *du'ā'* (act of supplicating Allah)? These acts of worship and dedication are ladders towards the higher which is within us. However, by our worship, we are not climbing up to the heavens. We are actually descending from the so-called ego towards the soul that is in us. As Rumi says, 'I have lived on the lip of insanity, wanting to know reasons, knocking on a door. It opens. I've been knocking from the inside.' Somebody I once knew loved to go to the *Ka'bah'*. For a short while, he had become the president of a country. On one visit, the presidents of several countries were taken inside the *Ka'bah'* and he loved it so much that he lingered behind. Everyone went out and they locked the door. This was at the time of King Faisal when the *Ka'bah'* would be ceremonially washed. He started banging on the door but because of the noise outside, they could barely hear him. He said the most frightening moment of his life was when he was locked up inside the *Ka'bah'*. You are inside the house! The light of Allah is within you, but are you courteous enough?

Allah says in *Surat al-'Alaq* (96:14): 'Does he not realize that Allah sees all?' It is all heard, seen, and known. Do you not fear that everything you do is known and is recorded? The Day of Reckoning is now. You need to be in a state of truly knowing that nobody can help you unless the Source or the energy from the emanation of the One inspires someone to help you. You say: 'There is no doer except He.' That is the beginning of *tawakkul* (reliance on Allah). We know from the story of *Nabi* Ibrahim (AS) when he was thrown into the fire, the angel came to him and said: 'Ask your Lord what you want. Ask me!' He said, 'You, I won't ask.' The angel said: 'Then ask your Lord.' He said: 'It is enough for me not to ask because He knows what state I am in.' You and I must not pretend to be *Nabi* Ibrahim (AS). He was *khalil'ullah* (friend of Allah). We may need to explicitly ask.

In another story, one of the great men of insight and knowledge asked Allah: 'Those who love you cry and plead, yet you do not

55

answer them. But you give to the biggest rascals before they even ask?' And the inspiration came, 'Because I do not want to hear them, I give them. But those whom I love, I want to hear.' Maybe you are amongst those who Allah loves to hear, so ask. Never pretend that you don't need to ask. You and I may need to ask and plead and be made to be seen asking. Don't be arrogant; crush your ego. Let it go and you will become a *rūh* (soul) and the *rūh* is *min amri Rabbi*, by the command of my Lord.

Allah is telling us that this life is only amusement and games. In truth, your real fun begins when you truly acknowledge that He is the only doer, the only existence, and the only destination. Thus, verse 1:5 says, 'You do we serve and from you do we seek help.'

اَهْدِنَاالصِّرَطَ ٱلْمُسْتَقِيمَ ﴿٦﴾

Guide us to the straight path. (1:6)

The root of the word *sirāt* is 'Sarata' which means to swallow whole. Look at the inner meaning of this verse. You will be swallowed in that Path. It will overwhelm you. This means you will be overtaken by it, from it, and unto it. You will be guided by it. The *sirāh* is straight from what? A dot, moved along one straight line, and without a shadow: that is the essence of *Sirāt al-Mustaqīm*, the straight and direct path, the shortest distance between two points, between subject and object, between man and Allah. That dot is from the *nun* in *kun* ('be'), the word from which everything emerged with the creational big bang. This verse means that I want to go back to that zone before creation where everything was not yet manifested when there was nothing other than Allah.

صِرَطَ ٱلَّذِينَ أَنْعَمْتَ عَلَيْهِمْ

The path of those You have blessed, (1:6)

Ni'mah (bounty, blessing) is another wonderful concept. It stands in contrast to *niqmah* (indignation, resentment, affliction). The verse also sheds light on its meaning. Some people are in a state of *niqmah* because they are lost, or they are removed from Allah. Allah says, 'I am closer to you than your jugular vein.' So why do we experience *ghadhab* (anger), feeling of being distant or cast out? It implies that we are not allowing the path to reform, and enlighten us and make us transcend the limitations of our physical existence. We do not deny physicality but to what extent are we acknowledging the divine light that gives rise to physicality? To what extent are we remembering and being aware of the essence of it?

Dhikr is the remembrance of Allah. Remembrance means that your awareness is perpetual, and you are also ready to perform your *salāt* (prayers) at any time. Without such mindfulness, we would be making false claims of being distinguished and chosen. However, you must question the identity of this 'you'? If it is your light, then it does not come into this dialogue of being elevated, reduced, extinguished, or distinguished. This light is *Nūr Allah* (Light of Allah), and it is timeless, having no beginning or end. As the *Quran* states, 'I breathed of My spirit into him.' It is the breath of Allah, so it is sacred, and it transcends the realm of discernment and hierarchy.

Discernment serves its purpose in matters of *sharī'a* (rules of conduct) and *dunyā* (this world), and without rules of conduct we would struggle to co-exist harmoniously. We would lead ourselves to perpetuate more injustice. The more we exercise justice, the closer we get to the Source of the ever-Present Divine justice.

If we witness outer injustice, we must turn to Allah. The reason behind such experiences is because Allah is *Al-'Adl* (The All Just) — it is an inherent attribute of Allah's. The fault does not lie with Allah, but with us. We are in a state of spiritual learning, akin to being in Allah's kindergarten, and in the process we must put out fires of wrongdoing and praise and reward the good. 'There is a reason for your life, O righteous ones!' The term righteous refers to the *abrār*, from *birr*, those who are true to their inner promise and remain true to the expansion of the inner heart, which is the *lubb* (the discerning heart; the inner kernel, the essence of being). Allah says in *Sūrat ale,-*

'Imrān (3:92): 'None of you will attain virtue unless you give out of what you cherish. Whatever you give, Allah knows about it very well'.

All the verses in the *Quran* are connected and intertwined with each other. We cannot simply recite without reading, lest we become parrots. We are commanded to *Iqra'* (read), and it is up to us to embody the essence of this command. When we say *'Qul'* (say), it should come from our hearts. In the state of *sajdah* (devotional prostration in prayer) our hearts are positioned above our heads. This signifies that your head (intellect) has accepted that there is only One Creator but that you are truly singing it from your heart. These heartfelt expressions have the power to touch hearts and elevate people. The purpose of repeating this chapter in every *salāt* (prayer) and at all times is to facilitate a shift from mere information to genuine transformation.

This chapter is called *Umm ul-Qur'an* (the mother of the *Qur'an*). When questioned about this significance, the response lies with the letter *bā*. When the *bā* moves along it transforms into *al-kitāb* (the book), encompassing and recording everything. It serves as the origin, progressing from *Umm ul-Qur'an* to *Ummul-kitāb*, and finally, to *al-kitāb* (the complete book). Through its shadows, it unveils the entirety of its existence. The shadows are indicators of the light. Always veer towards the One and you will discover the dualities, oppositions, and enmities, ultimately leading you to the One. As Allah says: 'And see our enemy as a close friend.' This is so that you transcend enmities and dualistic thinking, eliminating the notion of twos. Instead, view others as equals who have not had the same opportunities as you to realise that there is only One Creator and that the purpose of creation is to come to know the One Creator through *Al-Hamīd* (The Praiseworthy). In this way, you will transcend your identity and realise the ever-present sacred reality.

Chapter 5
SURAT AL-TIN

Quranic Verses

The Arabic text and the English translation of *Sūrat al-Tīn* follows immediately below. Thereafter I will focus my commentary on selected verses and words.

$$\text{بِسْمِ اللَّهِ الرَّحْمَٰنِ الرَّحِيمِ}$$

In the name of Allah, the Merciful to all, the Compassionate to each!

$$\text{وَالتِّينِ وَالزَّيْتُونِ}$$

1. *By the fig, by the olive,*

$$\text{وَطُورِ سِينِينَ}$$

2. *and by Mount Sinai,*

وَهَٰذَا ٱلۡبَلَدِ ٱلۡأَمِينِ ٣

3. by this safe town.

لَقَدۡ خَلَقۡنَا ٱلۡإِنسَٰنَ فِىٓ أَحۡسَنِ تَقۡوِيمٖ ٤

4. We indeed created Man in the fairest stature,

ثُمَّ رَدَدۡنَٰهُ أَسۡفَلَ سَٰفِلِينَ ٥

5. then reduced him to the lowest of the low.

إِلَّا ٱلَّذِينَ ءَامَنُواْ وَعَمِلُواْ ٱلصَّٰلِحَٰتِ فَلَهُمۡ أَجۡرٌ غَيۡرُ مَمۡنُونٖ ٦

6. Except those who believe and do good, so they shall have a reward never to be cut off.

فَمَا يُكَذِّبُكَ بَعۡدُ بِٱلدِّينِ ٧

7. What then can lead you to deny the Judgment?

أَلَيۡسَ ٱللَّهُ بِأَحۡكَمِ ٱلۡحَٰكِمِينَ ٨

8. Is not Allah the most just of judges

Commentary on Selected Verses

Sūrat al-Tīn is one of the shortest but immensely powerful Makkan chapters. Many of the chapters in the *Qur'an* take their name from a significant event or word in that chapter, and this one derives its name from *Tīn* (fig). We need to reflect upon these early, short Makkan chapters to see their multi-dimensionality. The chapter begins:

$$\text{وَٱلتِّينِ وَٱلزَّيْتُونِ} \quad ١$$

By the fig, by the olive, (95:1)

$$\text{وَطُورِ سِينِينَ} \quad ٢$$

and by Mount Sinai, (95:2)

$$\text{وَهَٰذَا ٱلْبَلَدِ ٱلْأَمِينِ} \quad ٣$$

by this safe town. (95:3)

The fig and olive trees, both ancient in existence, have come to us from thousands, if not hundreds of thousands of years ago. They propagate themselves by spreading out far and wide, and can be easily disseminated by taking cuttings and planting them elsewhere. The *Qur'an* mentions other trees such as the pomegranate and the grape which can also be grown from cuttings. The date palm, meanwhile, is propagated from seeds and by small baby plants that grow alongside the main tree. Date palms are grown in many parts of the world and their cultivation has significantly advanced in recent times. We now enjoy plump, succulent dates today thanks to interventions to aid their growth. This experimentation resembles a nursery, where we observe what is in front of us and have an idea of how we can improve on it and perfect it. This serves as a reminder of our journey back to the Garden. We are naturally drawn to the Garden, longing for its essence to be imprinted in our hearts.

This remarkable and concise chapter reminds us that there is continuity in this world and that the Prophet Muhammad's (S) appearance in Arabia was not a sudden occurrence. Prophethood had been an ongoing lineage for thousands of years, and in this, the clear reference is to the Abrahamic line. In the lands of what is now Syria, Palestine, Jordan and Israel, figs and olives were the mainstay of their sustenance. The people were beginning to cultivate grains but they could rely on dried figs and olives to get them through the winter months. The *zaytūn* (the olive) is particularly significant in their diet, as every part of the olive is used. Once the oil is extracted, the remains of the olive and the seed are used to produce a highly nutritious diet for cattle and other animals. Nothing is wasted. The pomegranate is similar. Every part of the fruit and the tree is usable and gives you goodness and is easy to keep, grow, dry, and reconstitute.

We take our sustenance from these amazing gifts of nature. Tribes of people of this region have come and gone, and civilisation began in these lands, bracketed on one side by Egypt and the other by Mesopotamia. Agricultural settlements emerged here thousands of years ago and from that, knowledge began to grow rapidly. The accumulation of knowledge occurs when people come together, leading to the advancement of civilisation, an improved quality of life, and sustainable goodness for everyone. In this profound chapter, Allah tells us to reflect upon our origins and our interconnectedness as humans. We are indebted to those who had profound insights and experienced a heightened state of consciousness as they expanded our understanding of human nature. Without those openings, we would not know as much as we know now about human nature and our basic flaws – our forgetfulness, volatility and unreliability. Regardless of our accomplishments, we constantly experience a sense of loss. Even in the most wonderful victory, a day will come when we can't sustain it. We yearn for enduring joy, not something that is fleeting. The people of the fig and olive trees remind us of this.

This chapter tells us by the evidence of the fact that caravans have come and gone through these ancient lands, that the Prophet Ibrahim (AS) traversed these lands. He travelled from what is now Southern Iraq to the north of what is now Turkey, down into Egypt before returning to Palestine, where he left this world. His progeny –Ismail, Ishaaq, and others—, thousands of them—, and of course, the famous Israelite Yaqoob and the sons of Yaqoob, continued his legacy. The chapter urges us to see how their story is the continuation of the story of Adam (AS) rising to discover his origin. We are given a great metaphor of how the Adamic consciousness arose and that it surpassed that of the angels. Allah says in the *Qur'an* that it is He and His angels who bless humankind, but it is us human beings who debase ourselves through our fears, anxieties, pettiness and our forgetfulness that we are here as temporary guests ultimately to return to Him.

This chapter asks us to reflect upon the land of Mount Sinai, these ancient lands of Palestine, the lands of religious teachings and unveiling, and to reflect upon these ethical connections throughout these thousands of years of the same teachings – to be courteous, correct, generous, and to depend on Allah. We relate to human beings and are correct towards them, knowing that Allah is the orchestrator of all affairs, for He is the doer. He gives us the energy to act. He is the Creator of the attributes that we love, the attributes of power, goodness and all His beautiful qualities. He is the very essence of it all. He is the beginning, He is the end. He is inward, and He is *Al-Dhāhir* (The Outward). Wherever you direct your gaze, there is a trace of Allah. These are the teachings that have come down over these hundreds of thousands of years.

$$\text{لَقَدۡ خَلَقۡنَا ٱلۡإِنسَٰنَ فِىٓ أَحۡسَنِ تَقۡوِيمٍ ٤}$$

We indeed created Man in the fairest stature, (95:4)

ثُمَّ رَدَدْنَٰهُ أَسْفَلَ سَٰفِلِينَ ۝

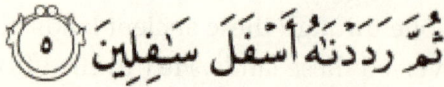

then reduced him to the lowest of the low. (95:5)

Reflect upon how human beings have been created as the culmination of the perfect design, with constant seeking as their purpose. Why are we here? Why have we been put into situations of trial? What is the purpose behind this paradox of give and take, good and bad?

Allah says: 'We created human beings physiologically, as well as metaphorically with the best of potentials, and everyone has that potential because everyone has the soul within.' Reflect upon this. The essence of all souls are the same, but the soul becomes obscured by one's personality, experiences, environment, culture, and other influences that have come along as you grow, giving you a different worldview. It is natural to have a different perspective and to accept what you have grown up with, but it is more important to reflect upon the pure light that resides within you.

The teachings of the Prophet Ibrahim (AS) and those before him tell us that our purpose in life is to perfect our worship. But how can we perfect our worship if we don't recognise perfection? How can we see perfection if the light within our hearts is dimmed by our own fantasies, anger, desires, imaginations, and love for power? We all want to be powerful because we love the All-Powerful but let us not be distracted. We all appreciate the wealth of the One who is beyond need, *Al-Ghanī* (The Rich Beyond Need) but let us not be distracted by our own wealth. Whatever comes to us, be it an increase or decrease, we will leave it behind. No matter how big, strong, or knowledgeable we may be, we will ultimately abandon it. What endures? What moves on? If in this life, we fail to gain certainty about our souls and the ongoing life beyond, then we have strayed from the path of the people of the fig and the olive!

The Abrahamic lineage teaches us that life unfolds in two distinct phases. The first phase is the worldly life that we experience here and now, and it is ever-changing. The second phase comes after our death. The entire *dīn* (life transaction; the way of life) of *Islām* (submission) revolves around this understanding. We are called to place our trust in the unseen while also fulfilling our responsibilities in the visible world. The seen world is but a fleeting glimpse, a fraction of the greater unseen reality.

If we have faith in the *ākhira* (the Next Life), then we are certain that what comes after our death is the continuation of this life. This belief depends on the state of our souls which can be burdened with our anxiety, thoughts, and life experiences. If a soul has not been burdened too much by the ego-self, then it is relatively easy. However, if it is heavily weighed down, then there is a need for purification. This entails reflecting on our actions and their consequences, whether leading to the extreme of the fire or the extreme of joy. We are told by the Prophet (S) that when death comes you begin to experience life exactly as a total human being you have been. Your life after death, the light of the soul in you, will experience the total extent of your readiness to declare that Allah is greater than anything, and smilingly leave, or smilingly stay a bit longer. As we age, it becomes important to prioritise our health. But what truly matters is our attitude. If we have come to perfect the knowledge of the One, then living a bit longer or a bit shorter will not matter. With this orientation, we have a reference point that can make even the biggest turmoil in this life more manageable. This is our spiritual map.

This verse, 'Then We reduced him down to the lowest of the low', highlights the law of life: what goes up must come down, whatever comes to life will also experience death. In our 30's and 40's our mind is still sharp and our memory reliable, but this changes as we age. The age of 40 is considered to be the peak; after that, it is downhill. Nowadays the entire world, particularly the West, is grappling with the challenges posed by greater longevity. People are living into their 80's, 90's and older, and younger generations struggle to care for them. This dynamic can disturb the fabric of society.

Once again, the *Qur'an* is exemplary: it gives us the roadmap to understand duality – the contrasting aspects of up and down, good and bad and what we like and dislike. And it also presents us with the exception to this duality. In reality, human beings are at a loss. The exception lies in those who are secure in their faith. They recognise that Allah brought us into this world and we will ultimately return to Him. So what is there to complain about? Why rush through life? After all, death is inevitable. Yet the rush stems from the desire to experience more of what you consider to be good, such as a few more pennies, and you don't know where to hide it or how to invest it. As soon as you do, the Euro goes down! That's why you have to laugh at the ego's relentless pursuits. The ego-self strives to assume the position of God, it wants to sit where the soul is, where the representative of Allah is, and where the light that has been given to us by Allah is. This is understandable in childhood, but by the time you are in your 40's or 50's, if you have not begun to wake up to the duality, within you, while seeking unity (which is the source of duality) then you are missing an opportunity for growth and understanding.

We chase instant gratification, instant wealth, and instant power. All of this already exists within us. But the light of the All-Powerful is also within us, but we don't access it because we are preoccupied. We become consumed by our desires, such as wanting a bigger house, but then we find ourselves burdened with the responsibilities that come with it. It is endless—one preoccupation brings you another, creating a never-ending cycle of distractions.

There are two hundred to three hundred words in the *Qur'an* which, in today's language, mean the opposite of how they were originally used. One of these terms is *isti'mar* which means 'occupied' (amongst other meanings including colonisation). Yet in the *Qur'an*, *isti'mar* means you have been allowed to come and put roots in this earth, and from it comes the beautiful word of *'ammara*, to develop, to build. This illustrates how we have deviated from the original *Qur'anic* Arabic. We have been 'colonised' by our mentality of 'more of that, let me do more,' and we are also exceptionally clever in always selecting half of the story. Let me first get wealthy because I have children to put through school, and before you know it the child is driving a car. Because you are a good father, you have bought him a sports car, and later on, he is involved in an accident. Very clever, very wise!

This carries on endlessly because we have failed to embrace the true benefits of our rituals. When we go into prostration, we must disappear and none of these fleeting matters will hold any significance. Similarly, when you go for *Hajj* (the Pilgrimage), you draft and sign your will and settle your affairs as though you may not return. All of these practices are perfect reminders that we are mere guests in this life. Allah is the only security, the only true reality. By Allah's grace, we have been granted a glimpse of that divine light. Now we must hasten towards that essence, towards the inner realm of light. It is not enough to simply believe; we must truly know that the Governor of all existence is *Al-'Adl* (The Just). So what is there to complain about? It is our fault for failing to see and anticipate this reality. If only we would stop for a moment and realise that the air which goes in may not come out. Are we prepared to leave this world cheerfully? Once we enter that realm of awareness, many of our mistakes are neutralised and we are less likely to repeat them.

Why do we repeat the same mistakes? Because we love ongoingness. We love to see that this is the most ancient tree or the oldest tradition. We love traditions because they have been doing it for thousands of years for us to imagine that time has stopped. After all, we are in time but not of time. The soul is not subject to space and time; it is in the infinite zone, and we love that. In the meantime, we try to mimic it. Then the reward is endless. If we do not have access to an endless inner reward, we are always in a state of agitation that whatever goodness we have may not last. Your health may not last, your relationship may not last, your family may not last, and nothing may last until you realise that within you lies that light that is beyond joy itself, which is forever. Then you realise that this life is temporary; a sample of that light within. What goes up comes down; and you realise that the entire creation is based on the balance between up and down, good and bad, living and dying or death.

Allah reminds us in this great chapter that our lives, traditions, and all of what we have come from is hanging onto this truth. Since we know there is a clear path to follow and that there are boundaries to accept, we can say 'I will not transgress because it will bring harm to myself, my neighbours, or humanity. So I will not be tempted.' If we don't have the *dīn* (life transaction; a way of life), boundaries, constant reflection, and awareness, then we will always be in a state of denial, accusation or blame. How can we deny the perfection of the path? If someone blames another, it means they are not taking responsibility for their actions. And why do we find ourselves at this place where people are quarrelling? Why aren't we in a place where people are calm and peaceful and reflecting upon the truth?

Temptation carried us; our ego carried us, and we point to this entity called *shaytān* (satan), which represents the ego-self. Many of esteemed *walis* (saints) say the biggest gift that Allah has given us is satan. Therefore we direct our blame to it. It is a powerful act to reject satan and spit at the ego-self! Nobody wants to blame themselves, at least blame satan; blame the ego-self, to begin with. Later, we come to realise that our ego-self was the source of the *waswās* (whispering, a *shaytānic* negative energy that whispers doubt into the hearts and minds of men) inside us.

Our heritage through the *Qur'an* and the Prophetic teachings is rich. Ibrahim (AS) exemplified *hanīf* (righteousness) as he worshipped only One. He was a Muslim, in submission to the truth. Are we in submission to the truth? Are we submitting to the truth that the ego-self tries to distract us from? Once you admit the truth of it, then you begin to discern the truth as it unfolds within our minds.

The *Qur'an* beautifully describes our minds as being in between the light of the Light and the shadow of the shadows. It reminds us to exercise caution, for the mind can also give us its destructions. If we want wealth, we justify it by saying, 'I want wealth to spend it on more mosques.' We may think we are being clever, by sanctifying our money through its association with a noble cause. Yet it is only Allah who is the ultimate, perfect, manifestation of justice and truth.

Allah reminds us so brilliantly in the *Qur'an* (51: 56): 'I created jinn and mankind only to worship Me!' How do we perfect our worship? We strive to do our best by being an active participant in our own life. Talk with people, perform *salāt* (prayers), nourish your body by eating and sleeping, but always remember that it is by Allah's mercy that you can do these things, and you are accountable to Him. This chapter uses the metaphor of the olive tree that gives you oil, and it is neither of the East nor the West. Without metaphors and similitudes of the unseen, we remain fixated on the earthly, material aspects of life. This story of the olives hanging on beautiful trees for thousands of years, when exploring the meaning behind it, it reveals the continuation of life. Life is continuous, and each generation has a greater advantage than the previous generation, but also greater risks of being distracted with gadgets, wealth, comfort, and ease, and forgetting that any day, any minute, we may leave this world. It is magnificent to contemplate the continuity these ancient creations symbolise.

Chapter 6

SURAT AL-IKHLAS

Quranic Verses

The Arabic text and the English translation of *Sūrat al-Ikhlās* follow immediately below. Thereafter I will focus my commentary on selected verses and words.

$$\text{بِسْمِ ٱللَّهِ ٱلرَّحْمَٰنِ ٱلرَّحِيمِ ١}$$

In the name of Allah, the Merciful to all, the Compassionate to each!

$$\text{قُلْ هُوَ ٱللَّهُ أَحَدٌ ١}$$

1. *Say: 'He is Allah, Unique,*

$$\text{ٱللَّهُ ٱلصَّمَدُ ٢}$$

2. *Allah, Self-sufficient.*

$$لَمْ يَلِدْ وَلَمْ يُولَدْ ٣$$

3.   He neither begetting nor begotten.

$$وَلَمْ يَكُن لَّهُۥ كُفُوًا أَحَدٌۢ ٤$$

4.   And none can be His peer.'

In every moment, the infinite, boundless unseen realm intersects with the physical, visible seen realm. The two are simultaneously and completely connected in the heart of the believer. Allah says in a *Hadeeth Qudsi*, 'The heavens and earth do not contain Me, but the heart of the believer contains Me.' The *rūh* (soul) is the *nūr* (light) of Allah. It contains in it all that I need to deliver me (the so-called me, the identifiable I) into my source, my origin, which is my Creator, Allah.

In this glorious chapter of the *Qur'an*, Allah shows us the myriad layers of the map of existence. He shows us how we as travellers are moving in a zone of twilight which combines the seen and the unseen, the known and the unknown, the outer and the inner, the higher and the lower. In this crucible of creation, He shows us how we can steer a course which delivers us to that which is the cause of our existence, from it, and by it. If we don't respond to the purpose of our life, we will fall short and we will end up in valleys where fires rage. There is a purpose to this life, a direction in this life, and that is to see the Life Giver's attributes, qualities, and intentions wherever we turn. Allah says in the *Qur'an* (2: 115): 'So, wherever you turn, there is the Face of Allah.'

See Allah's qualities in everything you observe! See Allah, who is *Al-Qawī* (the Most Strong), when animals fight fiercely, but also wait in watchfulness and see Allah's *sabr* (patience) in the animals. The Egyptian worship of many animals was a worship of attributes. The crocodile hibernates in stillness and patience for months on end, and then in a snap, it can catch its prey. These are Allah's attributes, Allah's glorious qualities. He is the First (*Al-Awwal*), the Last (*Al-Ākhir*), and the Self-Sufficient (*As-Samad*).

The purpose of this existence is to realise the Creator who exists behind, within, before and after everything. In this chapter, Allah says: 'Say!' commit to commanding our lower selves to proclaim this truth. The heavens and the earth bear witness to the fact that Allah is the One. It begins with the command of Allah: *Bismillah*, which signifies invoking the name and the radiance of the Creator of everything. Everything, including all the different manifestations of light and darkness, all proclaim that Allah is *Ahad*, the absolute singular. *Ahadiya* is for Allah only. From the *ahadiya* (singular oneness) comes all others, including the *wahadiya* (one, as in number). Allah is unique. He is not one of two. Allah is the most unique source.

The Prophet (S) advises us not to engage in debates, arguments or excessive discussions about God or Allah. It is permissible and encouraged to consider His attributes, qualities, manifestations, and His immensities because the discussions converge into that ultimate secret of secrets, which is the unknown and the unseen aspects of His being. Allah is noble through His qualities, His attributes, His manifestations, and His eternal presence, which we revere. We all love the All-Powerful, we all love He who has all the wealth, *Al-Ghanī* (The Rich Beyond Need), free from want. He is not only *Al-Ghanī* who is the Most-Wealthy but also *Al-Mughnī* (The Enricher) who can give and bestow wealth without relying on anyone.

As humans, we experience these qualities in fleeting moments. We may have experienced wellness, peace, and tranquillity, which is *Al-Salām* (The Bestower of Peace), however, it does not last because our situation and needs constantly change. As Allah's creation, we operate based on the fulfilment of needs, while He Himself is free of needs. We love Him who is completely self-sufficient. You and I have needs that keep us humble and reliant on Him.

$$\text{قُلْ هُوَ اللَّهُ أَحَدٌ ۝}$$

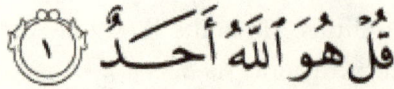

Say: 'He is Allah, Unique, (112:1)

Here Allah reminds us of His absolute uniqueness. The Prophet (S) emphasised the significance of *Sūrat al-Ikhlās,* and he reminded us that if we truly internalise it, we would have grasped one-third of the *Qur'an.* During many of the early battles which some of the leaders of the *Islāmic* community faced, nobody could have ever believed rationally that they could come out of it successfully. Their secret was the continuous recitation of this chapter. They placed their trust in *Al-Wāhid, Al-Ahad* (The One, The Absolute One). There are tremendous layers and waves of nourishment that you can get from delving into this chapter, if you truly go into it bereft, and following the command of Allah.

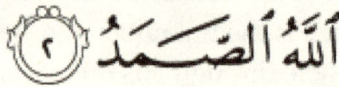

$$\text{اللَّهُ الصَّمَدُ ۝}$$

Allah, Self-sufficient. (112:2)

The word *Samad* holds a deep meaning. It signifies Allah's attribute of being self-sustaining, without the need for anything or anyone else. *Samad* implies remaining constant, steady and reliable, without wavering. We admire a person who is reliable, meaning constant. The source of that constancy is Allah. Allah is the Ever-Constant. There is a great description of a well-known Muslim being of light, Baba Farid Ganj Shakar, who is buried in Pakpattan, close to Multan in Pakistan. His last disciple was asked to give people a description of Baba Farid, and he replied that he was always the same. While we, as humans, may undergo changes in our external actions, being "the same" refers to maintaining inner consistency, always reflecting the higher, *Al-Samad* (the Ever-Present, the Ever Reliable, the One that has no need). People who embody this attribute are beloved to us.

The Prophet (S) said when we go to people to ask them for assistance or to help fulfil a need, they will run away. When we ask for donations, they may hesitate. Money holds a great attraction for people. That is why we feel lucky, even when we merely associate with the wealthy. The *Qur'an* warns against accumulating wealth excessively. It does not mean that you do not think about your provision for tomorrow. It is known that our glorious Prophet (S) made provision for members of his family for a few months, or up to a year. However, storing more than that constitutes hoarding, greed and obsession. Possessions and material wealth can become an endless pursuit. People on the path of enlightenment understand the important of change and transformation. They avoid staying in a place for more than three weeks. Change your habits! The mind should be open to change, while the heart remains focused on *Al-Samad* (the Eternally Self-Sufficient).

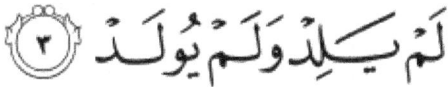

$$لَمْ يَـلِدْ وَلَمْ يُولَـدْ ﴿٣﴾$$

Neither begetting nor begotten. (112:3)

Allah does not beget in the sense of having children. This understanding is a source of confusion for Christians, the followers of Isa (AS) (Jesus). Allah is transcendent and beyond the process of procreation. He is not bound by time; rather, He is the Creator of time. Allah did not give birth to a biological son. The word son at that time meant 'from' in the Aramaic language, which was mostly spoken rather than written. When someone describes themselves as a son, it meant 'I am from.' Thus, when it was said that someone is the 'son of God', it implied a connection or origin rather than a literal biological relationship. The verse reiterates that we are all from Allah, by Allah, and unto Allah. Certainly, Allah does not give birth, nor was He a product of a birth. He is the Self-Creator, Self-Sustained, and Self-Effulgent.

وَلَمْ يَكُن لَّهُ كُفُوًا أَحَدُ ۝

And none can be His peer. (112:4)

The concluding statement of the verse, 'And no one or nothing is like Him,' Is of utmost significance *Kufuwan* is from *kāfa'a* meaning 'to be equal to, similar to or commensurate with.' There never was, nor will there ever be, anything like Allah. He is the most unique, the One without two. He is the One who has no beginning and no end; He is the One who has no needs. He is the One who created out of love and generosity, for all of us to realise that incredible treasure.

Allah was a hidden treasure, unknown. Out of His generosity, He created all of *Banī Ādam* (Children of Adam), so that through our hearts we would discover and realise the ultimate treasure of treasures – the knowledge and recognition of Allah Himself. Once you have begun to catch those incredible qualities of Allah in your heart, then you will find that what you cared for before, your so-called outer entertainment, becomes more about inner attainment, more self-reliant, God-reliant, divine reliance.

This does not mean we fail to relate to human beings. On the contrary, relationships between people can improve once we see others as potentially the same as us; if we recognise them as *arwāh* (souls). You do not see them solely on the basis of actions or outward appearance, as good or as bad. You see in them in the same light that you see in yourself; therefore, you respect that light. You may find a fellow to be a despicable liar, but you can also see in him or her, the higher potential of the original light that exists in all of us, which is the soul. Allah's mercy, generosity, and His bestowal of this boundless gift upon creation, ultimately manifest in the highest of creation, which is the human being. You are custodians of the ultimate gift, which is a spark of the original light of Allah within. You exist because of that battery of a soul, because of that energy in you. But that energy cannot be understood unless you are given to be inspired by the *nafs* (ego-self). Without the ego-self, the soul will not be known. The ego-self can be obedient, following the soul, or it can chase its shadows and suffer from them. Suffering is the way to the offering.

If you have difficulty and are suffering, know that it is Allah's love upon you, to turn you away from that which is going to destroy you. And if you find your path is easy for you, then you know it is from Allah's love for you, in that it is acknowledging that you are on the appropriate path with no resistance. When difficulty comes, you should see it as a gift from Allah to turn away from what has caused the difficulty so that you will only have ease in your heart. Allah tells the beloved Prophet (S) in the *Qur'an* that He did not bring upon him the glorious *Qur'an* to afflict him. Affliction is Allah's love upon him who is seeking the knowledge of Allah, to turn back and away from that which is causing him difficulty. If you seek reputation and admiration, Allah's love is such that He will send you people who will put you into disrepute. If you want to be loved by everyone else, Allah then sends people that will spit on you. Turn to the Creator, rather than chasing after creation. Creation includes His agents, to turn you back to Him. Read the message! Read the sign and you will be in gratitude and beyond gratitude. You will not know where to begin and where to thank Allah for His effulgence!

I remind myself and I remind you about our glorious heritage and the richness that we have in these chapters and in *Sūrat al-Ikhlās*. The more you read it, the more it will unveil itself to you. Read it as though it is the first time you are seeing it. Do not say I know it. Rather, claim ignorance and Allah will bestow His knowledge upon you, and His knowledge does not end. Our knowledge is limited because we have a beginning and an end.

I pray to Allah to make us truly worthy of the path of Islām (submission).

I pray to Allah to give us the delight of the ever-refreshing and ever-energising path of Imān (certainty and security that Allah knows and Allah sees).

I pray to Allah to thrill us and constantly humble us
with the light of Ihsān (inner and outer excellence in thought
and conduct).

Chapter 7

SURAT AL-MULK

Sūrat al-Mulk was likely revealed towards the latter part of the Makkan period and covers issues of earth and the heavens, as well as life, death, and the hereafter. There are at least seven key topics covered in this chapter which is only 30 verses long. A Over 20 other chapters are not too dissimilar from *Sūrat al-Mulk*, including *Sūrat an-Nisa'*, *Sūrat al-Al-Qiyāmah* and *Sūrat ar-Rahmān*. For example, in *Sūrat al-Qiyāmah* emphasis is placed on what comes after death, but it also touches upon the meaning of the human being, the purpose of this life, as well as the heavens and earth. In this chapter of the *Qur'an*, the emphasis is on our interaction with the earth and with nature, as well as certain aspects of ourselves.

Qur'anic Verses

The Arabic text and the English translation of *Sūrat al-Mulk* follows immediately below. Thereafter I will focus my commentary on selected verses and words.

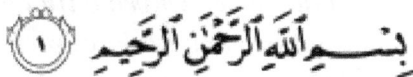

بِسۡمِ اللَّهِ الرَّحۡمَٰنِ الرَّحِيمِ ﴿١﴾

In the name of Allah, the Merciful to all, the Compassionate to each!

تَبَٰرَكَ ٱلَّذِى بِيَدِهِ ٱلْمُلْكُ وَهُوَ عَلَىٰ كُلِّ شَىْءٍ قَدِيرٌ ﴿١﴾

1. *Blessed is He in Whose hand is sovereignty, Who holds power over all things!*

ٱلَّذِى خَلَقَ ٱلْمَوْتَ وَٱلْحَيَوٰةَ لِيَبْلُوَكُمْ أَيُّكُمْ أَحْسَنُ عَمَلًا وَهُوَ ٱلْعَزِيزُ ٱلْغَفُورُ ﴿٢﴾

2. *Who created death and life that He may try you – which of you is best in deeds; and He is the Mighty, the Forgiving,*

ٱلَّذِى خَلَقَ سَبْعَ سَمَٰوَٰتٍ طِبَاقًا مَّا تَرَىٰ فِى خَلْقِ ٱلرَّحْمَٰنِ مِن تَفَٰوُتٍ فَٱرْجِعِ ٱلْبَصَرَ هَلْ تَرَىٰ مِن فُطُورٍ ﴿٣﴾

3. *Who created the seven heavens one above another; you see no incongruity in the creation of the Beneficent Allah; then look again, can you see any disorder?*

ثُمَّ ٱرْجِعِ ٱلْبَصَرَ كَرَّتَيْنِ يَنقَلِبْ إِلَيْكَ ٱلْبَصَرُ خَاسِئًا وَهُوَ حَسِيرٌ ﴿٤﴾

4. *Look again! And again! Your sight will turn back to you, weak and defeated.*

وَلَقَدْ زَيَّنَّا ٱلسَّمَآءَ ٱلدُّنْيَا بِمَصَٰبِيحَ وَجَعَلْنَٰهَا رُجُومًا لِّلشَّيَٰطِينِ وَأَعْتَدْنَا لَهُمْ عَذَابَ ٱلسَّعِيرِ ﴿٥﴾

5. *And We adorned the lower heaven with lamps, and made them things to stone Satans; and We have prepared for them the chastisement of the Blaze.*

وَلِلَّذِينَ كَفَرُوا۟ بِرَبِّهِمْ عَذَابُ جَهَنَّمَ وَبِئْسَ ٱلْمَصِيرُ ۝

6. *And to those who blasphemed their Lord there awaits the torment of hell – and a wretched destiny it is!*

إِذَآ أُلْقُوا۟ فِيهَا سَمِعُوا۟ لَهَا شَهِيقًا وَهِىَ تَفُورُ ۝

7. *When they are cast into it they will hear it sighing, the while it boils.*

تَكَادُ تَمَيَّزُ مِنَ ٱلْغَيْظِ كُلَّمَآ أُلْقِىَ فِيهَا فَوْجٌ سَأَلَهُمْ خَزَنَتُهَآ أَلَمْ يَأْتِكُمْ نَذِيرٌ ۝

8. *Almost bursting for fury. Whenever a group is cast into it, its keeper shall ask them: Did there not come to you a warner?*

قَالُوا۟ بَلَىٰ قَدْ جَآءَنَا نَذِيرٌ فَكَذَّبْنَا وَقُلْنَا مَا نَزَّلَ ٱللَّهُ مِن شَىْءٍ إِنْ أَنتُمْ إِلَّا فِى ضَلَٰلٍ كَبِيرٍ ۝

9. *They will reply, 'Yes' a warner did come to us, but we did not believe him. We said, 'Allah has sent down nothing: you are greatly misguided.'*

وَقَالُوا۟ لَوْ كُنَّا نَسْمَعُ أَوْ نَعْقِلُ مَا كُنَّا فِىٓ أَصْحَٰبِ ٱلسَّعِيرِ ۝

10. *And they shall say: 'Could we but hear or understand, we would not be among the dwellers of the Blaze.'*

فَٱعْتَرَفُوا۟ بِذَنۢبِهِمْ فَسُحْقًا لِّأَصْحَـٰبِ ٱلسَّعِيرِ ﴿١١﴾

11. *They will confess their misdeeds. Away with the inhabitants of the blazing fire!*

إِنَّ ٱلَّذِينَ يَخْشَوْنَ رَبَّهُم بِٱلْغَيْبِ لَهُم مَّغْفِرَةٌ وَأَجْرٌ كَبِيرٌ ﴿١٢﴾

12. *But they who fear their Lord in the Unseen shall obtain forgiveness and a great reward.*

وَأَسِرُّوا۟ قَوْلَكُمْ أَوِ ٱجْهَرُوا۟ بِهِ ۖ إِنَّهُۥ عَلِيمٌ بِذَاتِ ٱلصُّدُورِ ﴿١٣﴾

13. *Be secret in your speech, or proclaim it, He knows the thoughts within the breasts.*

أَلَا يَعْلَمُ مَنْ خَلَقَ وَهُوَ ٱللَّطِيفُ ٱلْخَبِيرُ ﴿١٤﴾

14. *How could He who created not know His own creation, when He is the Most Subtle, the All Aware?*

هُوَ ٱلَّذِى جَعَلَ لَكُمُ ٱلْأَرْضَ ذَلُولًا فَٱمْشُوا۟ فِى مَنَاكِبِهَا وَكُلُوا۟ مِن رِّزْقِهِ ۖ وَإِلَيْهِ ٱلنُّشُورُ ﴿١٥﴾

15. *He it was Who made the earth subservient to you, so roam its byways and eat of His provisions; to Him is the Resurgence.*

ءَأَمِنتُم مَّن فِى ٱلسَّمَآءِ أَن يَخْسِفَ بِكُمُ ٱلْأَرْضَ فَإِذَا هِىَ تَمُورُ ﴿١٦﴾

16. *Or are you confident that He Who is in heaven would not cause the earth to collapse beneath you, as it heaves in turmoil?*

أَمْ أَمِنتُم مَّن فِى ٱلسَّمَآءِ أَن يُرْسِلَ عَلَيْكُمْ حَاصِبًا فَسَتَعْلَمُونَ كَيْفَ نَذِيرِ ﴿١٧﴾

17. *Do you feel secure that He who is in heaven will not loose against you a squall of pebbles, then you shall know how My warning is?*

وَلَقَدْ كَذَّبَ ٱلَّذِينَ مِن قَبْلِهِمْ فَكَيْفَ كَانَ نَكِيرِ ﴿١٨﴾

18. *Those who went before them also disbelieved – how terrible was My condemnation!*

أَوَلَمْ يَرَوْا۟ إِلَى ٱلطَّيْرِ فَوْقَهُمْ صَٰٓفَّٰتٍ وَيَقْبِضْنَ مَا يُمْسِكُهُنَّ إِلَّا ٱلرَّحْمَٰنُ إِنَّهُۥ بِكُلِّ شَىْءٍ بَصِيرٌ ﴿١٩﴾

19. *Have they not observed the birds above them, with wings outstretched or clasped? None can restrain them but the All-Merciful. He sees full well all that exits.*

أَمَّنْ هَٰذَا ٱلَّذِى هُوَ جُندٌ لَّكُمْ يَنصُرُكُم مِّن دُونِ ٱلرَّحْمَٰنِ إِنِ ٱلْكَٰفِرُونَ إِلَّا فِى غُرُورٍ ﴿٢٠﴾

20. *Who is it who can act as your troops, to bring you aid, apart from the All-Merciful? The unbelievers are merely living in illusion.*

أَمَّنْ هَذَا الَّذِى يَرْزُقُكُمْ إِنْ أَمْسَكَ رِزْقَهُۥ بَل لَّجُّواْ فِى عُتُوٍّ وَنُفُورٍ ﴿٢١﴾

21. Or who is it who can provide for you if He withholds His provision? They have assuredly sunk deep in obstinacy and aversion from truth.

أَفَمَن يَمْشِى مُكِبًّا عَلَىٰ وَجْهِهِۦٓ أَهْدَىٰٓ أَمَّن يَمْشِى سَوِيًّا عَلَىٰ صِرَٰطٍ مُّسْتَقِيمٍ ﴿٢٢﴾

22. But What! Is he who goes prone upon his face better guided or he who walks upright upon a straight path?

قُلْ هُوَ الَّذِىٓ أَنشَأَكُمْ وَجَعَلَ لَكُمُ السَّمْعَ وَالْأَبْصَٰرَ وَالْأَفْـِٔدَةَ قَلِيلًا مَّا تَشْكُرُونَ ﴿٢٣﴾

23. Say: 'It is He Who brought you into being, Who provided you with hearing, sight and hearts, but little thanks do you give.'

قُلْ هُوَ الَّذِى ذَرَأَكُمْ فِى الْأَرْضِ وَإِلَيْهِ تُحْشَرُونَ ﴿٢٤﴾

24. Say: 'He it is Who multiplied you in the earth and to Him you shall be gathered.'

وَيَقُولُونَ مَتَىٰ هَٰذَا الْوَعْدُ إِن كُنتُمْ صَٰدِقِينَ ﴿٢٥﴾

25. They say, 'When shall this promise come to pass, if you speak truly?'

قُلْ إِنَّمَا ٱلْعِلْمُ عِندَ ٱللَّهِ وَإِنَّمَآ أَنَا۠ نَذِيرٌ مُّبِينٌ ۝

26. Say: 'The knowledge thereof is only with Allah and I am only a plain warner.'

فَلَمَّا رَأَوْهُ زُلْفَةً سِيٓئَتْ وُجُوهُ ٱلَّذِينَ كَفَرُوا۟ وَقِيلَ هَٰذَا ٱلَّذِى كُنتُم بِهِۦ تَدَّعُونَ ۝

27. But when they see it coming near, the faces of unbelievers will grow sorrowful, and it shall be said: 'This is what you asked for.'

قُلْ أَرَءَيْتُمْ إِنْ أَهْلَكَنِىَ ٱللَّهُ وَمَن مَّعِىَ أَوْ رَحِمَنَا فَمَن يُجِيرُ ٱلْكَٰفِرِينَ مِنْ عَذَابٍ أَلِيمٍ ۝

28. Say: 'Consider this. Should Allah make me perish, along with those who are with me, or else should He show us His mercy, Who shall offer refuge to the blasphemers from a painful punishment?'

قُلْ هُوَ ٱلرَّحْمَٰنُ ءَامَنَّا بِهِۦ وَعَلَيْهِ تَوَكَّلْنَا فَسَتَعْلَمُونَ مَنْ هُوَ فِى ضَلَٰلٍ مُّبِينٍ ۝

29. Say: 'He is the All-Merciful. We believe in Him, and in Him we put all our trust. Assuredly, you will soon, know who is in manifest error.'

قُلْ أَرَءَيْتُمْ إِنْ أَصْبَحَ مَآؤُكُمْ غَوْرًا فَمَن يَأْتِيكُم بِمَآءٍ مَّعِينٍ ۝

30. Say, 'Consider this. If your water is swallowed up by the earth, who will bring you water from a spring that is pure?'

Commentary on Selected Verses

$$\text{تَبَرَكَ ٱلَّذِى بِيَدِهِ ٱلْمُلْكُ وَهُوَ عَلَىٰ كُلِّ شَىْءٍ قَدِيرٌ} \quad (١)$$

Blessed is He in Whose hand is sovereignty, Who holds power over all things! (67:1)

A hand implies power, and in this verse it implies He who has control, management, and sovereignty over the entire cosmos. *Tabāraka* is from the word *baraka*, which means flowing grace. When you have done something good, goodness comes to you. For example, you have had a good meal, you slept well, and you performed your *salāt* (prayers) with devotion; these are all *barakas*. However, when it persists, it becomes a *baraka* from Allah, a divine blessing. It is also a term associated with camels, as is the case concerning at least a third of the *Qur'anic* terms. The root of the word *Baraka, baraka Jamilu*, is reminiscent of the demeanour of camels. Camels are typically restless, and they can be challenging to deal with and they can bite unless they are calmed into a sitting position. Camels were trained to sit to make it easier for people to utilise them effectively. Similarly, *Baraka Jamilu* is achieved through *'aql*, (reason), as it exemplifies tranquillity, akin to the camel's calm posture.

Mulk is a keyword, which implies kingdom, meaning ownership. *Mālik* is a king. There are at least 14 attributes of Allah threaded through this short chapter including *Al-Mālik* (The King), *Al-Qādir* (The Most Able), *Al-Latīf* (The Subtle), *Al-Khāliq* (The Creator), *Ar-Razzaq* (The Ever-Providing), *Al-Khabir* (The All Cognisant), *Al-'Alim* (The All-Knowing) and *Ar-Rahmān* (The All-Merciful).

$$\text{ٱلَّذِى خَلَقَ ٱلْمَوْتَ وَٱلْحَيَوٰةَ لِيَبْلُوَكُمْ أَيُّكُمْ أَحْسَنُ عَمَلًا وَهُوَ ٱلْعَزِيزُ ٱلْغَفُورُ} \quad (٢)$$

Who created death and life that He may try you – which of you is best in deeds; and He is the Mighty, the Forgiving, (67:2)

This verse holds profound wisdom and unveils new insights. It begins by saying: 'He created, He brought forth,' alluding to a time before the big bang, when there was no creation. There was only the light of Allah without the shadows of the earth, heavens, planets, the upper, and the lower. The verse declares: 'It is He who has created.' But what has been created? Intriguingly, the word is *mawt*, meaning physical death, is mentioned first, before *hayat* (life). 'It is He who created that which is dead.' This is a very unusual turn of phrase. Then Allah adds: 'and life.' It is a reminder to us that life emerges from the depths of death.

For people passing the peak of their lives, life gradually becomes more difficult. If you have been awakened to your inner light, then as you get older, you will be more joyful, rather than having a miserable lens. However, most people have not awakened to their inner light and so they become miserable as difficulties set in. There are numerous related verses, such as verse 28 of *Sūrat al-Baqarah* (chapter 2), which says: 'How can you deny in Allah when you were once dead, and He granted you life? He shall cause you to die, Then He shall resurrect you, Then to Him you shall return.' It starts with the reminder that you were dead and then you came to life and you will experience this in a personal way. Unless you take the *Qur'an* in its entirety, you will be puzzled.

It is He who created death. The earth was dead for billions of years before it was created, meaning there was no life in it. Then, through the interaction of light and energy, it began to exhibit the first signs of life, about 400 million years ago. What about those billions of years during which it was dead? He who created death first created the highest form of life, which is us human beings. Yet, we are puzzled about what is the purpose of life. After years of building your life, you have developed a few skills, you have a home, a spouse and children. Are you happier? If not, then you are not imbibing the original purpose of your life.

The purpose of your life is to know more about the Life Giver and to yield to the Essence of Life. Who is God's representative in you? It is your soul. If you haven't come to know your soul, then you are not following the prophetic teaching that 'He who knows himself knows his Lord,' meaning, if you don't know yourself, then you do not know your Lord. If you do not know that you are a composite of a lower self which is always in doubt, always uncertain and insecure, and the higher self which is ever secure, ever-illumined, joyful and is beyond the limitation of time and space, then you do not know your Lord. Your body and mind will die, so if you have identified yourself only with your body and mind then of course you will be worried and fearful of death. The essence of you, your soul, does not die.

How does it endure? With a certain colouration, meaning, a certain trace of your earthly identity. After death, we cannot act, or change our minds, or do anything. The more you prepare yourself while you are alive for that period in which you have no will and cannot act, the easier your flight back will be. As Allah describes, after that death, you come back to live in the *barzakh*, which is the interspace between the *Dunya* (the seen) and the *ākhira* (the Next Life, the unseen). Thereafter you return to the source, Allah. The more you prepare yourself joyfully, readily, cheerfully, and accept it with knowledge, the easier your life will be on this earth and after death.

ٱلَّذِى خَلَقَ سَبْعَ سَمَٰوَٰتٍ طِبَاقًا مَّا تَرَىٰ فِى خَلْقِ ٱلرَّحْمَٰنِ مِن تَفَٰوُتٍ فَٱرْجِعِ ٱلْبَصَرَ هَلْ تَرَىٰ مِن فُطُورٍ ﴿٣﴾

Who created the seven heavens one above another; you see no incongruity in the creation of the Beneficent Allah; then look again, can you see any disorder? (67:3)

Commentators say that in Arab culture, a reference to 'seven' means many. In this context, it refers to many levels of heaven. This chapter and various other verses in the *Qur'an* tell us that the heavens which we see are the lowest of the layers, meaning the rest do not have physical manifestations and they relate to subtler energies.

There are many other verses which are similar to this verse. I will only refer to a few of them from *Sūrat al-Hadid*. In verse *57:1* Allah says: 'Everything in the heavens and earth glorifies Allah' meaning everything is following His program and His design. In verse 57:2

Allah says: 'His is the dominion over the heavens and the earth; He grants life and deals death; and He has the power to will anything.' The verses of *Sūrat al-Hadid* continue brilliantly to show us again a major attribute of the creator. Allah is the first because He is not subject to time. He is the last because for Him time and space are insignificant; they do not exist except for our sake. We need to put things in perspective, otherwise, we become too rigid in the structured aspects of the *dīn* (life transaction; the way of life).

Human beings are bound by birth and death and we need boundaries in our lives, but we must also realise the truth that Allah is beyond boundaries. He has created boundaries for us to begin to look towards the horizons towards that which is boundless. This verse (67:3) says if you look back or if you look into it, you will not find any fault in Allah's creation. Otherwise, look back again. When you and I are confronted with a difficult issue, we say: 'This is not good.' Are you accusing the creator of creating it in a less-than-perfect way? As a human being we have an agenda: we want to have health, so we say, 'my health is not good,' but He says, 'take a deeper look.'

$$ ثُمَّ ٱرْجِعِ ٱلْبَصَرَ كَرَّتَيْنِ يَنقَلِبْ إِلَيْكَ ٱلْبَصَرُ خَاسِئًا وَهُوَ حَسِيرٌ ۝ $$

Look again! And again! Your sight will turn back to you, weak and defeated. (67:4)

He says, reflect on the underlying cause of your illness. How did it come to be? Perhaps you overdid it. You consumed excessive amounts of food or insufficient nutrients or have not had sufficient exercise, so your system is reporting to you. When we observe illness through the lens of perfection, we can discover layers of perfection within it. Our body harbours billions of viruses. But only when the immune system is weak do these viruses seize the opportunity to thrive. So how can you say this is not designed to perfection?

Do not deny the outer situation. For example, one might observe that a person is performing acts which are not conducive to the community's well-being. However, if you take a closer look you will find that his childhood was dysfunctional, society rejected him, so he turned out to be a criminal. Look behind the face and you will see natural perfection. But you must also respond to imperfections. What does the blood tell us? What do the emotions tell us? If you have a lot of headaches you should eradicate the sickness at its roots, not just treat the symptoms. Similarly, what is the purpose of imprisoning criminals if the root of the problem or the cause of unwholesome behaviour is not identified and remedied? If you fail to do this, society will produce more criminals.

وَلَقَدْ زَيَّنَّا ٱلسَّمَآءَ ٱلدُّنْيَا بِمَصَٰبِيحَ وَجَعَلْنَٰهَا رُجُومًا لِّلشَّيَٰطِينِ وَأَعْتَدْنَا لَهُمْ عَذَابَ ٱلسَّعِيرِ ۝

And We adorned the lower heaven with lamps, and made them things to stone Satans; and We have prepared for them the chastisement of the Blaze. (67:5)

This is a description of the heavens closest to us. There are over 100 billion galaxies and every galaxy has over 100 billion stars. However, in our immediate realm, we find the solar system, a small fragment of this grand tapestry. It consists of various components including one star which is the sun and a few planets which orbit around the sun. The *Qur'an* tells us this is the lowest heaven.

وَلِلَّذِينَ كَفَرُوا۟ بِرَبِّهِمْ عَذَابُ جَهَنَّمَ وَبِئْسَ ٱلْمَصِيرُ ۝

And to those who blasphemed their Lord there awaits the torment of hell – and a wretched destiny it is! (67:6)

We experience hell here and this includes disturbances in your work, with your partner, family or others. We are all thinking and reflecting animals so we will often respond to situations like a dog or a wolf. There is a beautiful line on this issue by Imam Shafi (RA): 'With most people, if you consider their motives regarding their worldly pursuits, they behave either like dogs barking, or like donkeys carrying things constantly to please people.' The truth is you know you will never be able to please anyone. A simple observation at business meetings will illustrate that he was right.

إِذَآ أُلْقُواْ فِيهَا سَمِعُواْ لَهَا شَهِيقًا وَهِيَ تَفُورُ ۝

When they are cast into it they will hear it sighing, the while it boils. (67:7)

تَكَادُ تَمَيَّزُ مِنَ ٱلْغَيْظِ كُلَّمَآ أُلْقِيَ فِيهَا فَوْجٌ سَأَلَهُمْ خَزَنَتُهَآ أَلَمْ يَأْتِكُمْ نَذِيرٌ ۝

Almost bursting for fury. Whenever a group is cast into it, its keeper shall ask them: Did there not come to you a warner? (67:8)

The word *nadhīrun* (warner) is important. Look at *Lā ilāha illā Allāh*; the warning is mentioned first, then the good news. If you accept the warning then you should establish outer and inner boundaries for yourself. Without these boundaries, you will never end up on the horizon of boundlessness.

قَالُواْ بَلَىٰ قَدْ جَآءَنَا نَذِيرٌ فَكَذَّبْنَا وَقُلْنَا مَا نَزَّلَ ٱللَّهُ مِن شَىْءٍ إِنْ أَنتُمْ إِلَّا فِي ضَلَٰلٍ كَبِيرٍ ۝

They will reply, 'Yes' a warner did come to us, but we did not believe him. We said, 'Allah has sent down nothing: you are greatly misguided.' (67:9)

Many verses in the *Qur'an* affirm this order, this hierarchy. First in the hierarchy is the warning that you hear and must then respond to. Your response should not be a dismissive one, driven by a desire for temporary pleasure. Instead, it should be a response rooted in seeking contentment and lasting happiness. Consider, for example, the verse regarding the Prophetic mission in *Sūrat al-Ahzab* verse 33:45, which says: 'O Prophet, We have sent you as a witness, a herald of glad tidings and a warner.' He was sent to witness how people yearn for the same result or ultimate destination but they often deviate from the correct path. The Prophet (S) was sent to warn human beings that if they don't begin to see the light of the One, refer to the light of the One, constantly calibrate their sight, their insight, with the Only Light, then they will be misguided. They may have some earthly wisdom but that is not enough. The heart has not come to its foremost joyfulness. The witnesser (*al-Shāhid*) testifies to the fact that all human beings, as the children of Adam, yearn for enduring goodness that lasts. They seek security in every aspect of their lives, yet the reality is that the world itself is not inherently secure. Verse 33:45 continues: 'and give them the good news.' What is the good news? The good news is that there is none other than the One, that you and I and everyone are seeking the same thing. Everything else is shadows that will pass. Nothing is important, except to realise the light of the One. Security ultimately lies in your own heart, in finding solace and contentment through a deep connection to the divine.

You are seeking the sacred light but in your own heart rests your soul. Your soul is a flash of that Sacred Light and you need to respond to it. If you respond only to your mind and your memory and all of the clever animals that are in you (for example, the fox, the wolf, the dog, and the donkey) then you will be overcome by the chaos of your inner zoo. If you respond to the light in your heart, then you will bask in the light of the Creator of all creation. Hear and use your mind but always turn to your heart and bask in the light which is within your heart. Throughout our *dīn* (life transaction; the way of life), we are taught the importance of maintaining a healthy body, nurturing the metaphysical donkey aspect of our being. Further, caring for our mental faculties is vital. However, above all else, nurture the quality of your heart because within that heart lies your soul. If the heart has been purified by a willingness to give away that which is not yours (your lifestyle, possessions and attachments) and if it is ready to move into the next phase, then you will be ready for the turning point of life and death which is the turning point from one phase of consciousness to another. In the womb, you were not conscious of this world so you didn't know that you must work, eat, bathe, and sleep. Birth is the turning point into the earthly consciousness. Similarly, death comes after another turning point into closed death consciousness. These transitions encompass different levels of consciousness.

The key point is that we will get to the same point. Every human being will taste the turning point in consciousness which we call death. Is that a big deal? Are you ready for it? If you are ready then it will not come to you as a shock, but if you are postponing it, delaying it, and scared of it, then of course it will come to you as a shock.

$$\text{وَقَالُوا لَوْ كُنَّا نَسْمَعُ أَوْ نَعْقِلُ مَا كُنَّا فِى أَصْحَابِ السَّعِيرِ ﴿١٠﴾}$$

And they shall say: 'Could we but hear or understand, we would not be among the dwellers of the Blaze.' (67:10)

After hearing, respond with *'aql*, meaning contain yourself, use your intellect. And, tether yourself. What does it mean to tether yourself? Hold yourself back. Ask yourself: why am I doing that, why am I eating too much or too little, or why am I not taking my medication? Put yourself within the boundaries of *'aql*. The origin of the word *'aql* is the number of camels that were used for blood money otherwise tribes would have killed other tribes in a never-ending cycle. The origin of *'aql* is *ma'aql* which is where the camels (which were intended to be given to the tribe as compensation and to stop bloodshed) were detained. *Ma'aql* also means detention centres such as those used by despotic rulers to detain people. In this context, the word *'aql* means that which is going to maintain appropriate boundaries.

$$\text{فَٱعْتَرَفُوا۟ بِذَنۢبِهِمْ فَسُحْقًا لِّأَصْحَـٰبِ ٱلسَّعِيرِ ﴿١١﴾}$$

They will confess their misdeeds. Away with the inhabitants of the blazing fire! (67:11)

The *Qur'an* says that they will ask: 'Why are we in this miserable state of hell?' It is because we did not hear, we did not use *'aql*, meaning we did not use intellect and reason. That is what connects human beings, all over the world. Use your reason. Ask: is it the right place and the right time?

The *Qur'an* takes us, urgently, to our state after death. It says: 'you did not do it then, so you are burning now.'

$$\text{إِنَّ ٱلَّذِينَ يَخْشَوْنَ رَبَّهُم بِٱلْغَيْبِ لَهُم مَّغْفِرَةٌ وَأَجْرٌ كَبِيرٌ ﴿١٢﴾}$$

But they who fear their Lord in the Unseen shall obtain forgiveness and a great reward. (67:12)

I do not want to do something which I will regret for years to come. I do not want to only have success in this world, instead, I want to always be with the light of triumph, which is my soul.

My soul is ever-victorious because it will not die. Allah is ever-triumphant. For this reason, I want to refer to Allah's measures, so that I don't suffer. If not, I will regret it. If I do not regret it in this life and correct my ways, then I will suffer forever after death.

$$\text{وَأَسِرُّوا۟ قَوْلَكُمْ أَوِ ٱجْهَرُوا۟ بِهِۦٓ إِنَّهُۥ عَلِيمٌۢ بِذَاتِ ٱلصُّدُورِ ﴿١٣﴾}$$

Be secret in your speech, or proclaim it, He knows the thoughts within the breasts. (67:13)

Allah knows our intentions, our actions, and our path, whether we choose to be open about it or conceal it. You may pretend you are a pious person and that you have the knowledge, but Allah knows whether you really have it. Your soul knows the truth and you know it. So, who are you hiding from? Don't engage in pretence. Be honest and be open. Admit your fears, acknowledge your flaws, and humbly ask for forgiveness by saying: 'I was fearful, I was in a bad state, and I made a mistake. Please forgive me.' Allah is ever-forgiving but if you keep your shortcomings buried, they will fester and manifest as a cancerous or ulcerous presence. It is crucial to have brothers and sisters whom you trust so that you can confide in them: 'I was silly. I thought I could buy others through money, but I now know I cannot do so.' If a relationship is not based on love and unconditional generosity, it will not lead to fulfilment.

أَلَا يَعْلَمُ مَنْ خَلَقَ وَهُوَ ٱللَّطِيفُ ٱلْخَبِيرُ ﴿١٤﴾

How could He who created not know His own creation, when He is the Most Subtle, the All Aware? (67:14)

This verse refers to two beautiful attributes of Allah namely *Al-Latif* (The Most Subtle) and *Al-Khabir* (The Cognisant, He who knows all, He who has all the wisdom, He who has all the expertise). Don't you know it is He who created you, He who has all those attributes?

هُوَ ٱلَّذِى جَعَلَ لَكُمُ ٱلْأَرْضَ ذَلُولًا فَٱمْشُوا فِى مَنَاكِبِهَا وَكُلُوا مِن رِّزْقِهِ ۖ وَإِلَيْهِ ٱلنُّشُورُ ﴿١٥﴾

He it was Who made the earth subservient to you, so roam its byways and eat of His provisions; to Him is the Resurgence.
(67:15)

In this verse, Allah reminds us of the inherent nature and beauty of the earth we inhabit. We are encouraged to behold its magnificence and to travel, while being mindful not to leave huge footprints or disturb its delicate balance. In Prophetic teaching, we have a great deal of interaction with nature and are taught not to disturb the ecological balance. We must not harm the bird that is singing. On the Day of Judgment, the slain bird will question why it was unjustly killed for enjoyment and sport, while it was singing Allah's praise.

Living our true life transaction; our way of life, according to the Prophet's (S) teachings, requires more than an occasional observance of prayer in congregation on a Friday. It requires us to delve into our spiritual journey, to connect with our inner selves, and to ensure that our words and actions emanate from a place of tranquillity rather than a troubled mind. The essence of our existence is about being aware of the sacred presence that permeates the earth and the heavens, our inner and our outer state as well as this life and death.

The second half of the chapter reminds us that nature, the earth, the heavens and all the seen and the unseen laws, are in perfect harmony. The verses ask us, 'what assurance do we have that the earth will not disintegrate, or that stones will rain upon us from the heavens, as it did for millions of years?'

This chapter gives us a lot of information about what is heaven, what is earth, the ways of Allah, the purpose of His creation and so on. It also provides prescriptions such as what to do to save ourselves from our stupidity, ignorance, and arrogance. There are descriptions, stories, parables and prescriptions in this regard. Here again, you have this idea that you are on earth but the earth is orbiting the sun and the galaxies are drifting at an incredible speed of over 100,000 kilometres an hour into space. With this in mind, what is the basis of your certainty?

وَلَقَدْ كَذَّبَ ٱلَّذِينَ مِن قَبْلِهِمْ فَكَيْفَ كَانَ نَكِيرِ ﴿١٨﴾

Those who went before them also disbelieved – how terrible was My condemnation! (67:18)

أَوَلَمْ يَرَوْا إِلَى ٱلطَّيْرِ فَوْقَهُمْ صَٰٓفَّٰتٍ وَيَقْبِضْنَ مَا يُمْسِكُهُنَّ إِلَّا ٱلرَّحْمَٰنُ إِنَّهُۥ بِكُلِّ شَىْءٍ بَصِيرٌ ﴿١٩﴾

Have they not observed the birds above them, with wings outstretched or clasped? None can restrain them but the All-Merciful. He sees full well all that exists. (67:19)

This second half of the chapter starts with a reminder for us to have *taqwā*, to be cautious, and to not be arrogant. What do you know about what is going to come? What do you know about the future of all humanity and the future of this little earth? There are numerous galaxies and every galaxy has millions of stars and the sun is only one of them. We have to truly take our mind to a point where, when we declare *Allāhu Akbar* (Allah is greater), we know that Allah is greater than we can ever imagine. Allah is beyond our minds. Allah is beyond our reckoning. Allah is beyond our calculation. Here it says: 'but human beings are in denial.'

We are then presented with a description of the nature of the ego-self. *Kadhaba* is to deny, to lie. The ego-self is quick to say no, much like a toddler whose first word is no. The ego-self, which is only a shadow of the soul, begins to have its own personality, so it says, 'no, I don't want to.' Rebellion is its nature. Therefore, verse 67:18 says: 'those before have rejected.'

The Prophetic purpose, the way of Muhammad (S), our life transaction; our way of life is to first witness things as they are. The Prophet (S) often used to pray to Allah to show me things, situations, and relationships as they are. I want to see perfection. How are they? How come they are perfect? Refer to verse 67:3. There is no imperfection. Look and you will find order in chaos. He wanted to see the light of Allah among the shadows of creation. That is *tawhīd* (Unity, Oneness of Allah). If you don't see the one, the two will be confusing as everybody is quarrelling with everybody else.

You need to have a healthy body and clear mind but if the heart is not clear and open, you will not get the light of the soul. Here again, the chapter suddenly takes us to another realm. The verse says, in reference to the birds: How is it that they are in balance? How are they caught with moving their wings up and down? How are they doing that? What is the software, the program in them? It is the command of Allah that makes them do that.

$$\text{أَمَّنْ هَٰذَا ٱلَّذِى هُوَ جُندٌ لَّكُمْ يَنصُرُكُم مِّن دُونِ ٱلرَّحْمَٰنِ ۚ إِنِ ٱلْكَٰفِرُونَ إِلَّا فِى غُرُورٍ ۝}$$

Who is it who can act as your troops, to bring you aid, apart from the All-Merciful? The unbelievers are merely living in illusion. (67:20)

The key part of this verse is contained in the last bit. Certainly, *kāfir* is he who covers up the truth. He denies the truth that we are here only to discover the light of Allah. How can you worship something or an entity unless you come to know it more? And how do you know it? He who knows himself knows his Lord. You know the lower self is treacherous and satanic but the light that shows us that it is satanic is from *Al-Rahmān* (The Merciful). This verse refers to those who deny the truth, those who cover up the truth and those who are in darkness. The noun *ghuroor* means *shaytān* (satan; ego-self) and it also implies pride, arrogance and status.

The biggest flaw that Christianity identified in the Romans was status and honour. Roman law included a governance system which involved having a representative of the population, called senators. For hundreds of years and in the peak of the Roman Empire, senators were honoured people in the land. They donated public baths, theatres, facilities and aqueducts to the people. And more importantly, they arranged entertainment, mainly using gladiators and the circus. For this, they held a high and lofty status. Eventually the senators were rebuked by the Christians who implored them to, 'be humble, you do not have to have honour, and you must not have pride.' But they could not work it out, so their solution was to kill the Christians. This continued until Constantine's reign in the year 312 when he found Christianity useful to get rid of the other emperors.

So, we are reminded to be wary of *ghururin* meaning pride and pompousness, of honour and superficial dignity. And yet, we Muslims crave honour and status. How often have you heard Muslims say 'Don't you know I am chief?' Imam Zain ul Abidin (AS) was often heard saying 'Oh Allah don't let them admire me and lift me unless I see within myself my faults, so I balance it.' We are all going to die and leave this world. What can we take with us? To what extent have we emptied ourselves (see *Surah as-Sharh* verse, 94:7, how empty are you?) to let the light in our souls guides us?

$$ أَمَّنْ هَٰذَا ٱلَّذِى يَرْزُقُكُمْ إِنْ أَمْسَكَ رِزْقَهُۥ ۚ بَل لَّجُّوا۟ فِى عُتُوٍّ وَنُفُورٍ ﴿٢١﴾ $$

Or who is it who can provide for you if He withholds His provision? They have assuredly sunk deep in obstinacy and aversion from truth. (67:21)

Rizq is provision for food, air, water, knowledge, light, understanding and conduct. The verse mentions that in spite of all of these provisions that come from Allah, people have persisted in insolence and aversion. They think: 'I am independent, I can do this, my father provides for me or the bank manager provides for me.' Yet nothing comes from anyone other than Allah. *Sūrat al-A'raaf* verse 7:188 states: 'Say: 'I have no power to do myself good or harm save as Allah wills.' Nobody can ever pretend to be independent. We are all dependent upon Allah, upon the light of Allah and upon Allah's agent in us which is the soul. He says if your provision is withheld, who is going to give it to you? Further, provision may be available but you may not benefit from it. Knowledge is around you, but you may not be able to receive it or be transformed by it. Food may be accessible, yet you may not be able to swallow it.

It takes a harmonious orchestration of circumstances for us to be able to benefit from the provision. We are all entirely dependent on the mercy of Allah. *Sūrat al-Mulk* says every aspect of governance and creational multiplicities are under His control. He is the ultimate ruler of these dominions, layer after layer, dominions on earth, heavens and in between. Can we contemplate that in an instant we could be rendered unable to swallow? Imagine if your throat passage suddenly blocked? I have known people who were suddenly unable to eat in the last few days of their lives and who succumbed to starvation despite being well until then. Is there a predictable time for leaving this world?

أَفَمَن يَمْشِى مُكِبًّا عَلَى وَجْهِهِۦٓ أَهْدَىٰٓ أَمَّن يَمْشِى سَوِيًّا عَلَىٰ صِرَٰطٍ مُّسْتَقِيمٍ ٢٢

What! Is he who goes prone upon his face better guided or he who walks upright upon a straight path? (67:22)

Allah is questioning whether it is the same for those who know – those who truly refer to Allah – relative to those who are absent-minded. Is their level of commitment and consciousness the same? Perhaps the latter group attend the masjid every Friday or once in a while they say *Astaghfiru'llah*. But can they be compared?

The *mithāl* (similitude) used here is beautiful. Can we consider a person who humbles themselves with their face on the ground in submission to Allah, to be the same as someone who walks upright, oblivious to the signs and messages around them? Can someone consumed by their ego be equated to one seeking the divine light?

Some want to know the light, while others remain confined to the limitations of a biological and physiological existence. But are you truly alive? Are you ready to say *Allāhu Akbar* (Allah is greater) and relinquish attachments because you believe in the continuation of life after death? If you are, then joy awaits you.

So what purpose does misery, anger and disappointment serve in our lives? That is the purpose of our *'ibadah* (worship), the purpose of our life transaction; our way of life. It is to awaken us to the truth that we are meant to exist in this world but not be consumed by it.

قُلْ هُوَٱلَّذِىٓ أَنشَأَكُمْ وَجَعَلَ لَكُمُ ٱلسَّمْعَ وَٱلْأَبْصَٰرَ وَٱلْأَفْـِٔدَةَ قَلِيلًا مَّا تَشْكُرُونَ ﴿٢٣﴾

Say: 'It is He Who brought you into being, Who provided you with hearing, sight and hearts, but little thanks do you give.
(67:23)

The most important word in this verse is *al-afidati*, the plural of *fu'ad*. *Fu'ad* is the innermost part of the *qalb* (heart, *qalb* is not a physical organ but an inner faculty). There are hundreds of verses about *qalb* which convey to us that there are at least nine different levels of the sickness of the heart. However, there are select references in the Qu'ran about *fu'ad* such as *Sūrat an-Najm* verse 53:11, The yearning heart (fu'ad) did not distort what it saw. The *fu'ad* will never lie to you and it is not affected by emotion. When people say 'my heart told me,' many do not know what they are talking about. Similarly, if you love something, you are blind because that love will make you blind (for example, a mother's love for her sick child).

Consider also *Sūrat al-Furqan* verse 25:32, which says: 'Those who disbelieve say: 'If only the Qur'an had been sent down upon him whole and undivided!' Rather, to confirm your heart (fu'ad) with it! And We made it to be chanted, a sublime chant! or *Sūrat al-Isra* verse 17:36, which says: 'hearing, sight and the heart (fu'ad) – all of these a person shall be questioned about.' *Fu'ad* is the ultimate level from which the soul shines because the dwelling place of the soul is the heart and the innermost recesses of the heart is *fu'ad*. It is a very important cosmology to realise.

قُلْ هُوَٱلَّذِى ذَرَأَكُمْ فِى ٱلْأَرْضِ وَإِلَيْهِ تُحْشَرُونَ ﴿٢٤﴾

'Say: 'He it is Who multiplied you in the earth and to Him you shall be gathered.' (67:24)

وَيَقُولُونَ مَتَىٰ هَٰذَا ٱلْوَعْدُ إِن كُنتُمْ صَٰدِقِينَ ﴿٢٥﴾

They say, 'When shall this promise come to pass, if you speak truly?' (67:25)

قُلْ إِنَّمَا ٱلْعِلْمُ عِندَ ٱللَّهِ وَإِنَّمَآ أَنَا۠ نَذِيرٌ مُّبِينٌ ﴿٢٦﴾

Say: 'The knowledge thereof is only with Allah and I am only a plain warner.' (67:26)

Here again, we have these three verses which tell us about the beginning and the end, life and death. Allah says: 'He, who has brought you into the earth, spread you out in the earth, to Him you will return or towards Him you will return.' Then the lower self, which is always in objection and denial, says, 'when will this happen?' The answer is: 'Only Allah knows, only He has knowledge of that timing.'

Denial is how we choose to live because we are not willing to die. If we are willing to die (as the Prophet (S) always reminds us to 'die before you die,') then every day is a bonus, every day is Eid, with another opportunity to embrace the truth. In this verse, Allah describes the Prophet (S) as 'a Warner for you'.

فَلَمَّا رَأَوْهُ زُلْفَةً سِيٓئَتْ وُجُوهُ ٱلَّذِينَ كَفَرُواْ وَقِيلَ هَٰذَا ٱلَّذِى كُنتُم بِهِۦ تَدَّعُونَ ﴿٢٧﴾

But when they see it coming near, the faces of unbelievers will grow sorrowful, and it shall be said: 'This is what you asked for.' (67:27)

قُلْ أَرَءَيْتُمْ إِنْ أَهْلَكَنِىَ ٱللَّهُ وَمَن مَّعِىَ أَوْ رَحِمَنَا فَمَن يُجِيرُ ٱلْكَـٰفِرِينَ مِنْ عَذَابٍ أَلِيمٍ ﴿٢٨﴾

Say: 'Consider this. Should Allah make me perish, along with those who are with me, or else should He show us His mercy, Who shall offer refuge to the blasphemers from a painful punishment?' (67:28)

Zul'fā is an important word which means closeness. We ask: 'When will this closeness manifest? When will it come?' The answer lies in other verses in the *Qur'an*, for example, *Sūrat Ash-Shu'ara* verse 26:90, 'The Garden shall be drawn near to the pious,' This signals that *Janna* and that state is close to those who are in cautious awareness. The state (the *Hāl*) that you experience which may be described as blissfulness, happiness, contentment, or serenity is already there, but we are otherwise occupied so we cannot plug into it. The *Qur'an* emphasises that at the point of death, or at the metaphorical death in this world, when we are ready to surrender ourselves completely, paradise becomes *uz'lifat*, meaning it becomes close to us (see also *Sūrat al-Qāf* verse 50:31).

Allah is the First (nothing precedes Him) and the Last (nothing is after Him), the Most High (nothing is above Him) and the Most Near (nothing is nearer than Him) (see *Sūrat al-Hadīd* verse 57:3). It is incorrect to say that Allah is far away. When we refer to Allah, many of us point to the heavens. What about the earth, what about the signs? We must recognise that there is nothing in existence, known and unknown, unless the light of Allah is in it, within it, preceding it and succeeding it. So, on the day of reckoning, who else is going to offer help or guidance to save the *Kāfirūn*? Who is going to help those who have in this life denied the truth of *Lā ilāha illā Allāh*? By referring to Allah, and by recognising His presence, we will dispel the inner *shaytān* (satan; ego-self).

قُلْ هُوَ ٱلرَّحْمَنُ ءَامَنَّا بِهِۦ وَعَلَيْهِ تَوَكَّلْنَا فَسَتَعْلَمُونَ مَنْ هُوَ فِى ضَلَٰلٍ مُّبِينٍ ﴿٢٩﴾

*Say: 'He is the All-Merciful. We believe in Him, and in Him
we put all our trust. Assuredly, you will soon, know who is in
manifest error.' (67:29)*

Aman is security, certainty, trust, and reliance – a state we aspire
to attain. It is a reliance upon that which is unseen, while recognising
that Allah has granted us the gift of sight. Allah is the seer, the perfect
seer, and I trust in that. This means I do what I can and I trust that
Allah will show me what I need to be shown. Consider the incident
when the Prophet (S) saw a man leaving his camel without tying it
and asked: 'How are you?' (or, more literally, what is your state?')
The man replied: 'I have *tawakkul*' (trust in Allah). The Prophet (S)
said: 'First tether your camel, do what you can as a caretaker of it
and then leave the rest to Allah. Do not carry the entire burden with
you thereafter.' We must strike a balance between taking action and
relying on Allah's guidance.

In life we may feel a sense of regret or wish we had done more.
However it is not our concern to burden ourselves with such thoughts.
Our focus should be on being present in the moment and practicing
hudhūr (presence). Don't be taken aback by adversity. Speak but
don't be shaken. Question what you are doing, and what your *niyya*
(intention) is and be accountable so you can be free from your lower
self.

قُلْ أَرَءَيْتُمْ إِنْ أَصْبَحَ مَآؤُكُمْ غَوْرًا فَمَن يَأْتِيكُم بِمَآءٍ مَّعِينٍ ﴿٣٠﴾

*Say, 'Consider this. If your water is swallowed up by the earth,
who will bring you water from a spring that is pure? (67:30)*

This incredible verse concludes this glorious chapter. What if
your water source runs dry or flows out beyond your reach? We have

witnessed how water disappears in the sand or the desert. It has no foundation. If it is not stable, you cannot make use of it. Imagine if nature was not based on the laws of gravity and viscosity? How would you have lived? This magnificent chapter tells us Allah is the ultimate authority over all creation. As human beings, when we recognise this, we gain profound insight.

We must develop insight. Begin by acknowledging the presence of pain and then delve deeper to discern its purpose, for within it lies perfection. In *Sūrat ash-Sharh* verse 94:6, Allah says: 'Truly where there is hardship there is also ease.' Herein lies the interplay between the heavens and the earth. We are earthly, made of mud, but we are also heavenly because we have a soul, elevating us in rank above the angels. We are capable of being lower than the lowest and we are also capable of being higher than the highest. Reflecting on our origins, we see that everything was once lifeless and then came the force that infused life into existence. Ultimately, all will return to the original state. That is the first thunderous disintegration and then again there will be the rise of life without will. At that point, we cannot do anything. However, we will be held accountable for what we have accumulated in our spiritual reservoir. The objectives we should aspire to achieve in this life are self-abandonment, soul submission, and the realisation that there is only one Master, one ultimate authority.

This chapter is truly remarkable. As I mentioned earlier, there are numerous other Makkan chapters such as *Sūrat ar-Rahmān* (chapter 55) and *Sūrat al-Insān* (chapter 76). While the number of Makkan chapters exceeds the number of Madinan chapters, they are much shorter in length and most of them address the issues of *haqīqah* and human responsibility. The Madinan chapters describe the structure of the life transaction; the way of life, and the obligation for us to perform our duties towards ourselves, our brothers and sisters, our communities, and humanity as a whole. With this we can become worthy of the title Muslims, and embrace the delight of being *mū'minin*(believers), and the ecstasy of living life as believers.

Chapter 8

SURAT AL-BALAD

Qur'anic Verses

The Arabic text and the English translation of *Sūrat al-Balad(90)* follows immediately below. Thereafter I will focus my commentary on selected verses and words.

$$\text{بِسْمِ اللَّهِ الرَّحْمَٰنِ الرَّحِيمِ ﴿١﴾}$$

In the name of Allah, the Merciful to all, the Compassionate to each!

$$\text{لَا أُقْسِمُ بِهَٰذَا الْبَلَدِ ﴿١﴾}$$

1. *No indeed! I swear by this City.*

$$\text{وَأَنتَ حِلٌّ بِهَٰذَا الْبَلَدِ ﴿٢﴾}$$

2. *While you live in this City!*

وَوَالِدٍ وَمَا وَلَدَ ۝٣

3. *By a begetter and what he begot!*

لَقَدْ خَلَقْنَا ٱلْإِنسَـٰنَ فِى كَبَدٍ ۝٤

4. *We have created man in hardship.*

أَيَحْسَبُ أَن لَّن يَقْدِرَ عَلَيْهِ أَحَدٌ ۝٥

5. *Does he imagine that none can over-power him?*

يَقُولُ أَهْلَكْتُ مَالًا لُّبَدًا ۝٦

6. *He says, 'I have squandered great wealth.'*

أَيَحْسَبُ أَن لَّمْ يَرَهُۥٓ أَحَدٌ ۝٧

7. *Does he think none has seen him?*

أَلَمْ نَجْعَل لَّهُۥ عَيْنَيْنِ ۝٨

8. *Did We not give him two eyes?*

وَلِسَانًا وَشَفَتَيْنِ ۝٩

9. *A tongue and two lips?*

وَهَدَيْنَهُ ٱلنَّجْدَيْنِ ﴿١٠﴾

10. And point out to him the two clear ways.

فَلَا ٱقْتَحَمَ ٱلْعَقَبَةَ ﴿١١﴾

11. Yet he has not attempted the steep path.

وَمَآ أَدْرَىٰكَ مَا ٱلْعَقَبَةُ ﴿١٢﴾

12. What will explain to you what the steep path is?

فَكُّ رَقَبَةٍ ﴿١٣﴾

13. It is to free a slave.

أَوْ إِطْعَـٰمٌ فِى يَوْمٍ ذِى مَسْغَبَةٍ ﴿١٤﴾

14. Or feeding, in time of famine.

يَتِيمًا ذَا مَقْرَبَةٍ ﴿١٥﴾

15. An orphan near in kin.

أَوۡ مِسۡكِينٗا ذَا مَتۡرَبَةٖ ﴿١٦﴾

16. *Or a poor person in distress.*

ثُمَّ كَانَ مِنَ ٱلَّذِينَ ءَامَنُواْ وَتَوَاصَوۡاْ بِٱلصَّبۡرِ وَتَوَاصَوۡاْ بِٱلۡمَرۡحَمَةِ ﴿١٧﴾

17. *Then he is of those who believe and charge one another to show patience, and charge one another to show compassion.*

أُوْلَٰٓئِكَ أَصۡحَٰبُ ٱلۡمَيۡمَنَةِ ﴿١٨﴾

18. *Such are they that have attained to righteousness;*

وَٱلَّذِينَ كَفَرُواْ بِئَايَٰتِنَا هُمۡ أَصۡحَٰبُ ٱلۡمَشۡئَمَةِ ﴿١٩﴾

19. *whereas those who disbelieve Our signs they are such as have lost themselves in evil.*

Commentary on Selected Verses

$$\lambda\bar{\imath} \,\text{...}$$

No indeed! I swear by this City. (90:1)

Sūrat al-Balad (The City) is an early Makkan chapter. Most historians and commentators say it is probably the fourth or fifth revealed chapter. That said, some say part of it was revealed later. The word *balad* means town, city, or country. In this chapter, City refers to Makkah and its surrounding area. The verse emphasises the significance of the city where Prophet Muhammad (S) was born. As the son of that city, he possesses a special responsibility and freedom to act in a manner that is appropriate for that city. His connection to the city is intertwined with his connection to the Creator, granting him freedom to fulfil his divine purpose within that context.

While you live in this City! (90:2)

Allah addresses the Prophet (S), saying: You are the voice of *Haqq* (truth), meaning you are only doing that which is appropriate. So you, oh Muhammad (S)—who has been appointed the recipient of the ever-present Divine Light, Divine Connection, Divine Command— are free because you are not speaking from yourself.

By a begetter and what he begot! (90:3)

'The begetter and the begotten,' in this verse is a reference to the cause-and-effect pattern that all situations in life follow. Here it does not reference a father or a mother; it means either because both are the root of a subsequent generation. Here the gender disappears, so the insinuation here could be *Nabi Allah*, Ibrahim (AS) because he was the founder or the builder of the first *Ka'bah* 4,000 years ago. It could also refer to Adam (AS), and could also, though it is less likely, be a reference to Prophet Muhammad (S). He was the founder of the new community that arose. The inner meaning (the *ishāra*) of this verse is that there cannot be a beginning without leading to something else. There cannot be a cause without an effect.

The *latīf* (the subtle, innate, sensitive) in every one of us is constantly producing or doing something that is the cause of something else. The truth, the *haqīqa*, is that Allah is the cause, the provider of the energy of every action. We are responsible for our actions but Allah designed those patterns in the unseen, and you and I must exercise caution. What are we planning to do? What are we going to say? We will be responsible for the action and the outcome of it, but Allah is the designer of it all.

$$\text{لَقَدْ خَلَقْنَا الْإِنسَٰنَ فِى كَبَدٍ ﴿٤﴾}$$

We have created man in hardship. (90:4)

The situation of the human being is one of toiling. *Insān* (Humankind) is he who seeks solace, ease and comfort. Its root word *anisa* (to be companionable, friendly, to like to be together) is similar to the word *nasiya*, which means 'to forget', denoting one aspect of man's nature. We are all forgetful and our forgetfulness teaches us humility and it shows us we are not infallible. Each one of us is likely to make an outer mistake but the more we refer to the inner light, the more we find that even our mistakes can be good. It can provide us with a useful lesson or an indication for us to return, which are mere reminders for us to be in constant awareness of

Allah's presence. We are a composite, meaning, a combination of *rūh* (soul) and *nafs* (ego-self). We are constantly being challenged in this world, constantly being given certain difficulties and afflictions, and its up to us to do what we can to help ourselves, in the outer sense. The *Qur'an* prescribes that once we have done so we should say 'Oh Allah, I do not know what to do, I have asked, I have taken counsel, I am helpless, you are the guide, the teacher. Please show me what to do.' We cannot deny that we are physical, material and biographical. We have a beginning and we have an end. Yet Allah tells us that our soul endures beyond that which our physical bodies can. So we are a combination of both physical and spiritual. This is why we experience *kabad* (difficulty). The liver, which is associated with the concept of *kabad*, purifies our blood. Similarly, this world is for us to learn how to discern and reject that which is not appropriate, and to embrace and affirm the foundation of *lā ilāha illā Allāh*. We must constantly purify ourselves by saying no to behaviour that leads to difficulty and afflictions and say yes to that which shows us, increasingly, the route to harmony and the inner heart, the foundation of *lā ilāha illā Allāh*.

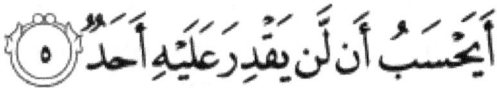

$$\text{أَيَحْسَبُ أَن لَّن يَقْدِرَ عَلَيْهِ أَحَدٌ ۝}$$

Does he imagine that none can over-power him? (90:5)

If you are in a good state, making good money, or are approved of by your family then you may think you are invincible. Many of us experience such moments from time to time. Even great leaders have gone through times when they have said: 'I thought that there was nothing that I could not do'. It may feel like heaven to have earth at your command, but of course, it does not last because heaven and earth belong to Allah. We may have been given a taste of heaven but we must never lose sight. Allah may have given you these gifts to test whether you are aware of the One. Are you mindful of the One? Are you maintaining your humility in the face of success? If not, the higher you fly the greater the fall.

113

يَقُولُ أَهْلَكْتُ مَالًا لُّبَدًا ٦

He says, 'I have squandered great wealth.' (90:6)

أَيَحْسَبُ أَن لَّمْ يَرَهُ أَحَدٌ ٧

Does he think none has seen him? (90:7)

Verse 90:5 says: Do you think that there is nothing higher than you? And verse 90:7 says: Do you think that nobody sees you? Here Allah is advising us to reflect upon ourselves and see ourselves in our inner mirror.

The inner heart contains the *raqib* (that which is recorded). Allah tells us in the *Qur'an* repeatedly: You are coming into reckoning with the *raqib*, with that which is recorded (see for example *Sūrat al-Ibrāhīm* verse 14:51). Let us reflect upon that before it is too late. How is it possible for us not to realise that we are constantly being watched by Allah? Allah sees us. Allah knows what is going on. It is also up to us to realise what is going on so that we do not develop a split personality. I think of something yet my heart wishes for something else or I say something and yet I mean something different. If you are not one, how can you talk about the One? Being on our path is about the One and only One.

Allah has given us the duality. But He created twos and multiples in order for us to realise that there is the One behind all. The entire package of our *dīn* (life transaction; way of life) is based on *tawhīd* (oneness). There is only One Creator, One Sustainer, One Maintainer, and from that One, comes infinite varieties of twos that appear to be opposing, good and bad. Allah transcends any small goodness or any small badness, because He is the epitome of goodness, the Absolute. Everything else is relative. Every relative light is a manifestation emanating from the Perfect Light. Do not deny the relativeness; understanding it is a step closer to the truth. However, Allah surpasses all those distinctions. By referring to this – and by recognising His supreme position – we are all humbled. In the bigger scheme of things, these dualities and relative matters are insignificant in the eye of Allah. But understanding them does help us maintain our reverence and humility.

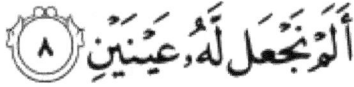

أَلَمْ نَجْعَل لَّهُۥ عَيْنَيْنِ ﴿٨﴾

Did We not give him two eyes? (90:8)

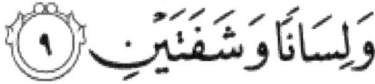

وَلِسَانًا وَشَفَتَيْنِ ﴿٩﴾

A tongue and two lips? (90:9)

So many of our faculties are in pairs. We have two hands, two legs, and two eyes and apart from the two physical eyes you also have sight and there is insight. But then, there are other organs that are one, such as the tongue, so that we don't fool around, instead speak with what is truly in our hearts. We are advised by the Prophetic teaching: 'let your tongue be behind your heart.' Don't just jabber. First question your head then see what is truly in your heart and thereafter you may speak. That is why the tongue is locked behind two lips and two sets of teeth, to remind you to be cautious. In addition, once you have said something you cannot retract it. How many times have you hurt other people by saying something that you did not mean? Isn't that unfortunate? It means you are distracted, and distraction is the door to destruction. Be aware of the impact of your words, be in *wudhū'* (a state of ritual ablution), and know that Allah sees you and that all you do and think is recorded in you. So, before you speak, consider whether it is the right time and the right place. Do you have the right intention? Do you speak with love for others who are less fortunate? Are you saying it out of love to uplift others? Reflect in this way so that you are constantly serving, meaning that you are constantly stepping beside yourself to reflect upon yourself.

$$وَهَدَيْنَٰهُ ٱلنَّجْدَيْنِ ﴿١٠﴾$$

And point out to him the two clear ways. (90:10)

$$فَلَا ٱقْتَحَمَ ٱلْعَقَبَةَ ﴿١١﴾$$

Yet he has not attempted the steep path. (90:11)

$$وَمَآ أَدْرَىٰكَ مَا ٱلْعَقَبَةُ ﴿١٢﴾$$

What will explain to you what the steep path is? (90:12)

The *Qur'an* tells us, that the reason for all of this is so that you can overcome obstacles. Yet how many people overcome these obstacles? Not many people can overcome the *'aqabah*. *'Aqabah* is a high ground which is difficult to climb and becomes restricted. From it comes *'iqāb* which also means punishment. Can you overcome the obstacle? The Prophet (S) teaches us repeatedly that the biggest obstacle in your life is that which is in your breast, meaning the *nafs*. How can I overcome my ego-self? By serving and helping others. How can I get out of my prison? By trying to help those enslaved by their attachments. Slavery is not a historical thing. It is not over. Most of us are enslaved by our work, our houses, our desires, and our status. There are various levels of enslavement including economic enslavement, political enslavement, social enslavement, and many others.

These forms of challenges are all part of the *'aqabah* and the *Qur'an* provides the solutions. Approach it in a bereft state because it is a treasure. The outer treasure is the classical Arabic description, however, if you want to discover the inner treasure then you must approach it as a *miskīn*, bereft and humble person, not as a challenger. Allah will not allow the test of challenge. You and I must give up. We must stop this pretence that we exist in separation from His control. We must yield; we must be in *Islām* (submission) and we must have *Imān* (certainty and security that Allah knows and Allah sees) and then the *Ihsān* (inner and outer excellence in thought and conduct) will prevail. Do you know what this *'aqabah* (high ground) is? The *Qur'an* answers it for us.

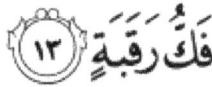

$$\text{فَكُّ رَقَبَةٍ} \quad (١٣)$$

It is to free a slave. (90:13)

You are a slave, so you have to free your neck from your illusions, delusions, and fantasies. In addition, if you find somebody who has been enslaved by any other means, traditionally, historically, or otherwise, then release the neck. Several verses in the *Qur'an* tell us when the neck has been lowered or weighed down by chains. When a person is heavily weighted down with debt, problems or troubles they will have their head lowered. Those who trust in the mercy of Allah and in experiencing the mercy of Allah, even when there is difficulty against them, have their neck up, meaning they are cheerful.

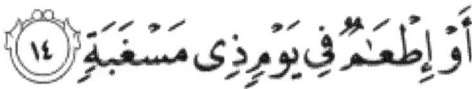

$$\text{أَوْ إِطْعَامٌ فِي يَوْمٍ ذِي مَسْغَبَةٍ} \quad (١٤)$$

Or feeding, in time of famine. (90:14)

There are four levels of nourishment implied in this verse. First, if somebody is hungry, they will not be able to see any other mercy, so begin with satisfying that hunger. Thereafter, one can satisfy the nourishment of the heart and nourishment of the mind. We are all concerned with our children's education. This refers to their nourishment of skills, knowledge, and information. Then there are higher levels of nourishment and the knowledge that Allah knows until you ultimately know *Haqq*.

These are all forms of nourishment. First, attend to the nourishment of the body and the basic need for shelter. There is more of the outer for us to attend to compared with the inner, so it is out of balance in a sense. The outer rituals, the outer *sharī'a* (revealed law or code of conduct) are essential, but if they are not complemented with inner awakening and transformation, we will end up out of balance. Imbalance in our lives is not the fault of the life transaction; the way of life, it is not the fault of the prophetic teaching, and it is not the fault of the *Qur'an*. It is our fault because we have not put the right balance together. Accept the outer until you are constantly concerned about the inner and then you will find the outer and the inner are never separable. Heaven and earth are never separated.

$$\text{يَتِيمًا ذَا مَقْرَبَةٍ} \,\, ١٥$$

An orphan near in kin. (90:15)

$$\text{أَوْ مِسْكِينًا ذَا مَتْرَبَةٍ} \,\, ١٦$$

Or a poor person in distress. (90:16)

Again, consider Allah's mercy. Some of the Prophets we know about in a biographical sense were orphans. They were sons of the community, the sons of Adam (AS), but they were not from strong families. They may have had a tribe or an extended family, but they did not have a nuclear family with a father and a mother, so they grew up in the care of uncles, aunts and others. Their concerns extended beyond themselves and encompassed society, their nation and all of humanity.

In truth, we are all *yatīm* (orphans). We have come to this world wanting to discover the true meaning of life, the correct guidance and the proper way to conduct ourselves. This doesn't negate the importance of our personal family situation but it emphasises that our families should expand to become communities, societies, nations, and into ultimately *rahmatal lil'aalameen* (a mercy to the world). We can't do this if our focus remains solely on our enclosed family unit, and if we fail to consider the well-being of our neighbours. Allah reminds us: 'Do not ever think that perpetrators of mischief will not afflict others who have no part in it but who are nearby (8:25).' It is our duty to try to put out fires and mischief, no matter where they are. We cannot have an ordered home while our neighbours are immersed in chaos and disorder.

Balad refers to a town, city, or nation. *Miskīn* (which is from *sakana* and means 'to be or become still, tranquil, peaceful; to calm down, repose, rest) is a person who has no home. However, you can also become metaphorically *miskīn* by confining yourself to your home and not showing regard for those around you, including your neighbours. Balance is crucial, meaning you need moments of relaxation and periods of activity. You need to sleep, and you need to be awake as everything in existence consists of two: active/inactive, outer/inner. The *Qur'an* also names outer and inner poverty, recognising different levels of material and spiritual destitution.

We must do our best to reduce outer poverty but we must recognise that the persistence of this issue is rooted in the inner poverty of many wealthy people. The inner impoverishment of rich nations is perpetuating global poverty, leading to a situation where 80% of the world's wealth is held by 5% of wealthy people. It is out of balance and unjust, but it is not advisable to respond by instigating chaos and revolutions. Instead, we must understand the principle that those who are trying to accumulate outer wealth are also in need of inner wealth. By cultivating greater inner wealth they will be inclined to distribute outer wealth more equitably. More is not always better, sometimes less is more.

$$\text{ثُمَّ كَانَ مِنَ ٱلَّذِينَ ءَامَنُواْ وَتَوَاصَوْاْ بِٱلصَّبْرِ وَتَوَاصَوْاْ بِٱلْمَرْحَمَةِ ۝}$$

Then he is of those who believe and charge one another to show patience, and charge one another to show compassion. **(90:17)**

Those who believe are those who have submitted to the truth and realise that Allah has created us in this world to realise that His *nūr* (light) penetrates everything. While each of us is like a walking city, it is only so by the grace of Allah who has put the light which is the soul, within our hearts. We need to be concerned about the external elements of life for us to grasp the internal aspects so that we see the unity of it all. Once we have this understanding, we are ready to detach ourselves from it all as Allah has brought us here to complete the *'ibadah* (adoration of Allah, worship). What does it mean to complete the worship? It is to behold the One amidst the duality. By recognising the One light that exists within, before and after all things, and by bearing witness to the pluralities, dualities, and opposing forces of existence, we are guided.

We all want to be certain that Allah's light is there. If we perfect our worship, are humble and ask Allah, the answers will come and all will be well. Rather than be in a state of anger and blame others, we ought to recognise them as messages from Allah. This is the difference and Allah describes it as follows:

$$\text{أُوْلَٰٓئِكَ أَصْحَٰبُ ٱلْمَيْمَنَةِ ۝}$$

Such are they that have attained to righteousness; **(90:18)**

This describes those who follow the right path. The two highways were mentioned earlier. One of them is the highway of righteousness and correctness and the other is of misery, affliction, denial (*kufr*) and blaming everybody else except ourselves. We must free ourselves from presumptions to be in the company of the companions of the right hand.

$$وَٱلَّذِينَ كَفَرُواْ بِـَٔايَـٰتِنَا هُمْ أَصْحَـٰبُ ٱلْمَشْـَٔمَةِ ۝١٩$$

whereas those who disbelieve Our signs they are such as have lost themselves in evil. (90:19)

The signs within us as well as the signs on the horizon are all Allah's signs. Whenever an experience or event has occurred, consider it a sign. Allah enabled it to occur. It may be a terrible event, but we must do something about it and then consider its roots and not expect an immediate remedy. We are witness to a rise in poverty, abuse, injustice and cruelty in this world, but we cannot put it right immediately. We can begin by working on what is closer to us which is our cruelty towards ourselves, our family, and others; and then it will begin to grow, as it did during the time of the Prophet (S). Within a period of less than 80 years, the entire world was illuminated by that light and then, later on, there were many other occasions when people lived their *Imān* and lived their *Qur'an*. In this way, we experience the garden here and now. The alternative is to experience hell, which we inadvertently create. This is Allah's mercy. He has given us this apparent choice but in truth, we have no choice for we all seek the garden.

I pray to Allah to make us people of the garden. I pray to Allah to make us worthy of our *Islām* (submission). I pray to Allah to make us all worthy of *Imān* (certainty and security that Allah knows, and Allah sees). I pray to Allah to make us be in that state of perpetual giving of that which we want to keep. In every way I pray for all of you as I pray for myself.

Chapter 9

SURAT AL INSAN

Sūrat al-Insān(76) is also referred to as *Sūrat ad-Dahr*. It is among the chapters which were revealed partly during the Madinah period and partly in Makkah. Interestingly, it encompasses both *haqīqah* (Truth, the realm of meaning) as well as *sharī'a* (the realm of senses); but it also highlights the story of humankind, the meaning of the human being, the purpose in this life, the awareness of the permanent and that which passes by. It's a great chapter which gives us a map of human nature.

My comments on some of the verses highlight how we can use the *Qur'an* as a manual on how to change our attitude, how information can lead to transformation, and how the voice of truth from beyond time and space can be applied in our lives within time and space.

Qur'anic Verses

The Arabic text and the English translation of *Sūrat al-Insān* follow immediately below. Thereafter I will focus my commentary on selected verses and words.

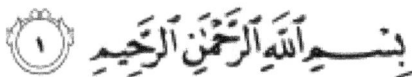

بِسۡـــمِ ٱللَّهِ ٱلرَّحۡمَٰنِ ٱلرَّحِيمِ ۝

In the name of Allah, the Merciful to all, the Compassionate to each!

هَلْ أَتَىٰ عَلَى ٱلْإِنسَٰنِ حِينٌ مِّنَ ٱلدَّهْرِ لَمْ يَكُن شَيْئًا مَّذْكُورًا ﴿١﴾

1. *Surely there came upon man a span of time, when he was a thing not worth remembering!*

إِنَّا خَلَقْنَا ٱلْإِنسَٰنَ مِن نُّطْفَةٍ أَمْشَاجٍ نَّبْتَلِيهِ فَجَعَلْنَٰهُ سَمِيعًا بَصِيرًا ﴿٢﴾

2. *We created man from a drop of mingled fluid to put him to the test; We gave him hearing and sight;*

إِنَّا هَدَيْنَٰهُ ٱلسَّبِيلَ إِمَّا شَاكِرًا وَإِمَّا كَفُورًا ﴿٣﴾

3. *We guided him upon the way, be he grateful or ungrateful.*

إِنَّا أَعْتَدْنَا لِلْكَٰفِرِينَ سَلَٰسِلَا۟ وَأَغْلَٰلًا وَسَعِيرًا ﴿٤﴾

4. *Surely, We have prepared for the unbelievers chains and shackles and a burning fire.*

إِنَّ ٱلْأَبْرَارَ يَشْرَبُونَ مِن كَأْسٍ كَانَ مِزَاجُهَا كَافُورًا ﴿٥﴾

5. *But the righteous shall drink from a cup mixed with choicest fragrance,*

عَيْنًا يَشْرَبُ بِهَا عِبَادُ ٱللَّهِ يُفَجِّرُونَهَا تَفْجِيرًا ﴿٦﴾

6. *A spring for Allah's servants, which flows abundantly at their wish.*

يُوفُونَ بِٱلنَّذْرِ وَيَخَافُونَ يَوْمًا كَانَ شَرُّهُ مُسْتَطِيرًا ۝٧

7. *They fulfil vows and fear a day the evil of which shall be spreading far and wide.*

وَيُطْعِمُونَ ٱلطَّعَامَ عَلَىٰ حُبِّهِ مِسْكِينًا وَيَتِيمًا وَأَسِيرًا ۝٨

8. *And they give food out of love for Him to the poor and the orphan and the captive:*

إِنَّمَا نُطْعِمُكُمْ لِوَجْهِ ٱللَّهِ لَا نُرِيدُ مِنكُمْ جَزَآءً وَلَا شُكُورًا ۝٩

9. *we only feed you for Allah's sake; we desire from you neither reward nor thanks:*

إِنَّا نَخَافُ مِن رَّبِّنَا يَوْمًا عَبُوسًا قَمْطَرِيرًا ۝١٠

10. *For we fear from our Lord a frowning day, inauspicious.*

فَوَقَىٰهُمُ ٱللَّهُ شَرَّ ذَٰلِكَ ٱلْيَوْمِ وَلَقَّىٰهُمْ نَضْرَةً وَسُرُورًا ۝١١

11. *So, Allah shall spare them the evil of that Day, and grant them splendour and joy.*

وَجَزَىٰهُم بِمَا صَبَرُوا۟ جَنَّةً وَحَرِيرًا ۝١٢

12. *And reward them, because they were patient, with garden and silk,*

مُّتَّكِئِينَ فِيهَا عَلَى ٱلْأَرَآئِكِ لَا يَرَوْنَ فِيهَا شَمْسًا وَلَا زَمْهَرِيرًا ۝

13. *they shall recline therein on couches, and therein shall experience neither burning sun nor piercing cold.*

وَدَانِيَةً عَلَيْهِمْ ظِلَٰلُهَا وَذُلِّلَتْ قُطُوفُهَا تَذْلِيلًا ۝

14. *With its shades spread above them and clusters of fruit hanging close at hand.*

وَيُطَافُ عَلَيْهِم بِـَٔانِيَةٍ مِّن فِضَّةٍ وَأَكْوَابٍ كَانَتْ قَوَارِيرَا۟ ۝

15. *They will be served with silver plates.*

قَوَارِيرَ۟ مِن فِضَّةٍ قَدَّرُوهَا تَقْدِيرًا ۝

16. *Crystal-like silver, perfectly proportioned,*

وَيُسْقَوْنَ فِيهَا كَأْسًا كَانَ مِزَاجُهَا زَنجَبِيلًا ۝

17. *and they will be given a drink infused with ginger,*

عَيْنًا فِيهَا تُسَمَّىٰ سَلْسَبِيلًا ۝

18. *rom a spring called Salsabil.*

وَيَطُوفُ عَلَيْهِمْ وِلْدَانٌ مُّخَلَّدُونَ إِذَا رَأَيْتَهُمْ حَسِبْتَهُمْ لُؤْلُؤًا مَّنثُورًا ﴿١٩﴾

19. *And round about them shall go youths never altering in age; when you see them you will think them to be scattered pearls.*

وَإِذَا رَأَيْتَ ثَمَّ رَأَيْتَ نَعِيمًا وَمُلْكًا كَبِيرًا ﴿٢٠﴾

20. *And when you see there, you shall see blessings and a great kingdom.*

عَلِيَهُمْ ثِيَابُ سُندُسٍ خُضْرٌ وَإِسْتَبْرَقٌ وَحُلُّوٓا أَسَاوِرَ مِن فِضَّةٍ وَسَقَاهُمْ رَبُّهُمْ شَرَابًا طَهُورًا ﴿٢١﴾

21. *Upon them shall be garments of fine green silk and thick silk interwoven with gold, and they shall be adorned with bracelets of silver, and their Lord shall make them drink a pure drink.*

إِنَّ هَٰذَا كَانَ لَكُمْ جَزَاءً وَكَانَ سَعْيُكُم مَّشْكُورًا ﴿٢٢﴾

22. *This shall be as a reward to you: Your venture was worthy of all praise.*

إِنَّا نَحْنُ نَزَّلْنَا عَلَيْكَ ٱلْقُرْءَانَ تَنزِيلًا ﴿٢٣﴾

23. *Surely, We have sent down the Qur'an to you descended in portions.*

فَٱصۡبِرۡ لِحُكۡمِ رَبِّكَ وَلَا تُطِعۡ مِنۡهُمۡ ءَاثِمًا أَوۡ كَفُورًا ﴿٢٤﴾

24. So, bear your Lord's verdict with patience, and obey not the
unbeliever or wicked among them.

وَٱذۡكُرِ ٱسۡمَ رَبِّكَ بُكۡرَةً وَأَصِيلًا ﴿٢٥﴾

25. And pronounce your Lord's name, morning and evening,

وَمِنَ ٱلَّيۡلِ فَٱسۡجُدۡ لَهُۥ وَسَبِّحۡهُ لَيۡلًا طَوِيلًا ﴿٢٦﴾

26. and part of the night; bow down before Him and magnify
Him through the long night.

إِنَّ هَـٰٓؤُلَآءِ يُحِبُّونَ ٱلۡعَاجِلَةَ وَيَذَرُونَ وَرَآءَهُمۡ يَوۡمًا ثَقِيلًا ﴿٢٧﴾

27. These people love the fleeting world, and turn their backs
upon a weighty Day.

نَّحۡنُ خَلَقۡنَـٰهُمۡ وَشَدَدۡنَآ أَسۡرَهُمۡ وَإِذَا شِئۡنَا بَدَّلۡنَآ أَمۡثَـٰلَهُمۡ تَبۡدِيلًا ﴿٢٨﴾

28. Yet We created them; We strengthened their constitution; if
We please, We can replace such people completely.

إِنَّ هَـٰذِهِۦ تَذۡكِرَةٌ فَمَن شَآءَ ٱتَّخَذَ إِلَىٰ رَبِّهِۦ سَبِيلًا ﴿٢٩﴾

29. This is a Reminder. Whoso wishes may follow a path to his
Lord;

وَمَا تَشَآءُونَ إِلَّآ أَن يَشَآءَ ٱللَّهُ إِنَّ ٱللَّهَ كَانَ عَلِيمًا حَكِيمًا ﴿٣٠﴾

30. *and you cannot so wish unless Allah wishes. Allah is All-Knowing, All-Wise.*

يُدْخِلُ مَن يَشَآءُ فِي رَحْمَتِهِ ۚ وَٱلظَّٰلِمِينَ أَعَدَّ لَهُمْ عَذَابًا أَلِيمًا ﴿٣١﴾

31. *For He admits into His mercy whomsoever He will; as for the evildoers, He has prepared for them a painful chastisement.*

Commentary on Selected Verses

هَلْ أَتَىٰ عَلَى ٱلْإِنسَٰنِ حِينٌ مِّنَ ٱلدَّهْرِ لَمْ يَكُن شَيْئًا مَّذْكُورًا ﴿١﴾

Surely there came upon man a span of time, when he was a thing not worth remembering! (76:1)

إِنَّا خَلَقْنَا ٱلْإِنسَٰنَ مِن نُّطْفَةٍ أَمْشَاجٍ نَّبْتَلِيهِ فَجَعَلْنَٰهُ سَمِيعًۢا بَصِيرًا ﴿٢﴾

We created man from a drop of mingled fluid to put him to the test; (76:2)

There was a time when humans did not have a physical identity or reality. Every human being was in oblivion, meaning we were not in the physical world. We were, if you like, in Allah's knowledge. We were light without being caught by matter as we are in this world. Human beings are a combination of a heavenly entity and reality; and an earthly being which has features that constantly change like personality and physiology. An aspect of us never changes and the other side of us is ever-evolving.

As the next verse says, it began with a drop of fluid and then Allah gave us hearing and sight.

In the *Qur'an*, the word 'hearing' comes before 'seeing' because the foetus can pick up sound vibrations. So the key meaning and effect of this chapter hinges upon the definition and identification of *insān* (humankind). *Dahr* refers to a period of time. There was a time when the cosmos and the earth did not even exist. There is only the *nūr* (light) of Allah, as the Prophet (S) says, 'above it and below it and beside it, there was only air and it was not seen, it was not known.'

That original light can only be understood by creation because it has all the elements of perfection. It is light that exists forever, it is constant and ever reliable, ever generous, and it has all of the divine attributes which we have within our heart, within our soul, and which we also love to show in our behaviour.

إِنَّا هَدَيْنَٰهُ ٱلسَّبِيلَ إِمَّا شَاكِرًا وَإِمَّا كَفُورًا ﴿٣﴾

We gave him hearing and sight; We guided him upon the way, be he grateful or ungrateful. (76:3)

Sabīl is a path. Allah says the path is obvious; it has been given to us. It has been instilled in us much like software within our hearts.

The path is within every one of us. We are either going to be in gratitude, contentment, joyfulness and celebration of the perfect *Rabb* (Lord) or we are in *kufr* (denial, ingratitude), and a state in which we blame others and run from pillar to post. The days pass and one's life is over before we have discovered that the way out is to elude the *nafs* (ego-self). The path of ease and the path of difficulty are already within the heart. But this cannot only be preached, it has to be lived. That is why information must move to affect us. It must be used as a tool of transformation. Then from within yourself you will be aware, you will have been warned and reminded, and you can check yourself for deviations and distractions.

إِنَّآ أَعْتَدْنَا لِلْكَٰفِرِينَ سَلَٰسِلَا۟ وَأَغْلَٰلًا وَسَعِيرًا ﴿٤﴾

Surely, We have prepared for the unbelievers chains and shackles and a burning fire. (76:4)

The verse uses strong language and imagery to describe the severe consequences that await those who fail to heed the guidance which comes from within us. The outer world also reinforces this truth. The guidance from within instructs us not to attach ourselves to worldly possessions. Do not identify with your wealth, your power, or your status because your situation is always transient. Identify with the *nūr* (light) in you because that light will continue even after your death, and if you fail to, the verse describes the punishment, difficulty, or the other outcomes of *kufr* (denial).

We find ourselves bound by heavy chains to something we have lost, and in this state, our heads hang low. We are miserable and in sa'īran which means in a great deal of agitation. Allah says if we don't remember the joy, the source of it, and the presence of it in our hearts, then we will find ourselves in a perpetual state of misery.

إِنَّ ٱلْأَبْرَارَ يَشْرَبُونَ مِن كَأْسٍ كَانَ مِزَاجُهَا كَافُورًا ﴿٥﴾

But the righteous shall drink from a cup mixed with choicest fragrance, (76:5)

عَيْنًا يَشْرَبُ بِهَا عِبَادُ ٱللَّهِ يُفَجِّرُونَهَا تَفْجِيرًا ﴿٦﴾

A spring for Allah's servants, which flows abundantly at their wish. (76:6)

131

يُوفُونَ بِالنَّذْرِ وَيَخَافُونَ يَوْمًا كَانَ شَرُّهُ مُسْتَطِيرًا ٧

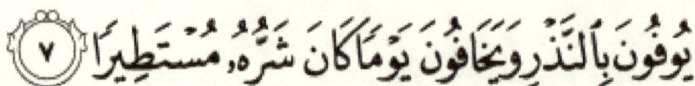

*They fulfil vows and fear a day the evil of which shall be
spreading far and wide. (76:7)*

The meaning of *abrār* is somebody who is completely, sincerely and
genuinely loyal. Loyal to whom? Were you aware of your existence
before you were created? Do you know when you will depart from
this world? We have to be loyal to He who created us, He whose
power is beyond all powers. We must be steadfast in our allegiance to
the source of all the virtues we hold dear, such as honesty, wellness,
generosity, goodness and health. Allah is the bestower of health, and
ultimately He is our orientation.

Then next verse (76:6) elaborates on this: this spring is a source
of nourishment for people as they crack it open. In other words, we
dig our own well for well-being. Each person has a unique set of
circumstances. Your problem is different from mine. The problem
you experienced yesterday is different from the problem you will
experience tomorrow. It is imperative to transcend those challenges
and immerse yourself into the well of wellness, into the original of
all lights. Otherwise, other sources of light will cast shadows, and
those shadows could instil fear within you.

We are all designed to seek permanence and everlasting joy. It
is no use having happiness for two seconds or being the king of the
world for one day. Everyone wants eternal security. That is the nature
of the soul. However, the ego-self can never find true security until it
yields to the soul. That is its submission and that is the foundation of
Islām (submission). The ego-self belongs to this world of space/time
where everything is in constant change, hence security (reliability,
stability) can never be found in this world.

Allah describes the *abrār*, those who fulfil their vows and promises,
as they embark on the path of becoming unified persons. Align one's
actions and words: don't say something and mean something else
and cheat this way or that way because, in the end, you are cheating

yourself. The *Qur'an* reminds us repeatedly that if we do good, it is beneficial for our own selves. So He describes and praises those who fulfil their promises and are genuinely and honestly loyal.

We must be mindful of the day when we will be rendered helpless, the day of reckoning, the day of death. It beckons us to remember that at any minute we may be in a vegetative state. We cannot do anything; we cannot even think. Fear of not being able to modify, improve, or groom the lower self must become urgent. How do we know we are going to live until tomorrow? Why not settle it now? If you have anger, rancour, and disappointment with other people, why not resolve it now before it is too late? Fear arises from the realisation that we may not have the opportunity to rectify the wrongs we have committed. It is vital to ensure our slate is clear. We can leave this world at any minute. If we follow this approach then whatever we pursue of this world is likely to be righteous.

$$ \text{وَيُطْعِمُونَ ٱلطَّعَامَ عَلَىٰ حُبِّهِۦ مِسْكِينًا وَيَتِيمًا وَأَسِيرًا ﴿٨﴾} $$

And they give food out of love for Him to the poor and the orphan and the captive: (76:8)

$$ \text{إِنَّمَا نُطْعِمُكُمْ لِوَجْهِ ٱللَّهِ لَا نُرِيدُ مِنكُمْ جَزَآءً وَلَا شُكُورًا ﴿٩﴾} $$

we only feed you for Allah's sake; we desire from you neither reward nor thanks: (76:9)

Most commentators say these verses were revealed in response to Imam Ali (AS) whose sons Imam Al Hassan (AS) and Imam Al Hussein (AS) were, at the time, very sick. He asked the Prophet (S) for guidance and the Prophet (S) recommended that he vow to fast for three days. This incident highlights the secret of abstention or self-restraint. In this world we are constantly taught more is better, but we discover that often less is better. By withdrawing from the world we open ourselves to health, replenishment and goodness.

On the first day of their fast, as they were about to break the fast, somebody knocked at the door and said: 'I am destitute (*miskīn*).' Five of them were fasting, including Fatima (RA) and their servant Fudlah. Each of them gave their piece of bread to the destitute person. The next day, again, as they were about to break fast the same thing happened. Somebody knocked on the door and said: 'I am an orphan, I have nowhere to go,' so each one gave their piece of bread to the orphan. On the third day, they did the same thing for a seer, someone who is not quite a prisoner of war, but who has been captured and incarcerated. He said: 'Nobody is feeding me.' Despite their own hunger, they gave their food to the seer.

When the Prophet (S) saw them, he was struck by their weakness and he did not know what to do. At that moment the above-referenced verses were revealed and their meaning remains applicable for all times. For this reason, it is often said, this chapter is more Madani than Makkih.

$$\text{إِنَّا نَخَافُ مِن رَّبِّنَا يَوْمًا عَبُوسًا قَمْطَرِيرًا ﴿١٠﴾}$$

For we fear from our Lord a frowning day, inauspicious. (76:10)

$$\text{فَوَقَىٰهُمُ اللَّهُ شَرَّ ذَٰلِكَ الْيَوْمِ وَلَقَّىٰهُمْ نَضْرَةً وَسُرُورًا ﴿١١﴾}$$

So, Allah shall spare them the evil of that Day, and grant them splendour and joy. (76:11)

The *abrār* are those people who live in a constant state of mindful awareness of Allah's presence and His all-encompassing knowledge. They understand that every thought, every action is known to Allah. This awareness drives them to give as much as they can, as often as they can, while constantly questioning themselves, saying, can we not do more for those who are less fortunate than us? That is how the early community of *Islām* grew so fast because everybody realised the way out of misery is to get out of their selfish and egotistic desires and demands for accumulation. They began to give to whoever they could, to relieve themselves from their lower selves. That was the hallmark of the people of that time. And so we see that within 70 years this small community of people, who were surrounded by two major empires (the Romans and the Persians), suddenly attracted attention in the Arabian Desert. This emergence was by *akhlāq* (refined conduct), by *suluk* a spiritual path of following both *haqīqa* (truth, the science of the inward) and *sharī'a* (the outer path, the realm of the senses), it was not by magic or chance. They were conscious of their role as *'Abd Allah*, meaning that they recognised that they are here to serve in the way of Allah, breaking free from the illusion of separateness. They understood that there is none other than Allah, *Lā ilāha illā Allāh*.

Therefore, this effulgence became a collective endeavour. It transcended individual piety and fostered a culture of sharing and caring, often measured by who would run further or be quicker to serve others. On the contrary, if you solely focus on doing things for yourself, the lower self can never be satisfied. As the Prophet (S) says, 'even if you were to fill the largest valley in the world with gold, it will not satisfy the greed of a single person.' This is the nature of the lower self.

In contrast, the higher self or your soul is ever content. So why not merge the two aspects of your being? In doing so you will begin to tap into the joy that is within you but you must crack open the shell that surrounds it. How do you crack it? By turning away from your obstructions and distractions that hinder your growth. You already have within you the light of *Al-Rahmān* (The Merciful), and you also have within you the *waswās* (whispering) of *shaytān* (satan; ego-self).

We find ourselves here in the middle, between heavens and earth. We have come into this world to return to that which is within us which is the heavenly domain of bliss and eternal light, the Divine Light. As human beings, we dwell between the realms of humanity and divinity. Humanity calls us to show compassion and apply reason, helping those in need. But divinity signifies that Allah's generosity and forgiveness surpass our limited understanding. So yield to Allah's grace and you will experience increased vitality and awakening. Allah will save those who are concerned about the day of reckoning and they will only see splendour and joyfulness.

Surūr is joyfulness while *Nazhr* pertains to seeing. Seeing what? Seeing the light of the One. It is through recognition that we gain discernment. We begin to understand what is good and what is bad, but we come to understand that what is good today may be the reverse tomorrow. See the One and you will come to realise that there is both worldly wisdom and heavenly wisdom. Heavenly wisdom is beyond us. It is for us to fulfil our responsibilities and then wait for higher *rahma* (mercy) and greater openings (there are only openings). See *Sūrat al-Fath* verse (48:1) which says: 'We have granted you a conspicuous victory.' Allah's openings are endless but if we cannot take it in, if we are not ready for it, it will not touch us.

Thus, a certain measure of readiness is required. You may have the electric fan all wired up, but if it is not plugged into its power source, it will not work. The same thing applies to us: we must be ready and open to receive it.

وَجَزَىٰهُم بِمَا صَبَرُواْ جَنَّةً وَحَرِيرًا ﴿١٢﴾

And reward them, because they were patient, with garden and silk, (76:12)

مُّتَّكِئِينَ فِيهَا عَلَى ٱلْأَرَآئِكِ ۖ لَا يَرَوْنَ فِيهَا شَمْسًا وَلَا زَمْهَرِيرًا ﴿١٣﴾

they shall recline therein on couches, and therein shall experience neither burning sun nor piercing cold. (76:13)

These are profound allegorical statements, and the *Qur'an* as a book of signs, facts, and allegorical wisdom presents them to us. Here it describes the beauty of the garden, where you are in a state of such ease that your mind does not dominate you. We are aware of how the body is affected by the mental state and our mental state is, in turn, affected by our spiritual state. There is a connection between the gross and the subtle. We cannot deny the unifying field or the unitive nature of the human being because that is the reflection of the unity of *Allah Azza wa Jal*.

وَدَانِيَةً عَلَيْهِمْ ظِلَٰلُهَا وَذُلِّلَتْ قُطُوفُهَا تَذْلِيلًا ١٤

With its shades spread above them and clusters of fruit hanging close at hand. (76:14)

وَيُطَافُ عَلَيْهِم بِآنِيَةٍ مِّن فِضَّةٍ وَأَكْوَابٍ كَانَتْ قَوَارِيرَا ١٥

They will be served with silver plates. (76:15)

The garden exists within every heart, and the soul recognises its connection with Allah through the question, '*alastu birabbikum*', 'Am I not your Lord?' (see *Sūrat al-A'rāf*, verse 7:172). Therefore it already knows the garden. It is a realm where there are no concerns, worries or anxieties. There is only presence. The ultimate garden is ever present, like different fields of energies available, but is your energy ready to enter that door? Or are you pre-occupied with the next deal, the next problem, or the fear and anxiety of losing what you think is yours? What truly belongs to you? What we have may be taken away from us, any day, at any minute. Our soul may leave the body at any minute. The more willing you are to surrender to that, the more you are in good balance and in justice, using what has been given to you, at the time it has been given to you. Start with outer balance, outer justice – question fairness, correctness and righteousness. Realise that Allah is *Al-'Adl* (The All Just), and original justice is utterly perfect. Although we make mistakes, Allah is All-Forgiving. We must play our part in this kindergarten of life, in order to be ready to return to the absolute. This verse is allegorical. There

137

are references to the garden and cups and objects like translucent silver. *Allah Azza wa Jal* likens this cup of silver to glass, as though it is just an illusion, meaning its existence is ephemeral, it is not physical. In other words, the notion of the Garden of Paradise is an allegory. We can (and do) experience paradise here in this life (not only after death). Just as we experience our consciousness in dreams, there are other realms beyond this world where our actions cease and our soul is there to lead and guide us. Our guidance will take us closer to, or further from where we have emanated. That's why we say *Innā lillāhi wa-innaā ilayhi rāji'ūn which means:* 'From Allah – To Allah – By Allah' (see *Sūrat al-Baqarah* (2:156). That is why the foundation lies in *Lā ilāha illā Allāh*. So the solution is to do what you can and leave the rest to Allah's divine will.

قَوَارِيرَأْمِن فِضَّةٍ قَدَّرُوهَاتَقْدِيرًا ﴿١٦﴾

Crystal-like silver, perfectly proportioned, (76:16)

وَيُسْقَوْنَ فِيهَا كَأْسًا كَانَ مِزَاجُهَا زَنجَبِيلًا ﴿١٧﴾

and they will be given a drink infused with ginger, (76:17)

عَيْنًافِيهَا تُسَمَّىٰ سَلْسَبِيلًا ﴿١٨﴾

from a spring called Salsabil. (76:18)

وَيَطُوفُ عَلَيْهِمْ وِلْدَانٌ مُّخَلَّدُونَ إِذَا رَأَيْتَهُمْ حَسِبْتَهُمْ لُؤْلُؤًا مَّنثُورًا ﴿١٩﴾

And round about them shall go youths never altering in age; when you see them you will think them to be scattered pearls. (76:19)

وَإِذَا رَأَيْتَ ثَمَّ رَأَيْتَ نَعِيمًا وَمُلْكًا كَبِيرًا ﴿٢٠﴾

And when you see there, you shall see blessings and a great kingdom. (76:20)

عَلِيَهُمْ ثِيَابُ سُنْدُسٍ خُضْرٌ وَإِسْتَبْرَقٌ وَحُلُّوا أَسَاوِرَ مِن فِضَّةٍ وَسَقَىٰهُمْ رَبُّهُمْ شَرَابًا طَهُورًا ﴿٢١﴾

Upon them shall be garments of fine green silk and thick silk interwoven with gold, and they shall be adorned with bracelets of silver, and their Lord shall make them drink a pure drink. (76:21)

إِنَّ هَٰذَا كَانَ لَكُمْ جَزَاءً وَكَانَ سَعْيُكُم مَّشْكُورًا ﴿٢٢﴾

This shall be as a reward to you: Your venture was worthy of all praise. (76:22)

All of these beautiful descriptions are of the state of the garden, as mentioned by *Allah Azza wa Jal*. Since we, as human beings, use language to express, these entities are described as eternal youths and of another nature, meaning they are made from a different light. They exist is the realm of the unseen, where lights and shadows intertwine, both unseen and seen. So it says, these are perfect beings, and they are translucent like pearls. And as we delve deeper we will uncover more and more of this wealth and blessings of Allah. That is why it is essential for us to engage in more meditation, reflection, increase our *salāt* (prayers), and perform *nawafil salāt* (optional prayer) until such time as we are constantly able to enter into a state of thoughtlessness with presence. It is so important for us to be present before we approach prayers. So, when you are doing your *wudhū'* (ritual ablution), leave all distractions behind and enter into the no-man's land between this world and the next. Then in verse 76:21 Allah mentions the provisions given to those in the garden, emphasising their purity. It is the first time He uses the word *Rabb*: 'and then their Lord will give them a pure provision.' Pure provision is indescribable as it emanates from the sacred. Then the verse continues: This is your reward, and whatever you strive for now, it is being acknowledged.

The remainder of the verses in this chapter are different. Up to now we have heard about human beings and the consequences of their actions. If they do not act righteously they will face unfavourable outcomes and endure suffering. The Prophet (S) and the *Qur'an* are intertwined and their message is complimentary. This book, or this treatise, or this *tanzīl* (this gift, this revelation), serves as our constant reference point, as our highway code to drive the ego-self back to its Original Creator through recognising the soul and through its purification.

إِنَّا نَحْنُ نَزَّلْنَا عَلَيْكَ ٱلْقُرْءَانَ تَنزِيلًا ﴿٢٣﴾

Surely, We have sent down the Qur'an to you descended in portions. (76:23)

فَٱصْبِرْ لِحُكْمِ رَبِّكَ وَلَا تُطِعْ مِنْهُمْ ءَاثِمًا أَوْ كَفُورًا ﴿٢٤﴾

So, bear your Lord's verdict with patience, and obey not the unbeliever or wicked among them. (76:24)

وَٱذْكُرِ ٱسْمَ رَبِّكَ بُكْرَةً وَأَصِيلًا ﴿٢٥﴾

And pronounce your Lord's name, morning and evening, (76:25)

وَمِنَ ٱلَّيْلِ فَٱسْجُدْ لَهُۥ وَسَبِّحْهُ لَيْلًا طَوِيلًا ﴿٢٦﴾

and part of the night; bow down before Him and magnify Him through the long night. (76:26)

إِنَّ هَٰٓؤُلَآءِ يُحِبُّونَ ٱلْعَاجِلَةَ وَيَذَرُونَ وَرَآءَهُمْ يَوْمًا ثَقِيلًا ﴿٢٧﴾

These people love the fleeting world, and turn their backs upon a weighty Day. (76:27)

Allah Azza wa Jal says this amazing *Qur'an* has been sent down to guide and lead the creation of *Banī Ādam* (Children of Adam) back to their intended purpose. He says in verse 76:24, 'The wisdom in this is to be patient, no more, no less.' If you exceed the bounds of patience, it can lead to anxiety. We have many examples in the *Qur'an* of this wisdom. For example, *Nabi Allah* Yunus (AS) desired a swift outcome but his impatience led him to darkness. We should strive to do what is in our capacity and leave the rest to Allah.

To truly understand the *Qur'an*, we must study it in the light of the *Qur'an* itself. The entire *Qur'an* is perfect, and as we delve deeper into its teachings we discover its inherent perfection. Reflect upon the signs of your Lord. Remember the names of your Lord (*Asmā' al-husnā*) Verse (76:25) says: 'And remember the Name of your Lord morning and evening' because it is from Him that we originated, by Him we are sustained, and to Him we will return. This will make sense to any person of intellect. Take this remembrance of Allah as the ultimate source of nourishment, understanding and connection. Remember the name of your Lord night and day, whenever you can. Stay awake during the night to remember the name of your Lord. How wonderful!

Verse 76:27 says most people still chase immediate pleasure and leave behind "a weighty day". This is the day when we do and say nothing. We can only see what we have done. All that we have done, or thought, or intended, will be presented in front of us and that is the only fuel or energy we have.

At present, you have a choice, energy and ability. You must take council. Reflect upon the excessive wastage and indulgence in the world. It has been consumed by excess and waste, because "Striving for more distracts you." (see *Sūrat at-Takāthur* 102:1). We constantly want more. The soul knows no limits. But the *nafs* desires the limitless even though it can only have the limitless if it dives into the soul and surrenders. Taking cover in Allah is one of the meanings of *Astaghfiru'llah*. Allah is all forgiving and His generosity is infinite. However, my generosity is limited. If I put my limited generosity alongside the limitless, it disappears. By aligning the relative with the absolute, the absolute will always prevail.

نَّحْنُ خَلَقْنَٰهُمْ وَشَدَدْنَآ أَسْرَهُمْ وَإِذَا شِئْنَا بَدَّلْنَآ أَمْثَٰلَهُمْ تَبْدِيلًا ﴿٢٨﴾

Yet We created them; We strengthened their constitution; if We please, We can replace such people completely. (76:28)

إِنَّ هَٰذِهِ تَذْكِرَةٌ فَمَن شَآءَ ٱتَّخَذَ إِلَىٰ رَبِّهِ سَبِيلًا ﴿٢٩﴾

This is a Reminder. Whoso wishes may follow a path to his Lord; (76:29)

وَمَا تَشَآءُونَ إِلَّآ أَن يَشَآءَ ٱللَّهُ إِنَّ ٱللَّهَ كَانَ عَلِيمًا حَكِيمًا ﴿٣٠﴾

And you cannot so wish unless Allah wishes. Allah is All-Knowing, All-Wise. (76:30)

$$\text{يُدۡخِلُ مَن يَشَآءُ فِى رَحۡمَتِهِۦۚ وَٱلظَّٰلِمِينَ أَعَدَّ لَهُمۡ عَذَابًا أَلِيمَۢا ﴿٣١﴾}$$

For He admits into His mercy whomsoever He wills; as for the
evildoers, He has prepared for them a painful chastisement.
(76:31)

The last three verses sum up the entire lesson of the meaning
of this great chapter. It says: This is a reminder (*Tadhkirah*), which
is from the same root as *dhikr* (remembrance of Allah). *Tadhkirah* is
also likened to a ticket in Arabic. It means this is your passport or a
reminder for you 'and he who wants to benefit from this will find a
way towards his Lord.' How does one find a way? By serving others,
helping others, and learning from others until you realise this is
Allah's kindergarten and we have come from the higher unknown.
This is a reminder that brings urgency. Don't postpone it because
there may not be a tomorrow. Find a way that gets you closer to the
knowledge that is within you, that is closer to you than your jugular
vein. Whatever we wish for must fit within the Divine Will. I have
my will; I want to teach, I want to help, I want to benefit myself,
and I want to have a good life, but that must fit within the Divine
patterns. The Divine patterns are unchangeable, while my destiny
is subject to change. The way Allah designs patterns in the cosmos,
in the development of the foetus, in the body and in relationships
reflect His unconditional love. What use is a bit of wealth now and
being impoverished for the rest of my life? I want inner wealth that
never diminishes. That is why addressing poverty goes well beyond
external circumstances. You cannot just be concerned with outer
poverty, what about inner poverty? Most of the world is impoverished.
You must be self-contained, self-reliant, self-accountable, and open
to others and then a society that is wholesome, decent, and worthy
of calling themselves *Banī Ādam* (Children of Adam) will arise. And
that is how Allah's *rahma* (mercy) will permeate. *Allah Azza wa Jal* says
in the *Qur'an* that His *rahma* is above everything and it encompasses
everything. But verse 76:31 says it's important that we recognise

Allah's mercy. Sometimes having less can be a great mercy. Do you recognise it? When you are ill, do you recognise it as His mercy? If you don't, then reflect again.

Sūrat al-Mulk tells us to look back again. Delve within yourself, for you will find that what you once disliked is actually beneficial for your inner state in the long term. Embracing limitations and surrendering can be advantageous.

We human beings are the same. *Sūrat ad-Dahr* tells us that there was a time when we did not have a mentionable identity; but the soul existed within Allah's knowledge. We need to recognise that the truth in us has no beginning or end and that it is a soul. The way to recognise you are a soul is not to deny the lower self but to acknowledge it and put it in its place. Say: 'I cannot do this because it is beyond what I consider to be wholesome, acceptable, or good.' In this way, you limit the ego and allow the soul to be ever-shining, ever-boundless and ever-glorious. This is our life transaction; our way of life. It is about recognising the cosmology of the human being and living according to that. Do not deny the lower, acknowledge the higher and recognise that all of it belongs to Allah. See *Sūrat al-Hadīd* verse 57:2 which means 'whatever you have has been loaned to you.' All that you are, whatever you have, has been loaned to you.

Ask yourself what you are doing. Is it afflicting or liberating you from your selfishness and stupidity? If it is liberating you, then it is good wealth, and if not, then it is detrimental. So the position of the human being is between the heavens and the earth, between this life and the next. The more we remember, the more we remind each other, the more we are living our life transaction; our way of life, the more we are truly in *Islām* (submission) and the more we relish and enjoy our *Imān* (certainty and security that Allah knows, and Allah sees) and the closer we are to the entry of the joyfulness of *Ihsān* (inner and outer excellence in thought and conduct).

Chapter 10

SURAT AL-IQRA'

This chapter is referred to either as *Sūrat al-Iqra'* or *Sūrat al-'Alaq*. It is accepted that the first five verses of this chapter were revealed to the Prophet (S) during the last ten days of *Ramadhān* (the month of abstention). In those days they were not instructed to fast. The Prophet (S) would go to the cave in Hira and spend at least a month if not longer, in abstention and restriction with the intention of getting out of his habits. The first five verses of this chapter, according to all classical historical commentators, were the ones which were revealed to him at that time.

Muslims consider this chapter or the five verses as the very beginning of revelation of the *Qur'an*. There are 19 verses in this chapter and according to most historians and commentators who follow the sequence in which the verses were revealed, the remaining verses were revealed about one year after the first five verses.

Qur'anic Verses

The Arabic text and the English translation of *Sūrat al-Iqra'* follow immediately below. Thereafter I will focus my commentary on selected verses and words.

بِسۡمِ ٱللَّهِ ٱلرَّحۡمَٰنِ ٱلرَّحِيمِ

In the name of Allah, the Beneficent, the Merciful.

اقۡرَأۡ بِٱسۡمِ رَبِّكَ ٱلَّذِى خَلَقَ ﴿١﴾

1.   *Recite, in the name of your Lord! He Who created!*

خَلَقَ ٱلۡإِنسَٰنَ مِنۡ عَلَقٍ ﴿٢﴾

2.   *He created man from a clinging substance.*

اقۡرَأۡ وَرَبُّكَ ٱلۡأَكۡرَمُ ﴿٣﴾

3.   *Recite! Your Lord is most bountiful,*

ٱلَّذِى عَلَّمَ بِٱلۡقَلَمِ ﴿٤﴾

4.   *who taught by the Pen.*

عَلَّمَ ٱلۡإِنسَٰنَ مَا لَمۡ يَعۡلَمۡ ﴿٥﴾

5.   *Taught man what he knew not.*

كَلَّا إِنَّ ٱلۡإِنسَٰنَ لَيَطۡغَىٰ ﴿٦﴾

6.   *No! man is most surely inordinate,*

أَن رَّءَاهُ ٱسْتَغْنَىٰ ۝ ٧

7. for he thinks himself self-sufficient.

إِنَّ إِلَىٰ رَبِّكَ ٱلرُّجْعَىٰ ۝ ٨

8. Surely to your Lord is the return.

أَرَءَيْتَ ٱلَّذِى يَنْهَىٰ ۝ ٩

9. Have you seen the man who forbids,

كَلَّا لَئِن لَّمْ يَنتَهِ لَنَسْفَعًا بِٱلنَّاصِيَةِ ۝ ١٥

10. a worshipper as he prays?

أَرَءَيْتَ إِن كَانَ عَلَى ٱلْهُدَىٰ ۝ ١١

11. Have you seen whether he is rightly guided

أَوْ أَمَرَ بِٱلتَّقْوَىٰ ۝ ١٢

12. or commands to piety?

$$\text{أَرَءَيْتَ إِن كَذَّبَ وَتَوَلَّى ﴿١٣﴾}$$

13. *Have you seen whether he denies the truth and turns away from it?*

$$\text{أَلَمْ يَعْلَم بِأَنَّ اللَّهَ يَرَى ﴿١٤﴾}$$

14. *Does he not realize that Allah sees all?*

$$\text{كَلَّا لَئِن لَّمْ يَنتَهِ لَنَسْفَعًا بِالنَّاصِيَةِ ﴿١٥﴾}$$

15. *No! If he does not stop, We shall drag him by his forehead,*

$$\text{نَاصِيَةٍ كَاذِبَةٍ خَاطِئَةٍ ﴿١٦﴾}$$

16. *a lying, wicked forehead.*

$$\text{فَلْيَدْعُ نَادِيَهُ ﴿١٧﴾}$$

17. *Let him summon his gang,*

$$\text{سَنَدْعُ الزَّبَانِيَةَ ﴿١٨﴾}$$

18. *We shall summon the guards of Hell.*

$$\text{كَلَّا لَا تُطِعْهُ وَٱسْجُدْ وَٱقْتَرِب} \quad \textbf{۱۹}$$

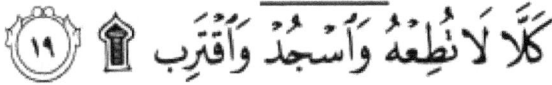

19. No! Do not obey him, but kneel down, and draw near!

Commentary on Selected Verses

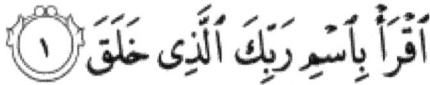

$$\text{اقْرَأْ بِٱسْمِ رَبِّكَ ٱلَّذِى خَلَقَ} \quad \textbf{۱}$$

Recite, in the name of your Lord! He Who created! (96:1)

The word *iqra'* has multiple meanings, including to know, to gather or to read. The word *Qur'an* comes from the same root. *Qur'an* is the compilation of divine revelations which were revealed to the Prophet Muhammad (S) during his years of Prophethood. This verse was revealed when he was 40 years old. For 23 years, the verses were compiled (as they descended) and arranged into a special order which the Prophet (S) formulated himself (rather than in chronological order) thus resulting in the *Qur'an* as it is today.

The *Qur'an* is a remarkable bouquet of knowledge which was revealed in stages or waves. The word *Qur'an* can be understood to mean that which contains all the truths that are possible or available, emphasising its comprehensive and encompassing nature.

When Allah commanded the Prophet (S) to read, an extraordinary surge of spiritual energy descended upon him. His first response to this experience was: 'I do not read.' Some commentators suggest that his response stemmed from his understanding that he knew he could do nothing, because all of it is from Allah. The implication is, that he could only read if the One who granted him the ability to read also enabled him to do so.

Jibrāīl (AS) (Angel Gabriel) returned to the Prophet (S) with the same request three times, eventually leading him to read and receive the divine message. This encounter exhausted him because it opened up his heart to the Universal Heart, to the Ultimate Sacredness that prevails. It was a transformative event in his life instantly establishing a profound connection between the seen and the unseen. We also say the entire *Qur'an* descended on the Night of *Qadr* (Power) but it unfolded over 23 years.

Consider this analogy: if you have been under water all your life you have not seen the magnificent islands, trees, birds and flowers that exist above the surface. Once your head is above water, you see incredible scenery, however, it will take some time for you to describe and comprehend it. The *Qur'an* descended similarly. The Prophet (S) already knew that the power, knowledge, and the attributes of Allah were always present. However, the unfolding of the divine message needed the constraints of human existence within space and time

The term *bi-is'mi* holds significant meaning in the context of revelation. Some commentators say that the revelation included the *bismillah* along with *iqra'* (read) because *bismillah* is the permission under which the revelation opened up for the Prophet (S). *Bi* means by permission of, through the means of and in the name of Allah.

The name of Allah is the key to everything possible within the cosmos. Everything is from the One, by the One, unto the One. If we say *bismillah*, it is a most powerful and amazing invocation because *bismillah* implies that you have not identified yourself as the actor but that you are invoking the ultimate power that prevails upon all powers, known and unknown.

Rabb means Lord, and it signifies the nurturing and sustaining aspect of Allah's authority. Anything that happens, anything that grows or begins, anything that is earthly or heavenly is under the *rubūbīyah* (lordship) of Allah. One of the most important aspects of our *dīn* (life transaction; a way of life) is to give people the right quality of conduct, character, and behaviour all of which amount to *tarbiyya*, which means upbringing and development of individuals in a manner that aligns with the values of Islam.

The command – to all of us as *Banī Adam* (children of Adam) – is 'read by permission, by the power of, by the courtesy, by the generosity of your Lord' who has created. We are all *khalaqa* (creation) and Allah is *Al-Khāliq* (The Creator). Our connection to *Al-Khāliq* is through our *rūh* (soul) which is described in the *Qur'an* as, 'when all of the *nufus* (ego-selves) have been exposed to their Lord and they were asked *alastu birabbikum* (Am I not your Lord)?' They answered 'Yes' (Sūrat al-A'rāf 7:172). In this context the *nafs* refers to the *rūh* (soul) itself because it is the higher aspect of the *nafs* (ego-self). The soul inherently knows its Lord. Humans are a composition of a growing ego from infancy to maturity, back towards the inner delight and light of our soul. This composition is called *insān* (humankind).

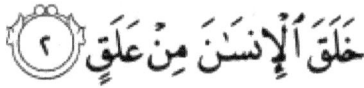

خَلَقَ ٱلْإِنسَٰنَ مِنْ عَلَقٍ ﴿٢﴾

2. He created man from a clinging substance. (96:2)

The word *'Alaqah* is an important word which means a little snail or a leech and it signifies something that adheres or is attached. In this context, it refers specifically to a blood clot, but consider what the word itself conjures in the mind: 'anything that hangs on.' From a physiological and biological sense, our lives begin as a tiny multiplying cell, which develops into a foetus, which in a sense hangs on, leech-like, to the womb. But even after birth, we continue to cling on. We depend on the air we breathe, our ability to think, our minds and our ability to move.

ٱقْرَأْ وَرَبُّكَ ٱلْأَكْرَمُ ﴿٣﴾

Recite! Your Lord is most bountiful, (96:3)

Read the incredible books and access the knowledge that we have, including treaties on the heavens and on earth. Read the signs, by permission of *Al-Karīm* (The Most Generous). What more could we possibly desire, other than reading the book of life, the book of knowledge? Consider the discoveries we are making through geneticists, such as DNA or gene sequencing. Read, read, read! If you were to compile the book on the human genome, it would consist of about three trillion letters, taking on average of over 80 years to read.

This is just one book. What about the other books? That is why we have wonderful descriptions of these things in the *Qur'an*. There are over 300 verses which mention the word book, *kitāb*. See for example *Sūrat al-Ahzab* verse 33:6 which signifies that everything that is written, known and unknown is encompassed within a book.

The *Qur'an* tells us that nothing, whether small or large, exists except that it is recorded in the *Kitāb al Mubīn* (the Clear Book). Once again, we have wonderful verses about the Day of Reckoning, like *Sūrat Al-Isra* verse 17:13, which says on the Day of Reckoning you will have a book that is open to you. It will tell you who you are, what you did, what you thought, what you hid, what you lied about, the hypocrisy you manifested, if you embodied multiple personas or were one authentic person. The very next verse (17:14) says 'now read' *aqra* again, read now, now you have read; now you have no option.

We may have the inclination to resist and say, no, I don't want to confront this, this is the negative side of me, this is the mean side of me that I don't like to acknowledge. However, on the day of reckoning we will be held accountable for our actions and there will be nowhere to hide, nowhere to escape?

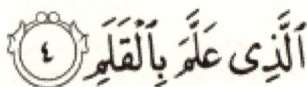

$$ ٱلَّذِى عَلَّمَ بِٱلْقَلَمِ ﴿٤﴾ $$

who taught by the Pen. (96:4)

The word *qalam* means pen. *Qalam* also means to cut or sharpen something, to clip or prune. Additionally, it signifies leaving a mark on clay, which was the method of writing in ancient times. Writing involved using a hard object with a sharp end to make imprints on soft clay.

Whatever comes from the unseen will be expounded upon, is going to be shown, in all its attributes and differentiation by *qalam*, by being sharpened and cut to leave its mark. It will be expressed through the medium of writing. *Sūrat al-Qalam* 68:1 mentions: 'By the Pen, and by what they trace in lines!'. Addressing the Prophet (S), it continues (68:2): 'You are certainly not covering up the great *ni'mah* (grace, favour of your Lord) that has come upon you.'

The word *qalam* comes again, brilliantly, in *Sūrat al-Luqmān* verse (31:27): If you take all of the trees on earth and make them into pens, and if the oceans are extended into seven more oceans beyond them, the commands, words, energy modules, or beams of Allah will not end.

Allah is the Enabler, the Giver, and *Al-Akram* (the Most Generous) who has enabled us to read what is not physically written. That is why these great beings, especially the Prophet Muhammad (S), could read that which was unknown to us, and that is why we say it is revealed. We may be inspired when the heart is crystal clear when the mind is healthy and receptive and there are no concerns, then we can read that which is beyond the ordinary human limitations.

Consider *Sūrat ar-Rahmān* verse *(55:1-2)*: '*Ilm* is knowledge. It is by *qalam* that we differentiate and have accumulated so much information and knowledge over hundreds of years. It is the way in which the magnificent unseen is unfolding itself.

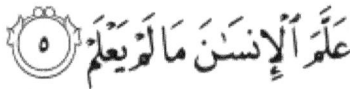

$$عَلَّمَ ٱلْإِنسَـٰنَ مَا لَمْ يَعْلَمْ ۝٥$$

Taught man what he knew not. (96:5)

Some scholars say the reason the Prophet (S) initially said 'I cannot read this,' was because he recognised that his source of knowledge was not based on conventional learning but rather on divine transmission and the command of Allah. That is why he later said: 'Allah has given me more than whatever anybody can ever imagine, which is the source of the contentment of the believer. Allah will give you what you need, not what your whims tell you, or where your silly mind drives you. These are all distractions and most distractions bring about destruction. The next verses describe our pathology: they tell us who we are.

$$كَلَّا إِنَّ ٱلْإِنسَـٰنَ لَيَطْغَىٰ ﴿٦﴾$$

No! man is most surely inordinate, (96:6)

$$أَن رَّءَاهُ ٱسْتَغْنَىٰ ﴿٧﴾$$

for he thinks himself self-sufficient. (96:7)

Certainly, human beings will always transgress. We are always arrogant, especially when we have health, power and wealth, we believe: 'I can do anything.' With such people, we hope that one day they will realise that there is nothing that we can possess. Allah is the possessor of it all. That is why we have this magnificent practice of lifting our hands by saying *Allāhu Akbar*, meaning Allah is greater than whatever I can think and do. We are dependent; we are hanging on to this energy, which is the soul. It gives us a mind, ability, memory, and all of our history, of who I am and who you are and how different we are, when in essence we are all the same. It gives us goodness that does not come and go and joy that is ever-constant.

So this is the warning: if you want to *Iqra'* (read), then take heed. Human beings will be arrogant. Here the *Qur'an* is reminding us: whenever they feel they are now self-sufficient, self-content, proud, denying dependence upon the unseen, they become susceptible to that arrogance and spiritual blindness. Our failure is that we don't connect the seen with the unseen. Because in that connection, we enter a safe harbour. *Sūrat al-Baqarah* verse 2:3 tells us to: 'take refuge in the unseen.' However, we tend to rely solely on the tangible and visible aspects of life, clinging to our perceived security.

The example of the devastating floods in Pakistan a few years ago illustrates the fragility of our material security. Over 20 million people were left destitute in less than three weeks. Unforeseen events can disrupt our lives and strip away our sense of security. Absolute security is unattainable. We must do our best to have some measure of security, health, a clear mind, and a pure heart. For the rest, you must plead to Allah and put your trust in Him, because here again, we are reminded:

$$\text{إِنَّ إِلَى رَبِّكَ ٱلرُّجْعَىٰ ﴿٨﴾}$$

Surely to your Lord is the return. (96:8)

The term 'return' is important. If you acknowledge your return to nothingness as far as the physical side is concerned and perpetuity as far as your soul is concerned, then you are in a state of balance.

The wonderful divine attributes in this surah are quite critical. They include *Al-Rabb* (The Lord), *Al-Khāliq* (The Creator), *Al-Karīm* (The Most Generous), *Al-'Alim* (The All-Knowing), *Al-Hādī* (The Guide), *Al-Basīr* (The All-Seeing).

$$\text{أَرَءَيْتَ ٱلَّذِى يَنْهَىٰ ﴿٩﴾}$$

Have you seen the man who forbids? (96:9)

$$\text{كَلَّا لَئِن لَّمْ يَنتَهِ لَنَسْفَعًا بِٱلنَّاصِيَةِ ﴿١٥﴾}$$

a worshipper as he prays? (96:10)

These verses say: Don't you see, he who objects when someone is praying. In the early days of his prophethood, there were those who went up against Muhammad (S), and his enemies included his closest relatives. This verse – in terms of its historical descent – is about Abu Jahal who would object whenever he saw the Prophet (S) doing his rituals.

أَرَءَيْتَ إِن كَانَ عَلَى ٱلْهُدَىٰٓ ﴿١١﴾

Have you seen whether he is rightly guided? (96:11)

This verse says: can't they see, that this being is on guidance? He is connecting the seen and unseen, he is reading, he is performing *Iqra'*, he is reading the truth, that 'I must admit my dependence upon Allah and I am going into prostration.'

أَوْ أَمَرَ بِٱلتَّقْوَىٰٓ ﴿١٢﴾

or commands to piety? (96:12)

Taqwā refers to constant awareness or God-consciousness, that if I am not doing the right thing, I may be doing wrong. Ask yourself who you have chosen to do something. Is it the right time? Is it the right place? Is it among the right people, or does acting in this way gain you status because it looks as if you know a bit more than others? Are you becoming arrogant? Take heed.

أَرَءَيْتَ إِن كَذَّبَ وَتَوَلَّىٰٓ ﴿١٣﴾

Have you seen whether he denies the truth and turns away from it? (96:13)

$$\text{أَلَمْ يَعْلَم بِأَنَّ ٱللَّهَ يَرَىٰ ﴿١٤﴾}$$

Does he not realize that Allah sees all? (96:14)

These verses remind us: 'Don't you see he who lies and eventually leaves and goes away?' Doesn't he know? As human beings who are intelligent and have sight, we should also recognise and reflect upon a being who possesses far greater insight and understanding. He is *Al-Baṣīr* (The All-Seeing), and *As-Sami* (The All-Hearing). We may have some capacity to see and hear, but our abilities fall short in comparison to His. His are beyond measure. We can hear a little bit and we thank God. Otherwise, you hear so much noise. For this reason, a limitation is also protection.

$$\text{نَاصِيَةٍ كَٰذِبَةٍ خَاطِئَةٍ ﴿١٦﴾}$$

a lying, wicked forehead. (96:16)

Nāsiya is forelock, implying the forehead. This is the Adamic rise. We are led by the forelock to the higher consciousness. It says if he is not going to yield, he will be pulled down by the scruff of his neck, so to speak. *Nadiyah* is where the Arabs used to meet, next to the *Ka'ba*; *nadi* the verb means 'to call' and the noun, pronounced the same way, means 'club' (for example a club of elders). He, the Original Cause, says, let them call their council; let them go to their club, let them see what they can do because it was already decided in the unseen that Muhammad (S) would prevail, whether they like it or not.

$$\text{(١٨)} \; \text{سَنَدْعُ ٱلزَّبَانِيَةَ}$$

18. We shall summon the guards of Hell.

Historically, the time was ripe for change in 7th century Arabia. The two great empires — the Persian and the Romans — had exhausted each other. There was a vacancy for spirituality. Christianity had become decadent and abusive. There was a natural, correct timing for an awakening and that is what happened. It was very clear that this *dīn* and this truth will prevail.

$$\text{(١٩)} \; \text{كَلَّا لَا تُطِعْهُ وَٱسْجُدْ وَٱقْتَرِب}$$

No! Do not obey him, but kneel down, and draw near! (verse 96:19)

The chapter concludes with this amazing word, *wa-us'jud* (prostrate). When we Muslims hear it, we are expected to enter into that stage of *sajdah* (devotional prostration in prayer), a stage of oblivion and disappearance from the scene.

Wa-uq'tarib (draw close to Allah) is another remarkable word. *Qurb* means closeness. Allah repeatedly says, 'I am closer to you than your jugular vein, so call on Me.' When you call Me from the heart when you are bereft and you have no one else that you may call upon other than the One and Only, the Creator, then invariably you will feel better by calling and you will feel doubly better by knowing that you will be answered, because as verse 96:3 reminds us, Allah is most generous, beyond what we think is generosity.

Allah knows better than we do about what is good for us. We should be mindful of this when we made du'a. We ask Allah: 'I believe that I need this but you know best. So I leave it to you and I am going to listen to your decree so that I have a perfect destiny; so that I am always inwardly content, outwardly doing my best and to do the most I can.' Otherwise, I will be only serving my lower ego and getting myself into that dungeon of the darkness of the inner *shaytān* (satan; ego-self). We all love the light of His Mercy, but the way of that light is that we first recognise the darkness, turn away from it and then hold on to *Bismillah*. Then you know He is *Al-Rahmān* (The All-Merciful), He is Al-Rahīm (The All-Compassionate) and you have the best of times at all times as a prelude to returning to the garden.

Chapter 11
SURAT AN-NABA

In this chapter (78), the emphasis is on finality, and that is why it is called *Nabā*. *Nabā* also means the news; some translators use the word tiding. *Nabi* is from the same root. It means to give you the news. *Nabi* means the prophet, *Rasul* means messenger. What is the news? This chapter explains it.

Qur'anic Verses

The Arabic text and the English translation of *Sūrat an-Nabā* follow immediately below. Thereafter I will focus my commentary on selected verses and words.

بِسْمِ اللهِ الرَّحْمَنِ الرَّحِيمِ

In the name of Allah, the Merciful to all, the Compassionate to each!

عَمَّ يَتَسَاءَلُونَ ﴿١﴾

1. What is it that they question each other about?

عَنِ ٱلنَّبَإِ ٱلْعَظِيمِ ﴿٢﴾

2. *The momentous announcement*

ٱلَّذِى هُمْ فِيهِ مُخْتَلِفُونَ ﴿٣﴾

3. *about which they differ?*

كَلَّا سَيَعْلَمُونَ ﴿٤﴾

4. *No indeed; they shall soon know!*

ثُمَّ كَلَّا سَيَعْلَمُونَ ﴿٥﴾

5. *Again, no indeed; they shall soon know!*

أَلَمْ نَجْعَلِ ٱلْأَرْضَ مِهَٰدًا ﴿٦﴾

6. *Did We not make the earth smooth*

وَٱلْجِبَالَ أَوْتَادًا ﴿٧﴾

7. *and the mountains as pegs?*

وَخَلَقْنَاكُمْ أَزْوَاجًا ﴿٨﴾

8. *And We created you in pairs,*

وَجَعَلْنَا نَوْمَكُمْ سُبَاتًا ﴿٩﴾

9. *give you sleep for rest,*

وَجَعَلْنَا ٱلَّيْلَ لِبَاسًا ﴿١٠﴾

10. *the night as a cover,*

وَجَعَلْنَا ٱلنَّهَارَ مَعَاشًا ﴿١١﴾

11. *and the day for your livelihood?*

وَبَنَيْنَا فَوْقَكُمْ سَبْعًا شِدَادًا ﴿١٢﴾

12. *Did We not build seven strong above you,*

وَجَعَلْنَا سِرَاجًا وَهَّاجًا ﴿١٣﴾

13. *and have placed a lamp full of blazing splendour?*

وَأَنزَلْنَا مِنَ ٱلْمُعْصِرَٰتِ مَآءً ثَجَّاجًا ﴿١٤﴾

14. *And We send down from the clouds water pouring forth abundantly,*

لِنُخْرِجَ بِهِۦ حَبًّا وَنَبَاتًا ﴿١٥﴾

15. *that We may bring forth thereby grain and plants,*

وَجَنَّٰتٍ أَلْفَافًا ﴿١٦﴾

16. *and gardens intertwined?*

إِنَّ يَوْمَ ٱلْفَصْلِ كَانَ مِيقَٰتًا ﴿١٧﴾

17. *A time has been appointed for the Day of Decision:*

يَوْمَ يُنفَخُ فِى ٱلصُّورِ فَتَأْتُونَ أَفْوَاجًا ﴿١٨﴾

18. *the Day when the trumpet is sounded and you all come forward in multitudes;*

وَفُتِحَتِ ٱلسَّمَآءُ فَكَانَتْ أَبْوَٰبًا ﴿١٩﴾

19. *and when the skies are opened and become gates.*

وَسُيِّرَتِ ٱلۡجِبَالُ فَكَانَتۡ سَرَابًا ﴿٢٠﴾

20. *When the mountains will vanish like a mirage.*

إِنَّ جَهَنَّمَ كَانَتۡ مِرۡصَادًا ﴿٢١﴾

21. *Hell lies in ambush,*

لِّلطَّٰغِينَ مَـَٔابًا ﴿٢٢﴾

22. *For the insolent a resort.*

لَّٰبِثِينَ فِيهَآ أَحۡقَابًا ﴿٢٣﴾

23. *In it shall they remain for a long time.*

لَّا يَذُوقُونَ فِيهَا بَرۡدًا وَلَا شَرَابًا ﴿٢٤﴾

24. *Therein they taste neither coolness nor anything to drink,*

إِلَّا حَمِيمًا وَغَسَّاقًا ﴿٢٥﴾

25. *save boiling water and pus.*

جَزَآءً وِفَاقًا ﴿٢٦﴾

26. *for a suitable recompense.*

إِنَّهُمْ كَانُواْ لَا يَرْجُونَ حِسَابًا ﴿٢٧﴾

27. *They indeed hoped not for a reckoning,*

وَكَذَّبُواْ بِآيَٰتِنَا كِذَّابًا ﴿٢٨﴾

28. *and they rejected Our messages as lies.*

وَكُلَّ شَىْءٍ أَحْصَيْنَٰهُ كِتَٰبًا ﴿٢٩﴾

29. *But We have placed on record every single thing.*

فَذُوقُواْ فَلَن نَّزِيدَكُمْ إِلَّا عَذَابًا ﴿٣٠﴾

30. *So, taste it! For We shall only increase you in torment.*

إِنَّ لِلْمُتَّقِينَ مَفَازًا ﴿٣١﴾

31. *Surely, for those who are cautiously aware is achievement,*

حَدَائِقَ وَأَعْنَٰبًا ﴿٣٢﴾

32. *Gardens and vineyards,*

وَكَوَاعِبَ أَتْرَابًا ۝ ٣٣

33. *companions, shapely and alike of age,*

وَكَأْسًا دِهَاقًا ۝ ٣٤

34. *and an overflowing cup.*

لَا يَسْمَعُونَ فِيهَا لَغْوًا وَلَا كِذَّابًا ۝ ٣٥

35. *No empty talk will they hear in that nor any lie.*

جَزَاءً مِّن رَّبِّكَ عَطَاءً حِسَابًا ۝ ٣٦

36. *A reward from your Lord, a gift according to a reckoning:*

رَّبِّ السَّمَوَاتِ وَالْأَرْضِ وَمَا بَيْنَهُمَا الرَّحْمَنِ لَا يَمْلِكُونَ مِنْهُ خِطَابًا ۝ ٣٧

37. *From the Lord of the heavens and earth and everything between, the Lord of Mercy. They will have no authority from Him to speak.*

يَوْمَ يَقُومُ الرُّوحُ وَالْمَلَائِكَةُ صَفًّا لَّا يَتَكَلَّمُونَ إِلَّا مَنْ أَذِنَ لَهُ الرَّحْمَنُ وَقَالَ صَوَابًا ۝ ٣٨

38. *The day on which the spirit and the angels shall stand in ranks; they shall not speak except he whom the Beneficent Allah permits and who speaks the right thing.*

ذَلِكَ ٱلْيَوْمُ ٱلْحَقُّ فَمَن شَآءَ ٱتَّخَذَ إِلَىٰ رَبِّهِۦ مَـَٔابًا ﴿٣٩﴾

39. *That is the Day of Truth. So, whoever wishes to do so should take the path that leads to his Lord.*

إِنَّآ أَنذَرْنَـٰكُمْ عَذَابًا قَرِيبًا يَوْمَ يَنظُرُ ٱلْمَرْءُ مَا قَدَّمَتْ يَدَاهُ وَيَقُولُ ٱلْكَافِرُ يَـٰلَيْتَنِى كُنتُ تُرَٰبًۢا ﴿٤٠﴾

40. *We have warned you of imminent torment, on the Day when every person will see what their own hands have sent ahead for them, when the disbeliever will say, 'If only I were dust!'*

Commentary on Selected Verses

عَمَّ يَتَسَآءَلُونَ ﴿١﴾

What is it that they question each other about? (78:1)

عَنِ ٱلنَّبَإِ ٱلْعَظِيمِ ﴿٢﴾

The momentous announcement. (78:2)

ٱلَّذِى هُمْ فِيهِ مُخْتَلِفُونَ ﴿٣﴾

about which they differ? (78:3)

كَلَّا سَيَعْلَمُونَ ﴿٤﴾

No indeed; they shall soon know! (78:4)

ثُمَّ كَلَّا سَيَعْلَمُونَ ﴿٥﴾

Again, no indeed; they shall soon know! (78:5)

أَلَمْ نَجْعَلِ ٱلْأَرْضَ مِهَٰدًا ﴿٦﴾

Did We not make the earth smooth (78:6)

$$وَٱلۡجِبَالَ أَوۡتَادًا ٧$$

and the mountains as pegs? (78:7)

'*Amma* means 'about what?' What is it that concerns human beings? What is it that we are disturbed about? What is it that we ask each other? What happens after death? What is the meaning of death? What is the purpose of this? What is the beginning? What is birth? What is death? Verse 78:2 refers to the great news, which is the addressing, focusing, speculating, or wondering about the end. We all want comfort, ease, security, wellbeing and happiness throughout our lives. The life that we live is nothing other than a practice of how to be content at heart despite knowing that the outer world will never be constant, steady, or only give us good news.

Wherever there is pleasure, there is displeasure. Wherever there is wealth there is also poverty in another form. You may be rich in financial terms or you may have outer power, but you may feel impoverished in your heart meaning you are not joyful, you are not content, and you are not in a state of bliss. One of the biggest industries in the world is alcohol and drug-related. Nearly 40% of global wealth is derived from the sale of substances which are aimed at getting people out of their normal state of minds. We seek an escape from a mind we are stuck with and which presents us with troubles. Yet, it is not the mind that is the issue. It is our will and discipline which is lacking.

Over the course of thousands of years, there were numerous prophetic unveilings. The biggest effulgence of the unveilings was with the Prophet Ibrahim (AS) about 4,000 years ago. For him, it became clear that there is none other than the One. He spent quite a bit of time in pharaonic Egypt. The greater the Pharaoh, the more emphasis was placed on the second, unseen journey. Tombs would be filled with treasures for this second journey.

Many other cultures believed in life after death, and there is some evidence of this. Mummified birds, considered a big sacrifice 3,000 years ago, was a big industry. Birds were a symbol of regeneration. Those who could afford it would buy the birds from a priest. Upon their death, the birds would be buried in their graves. The idea of the journey after death was prominent.

The Judaic period and the Christian era followed this; and then subsequently all of the great Prophets until finally, the world received the Prophet Muhammad (S).

The *Qur'an* gives us a clear picture. You will die according to the state you are in, according to your accumulated intention and actions. This is who you are, and you experience it afterwards. The question arises as to how long the suffering, or this *barzakh* (the interspace between *Dunya* and *ākhira* (the Next Life) lasts. Is it forever or is it short? This chapter tells us in verse 78:4 that certainly they will come to know. Every one of us will experience death, nobody can escape it. The emphasis, on 'coming to know' is repeated in verse 78:5. Certainly, every person who has asked the question, 'what is going to be my state after death?' will experience it. Verse 78:6 tells us that the earth is a nursery for us to discover the light of Allah in our hearts to make it easy for us. Verse 78:7 refers to mountains as pegs holding part of the gravitational story of the earth's field.

$$وَخَلَقْنَـٰكُمْ أَزْوَٰجًا ۝٨$$

And We created you in pairs, (78:8)

$$وَجَعَلْنَا نَوْمَكُمْ سُبَاتًا ۝٩$$

give you sleep for rest, (78:9)

$$وَجَعَلْنَا ٱلَّيْلَ لِبَاسًا ۝١٠$$

the night as a cover, (78:10)

وَجَعَلْنَا ٱلنَّهَارَ مَعَاشًا ۝

and the day for your livelihood? (78:11)

وَبَنَيْنَا فَوْقَكُمْ سَبْعًا شِدَادًا ۝

Did We not build seven strong above you, (78:12)

وَجَعَلْنَا سِرَاجًا وَهَّاجًا ۝

and have placed a lamp full of blazing splendour? (78:13)

وَأَنزَلْنَا مِنَ ٱلْمُعْصِرَاتِ مَآءً ثَجَّاجًا ۝

And We send down from the clouds water pouring forth abundantly, (78:14)

لِّنُخْرِجَ بِهِۦ حَبًّا وَنَبَاتًا ۝

that We may bring forth thereby grain and plants, (78:15)

وَجَنَّٰتٍ أَلْفَافًا ۝

and gardens intertwined? (78:16)

This section, until verse 16, presents a few sub-sections. One is the challenge: What are you asking for? What are you concerned about? You want to constantly find out what is the final point. What is the end of this relationship? In a friendship, you want to know that it is going to last for a long time. When you build a house, you want to make sure it is secure for many years to come. The focus is the end. Every intelligent human being is concerned about the end. This is the first part. Then comes the story of duality.

Verse 78:8 explains that nothing exists unless it is one of two. Good and bad, up and down, man and woman, day and night, happy and miserable. You cannot have any possibility in this life without plurality. We created everything from pairs, and we created, as verse 78:9 says, 'sleep as a rest.' *Subāt* is hibernation. You must let go so that the mind, the subconscious, and other levels of consciousness work themselves out because you had a lot of overloads during the day. Sleep is the other half of wakefulness. These are the two parallels or pluralities.

Verse 78:11 continues, 'And We have made the day for seeking livelihood.' We must interact with the outer world, with the earth, with plants, with animals, with food, and with rest. We are also put through incredible challenges. How does *Allah Azza wa Jal* create? How does He maintain the entire cosmos and billions of galaxies? You and I are one person, two people, perhaps a family, perhaps 20 or 50 people, and we say, 'my God this is a lot of trouble.' Consider the incredible *Rabb* (Lord).

'Seven strong ones' in verse 78:12 refers to the different layers of the cosmos or the heavens above us. Then, verse 78:13 refers to the sun. The sun is always referred to as *sirāj* (self-effulgent) and the moon as *nūr* (light). Verse 78:14 refers to the rain that comes down, and then verse 78:15, from water comes life. If water is polluted it can also be the taker of life. Isn't that amazing? The ultimate goodness comes from water and it also presents incredible challenges, thus verse 78:16, 'And gardens of thick foliage.'

Now we come to the next section, which is the essence of this chapter.

إِنَّ يَوْمَ ٱلْفَصْلِ كَانَ مِيقَٰتًا ۝

A time has been appointed for the Day of Decision: (78:17)

يَوْمَ يُنفَخُ فِى ٱلصُّورِ فَتَأْتُونَ أَفْوَاجًا ۝

the Day when the trumpet is sounded and you all come forward
in multitudes; (78:18)

وَفُتِحَتِ ٱلسَّمَآءُ فَكَانَتْ أَبْوَٰبًا ۝

and when the skies are opened and become gates. (78:19)

وَسُيِّرَتِ ٱلْجِبَالُ فَكَانَتْ سَرَابًا ۝

When the mountains will vanish like a mirage. (78:20)

إِنَّ جَهَنَّمَ كَانَتْ مِرْصَادًا ۝

Hell lies in ambush, (78:21)

لِّلطَّٰغِينَ مَـَٔابًا ۝

For the insolent a resort. (78:22)

لَّبِثِينَ فِيهَآ أَحْقَابًا ﴿٢٣﴾

In it shall they remain for a long time. (78:23)

لَّا يَذُوقُونَ فِيهَا بَرْدًا وَلَا شَرَابًا ﴿٢٤﴾

Therein they taste neither coolness nor anything to drink, (78:24)

إِلَّا حَمِيمًا وَغَسَّاقًا ﴿٢٥﴾

save boiling water and pus. (78:25)

جَزَآءً وِفَاقًا ﴿٢٦﴾

for a suitable recompense. (78:26)

إِنَّهُمْ كَانُوا۟ لَا يَرْجُونَ حِسَابًا ﴿٢٧﴾

They indeed hoped not for a reckoning, (78:27)

وَكَذَّبُوا۟ بِـَٔايَـٰتِنَا كِذَّابًا ﴿٢٨﴾

and they rejected Our messages as lies. (78:28)

وَكُلَّ شَىْءٍ أَحْصَيْنَـٰهُ كِتَـٰبًا ﴿٢٩﴾

But We have placed on record every single thing. (78:29)

$$\text{فَذُوقُواْ فَلَن نَّزِيدَكُمْ إِلَّا عَذَابًا (٣٠)}$$

So, taste it! For We shall only increase you in torment. (78:30)

These verses present the concept of *Yawm al faṣl,* which is the news, the day of separation, the day of the end of *Furqān* (discrimination). This tells us that we can think and act now but we cannot do so after death. *Yawm al fasl* refers to the latter part of life after we leave this earth and there is no longer indecision. Verse 78:18 tells us this is like a blow-up, the end of light as we understand it, or another energy bang that takes place announcing the beginning of the end of this cycle.

Verse 78:19 says there will be patterns in the sky, energy patterns, and consciousness patterns. Verse 78:20 continues, 'And the mountains will be set in motion as if they were a mere *sarāb* (mirage).' He says the mountains will be set in motion as if they are floating. Then verse 78:21, 'Surely, Hell lies in wait.' *Mir'sād* means 'is focused upon.' *Jahannam* (hell) is a wonderful Arabic word which has many derivatives such as *Janna* (heaven). In classical Arabic, it means a bottomless pit. It means there is no security in it, there is no gravitational resting in it, it is endless, and it is turmoil.

Verse 78:22 references transgressors in this world, and verse 78:23 describes *Ahqāb* (periods). Allah tells us that hell and paradise are not forever. If I had been wayward in this life, not giving enough time to purify my inner core, my intention, and my heart, if I had not been able to get to my innermost, which is my soul, then I still need to be purified. Purification is important when we consider what comes after death.

In verse 78:24, Allah says, 'they will not taste.' If you taste the inner joy, then you have accessed another zone of comprehension. As humans we need to be purified after our death if we have not already done it ourselves sufficiently. They asked the Prophet (S) what about those who are righteous? What is the state of their account?

He says it is easy, it is swift; you know you don't need to be shaken too much, as you would do in muddy water which will need to be filtered many times.

Verse 78:27 explains, 'because they were not considering the fact, and the truth that whatever you do will have its account.' *Hisāb* means account, reckoning. Is your action for *Bismillah* or *Fī sabīl Allāh* (in the path of Allah, for the sake of Allah)? If yes, then you are freeing yourself from your lower self.

Then verse 78:28, which means 'they denied all the signs in this world.' We do not see all the signs around us such as the need for us to eat, drink, rest, care for others, and relate to other human beings. If you do not accept these signs as a nursery for what comes later, then we have missed it.

The key verse in this section is 78:29, 'And We have recorded everything in a Book,' there is no wastage in this world. According to the first law of thermodynamics, there is no addition or subtraction in the energy which is in this world. The second law of thermodynamics is that any system will lose its efficiencies until it gives out. The same principle applies to a child who is full of energy, compared to a 50 year-old who starts to fall ill occasionally. You must be ready for it, embracing it joyfully, and not in misery. We ask: 'Why am I going to die?' The moment you were born you were one moment closer to death. This realisation is good news. Smile at it and do your best, care for others, share and interact with this world, constantly remembering that the world has no beginning and no end.

How do you access it? We have many rituals. If you don't know how to separate yourself from the worries of day-to-day life then go into your *sajdah* (devotional prostration in prayer), disappear, be mindless and be free of thoughts. It is a matter of practice. The section concludes with verse 78:30, 'So taste! For We shall not add to you anything but punishment.'

إِنَّ لِلْمُتَّقِينَ مَفَازًا ﴿٣١﴾

Surely, for those who are cautiously aware is achievement, (78:31)

حَدَائِقَ وَأَعْنَابًا ﴿٣٢﴾

Gardens and vineyards, (78:32)

وَكَوَاعِبَ أَتْرَابًا ﴿٣٣﴾

companions, shapely and alike of age, (78:33)

وَكَأْسًا دِهَاقًا ﴿٣٤﴾

and an overflowing cup. (78:34)

لَا يَسْمَعُونَ فِيهَا لَغْوًا وَلَا كِذَّابًا ﴿٣٥﴾

No empty talk will they hear in that nor any lie. (78:35)

جَزَاءً مِّن رَّبِّكَ عَطَاءً حِسَابًا ﴿٣٦﴾

A reward from your Lord, a gift according to a reckoning: (78:36)

رَّبِّ ٱلسَّمَٰوَٰتِ وَٱلْأَرْضِ وَمَا بَيْنَهُمَا ٱلرَّحْمَٰنِ لَا يَمْلِكُونَ مِنْهُ خِطَابًا ۝

From the Lord of the heavens and earth and everything between,
the Lord of Mercy. They will have no authority from Him to
speak. (78:37)

This is the story, the news, the *nabā*. It is the ultimate map of what we will experience after we leave this so-called normal consciousness. Verse 78:31 explains, certainly, for those who are in cautious awareness or God consciousness, those who are aware that any minute they may leave, and they are therefore accountable, their account is always brought up to date and there is *mafāza'* (victory). If you are constantly aware that this day may be your last day, this minute may be your last minute, then you will certainly be victorious.

Verse 78:33 refers to companions that are of the right companionship. In other words, they are all looking for companions in this world, whether it be through spouses, wives or friends. We all seek perfect compatibility. You experience it occasionally but not consistently because that is the nature of this life. You experience goodness, love, and compassion, but it is not permanent.

He was wonderful on the wedding day but five years later she says: 'My God you were so kind to me then, but now you don't notice me.' This is the nature of the world. The poor fellow is forgetful. He has so many demands made on him. The poor woman has children and other responsibilities. Therefore, the idea is that in this world you will have just a taste of that perfect compatibility, perfect joy and perfect bliss.

Verse 78:34 means a cup that overflows with joy. When you experience a form of worship or *Hajj* (the Pilgrimage), you truly experience bliss. How do you prolong it? By the practice of leaving yourself aside which means leaving aside self-concern and getting out of the box of the mind without drugs. Consider our practices of worship: the Prophet (S) described *sajdah* (devotional prostration in prayer) as *mi'rāj al mu'min* (ascension of the believer). *Mi'rāj* is taking off beyond the zones of the norm, into other heavens. If you have faith and trust in your creator and the light in your heart, then you are in your *mi'rāj* (ascension).

For this reason, this life cannot be fully accepted unless you recalibrate all the time, by stepping out of your mind and into the heart and the original light that is already with you. What more can Allah give as a gift to human beings? This is the good news. This is the *bushrā*. The *bushrā* is that the light of the creator is in your heart. If you fall into the abyss of the darkness of creation, it is your own fault. Who told you to go there and fall into it? Come back, climb back, dust yourself off and redo your commitment.

Bismillah is the beginning of endless joy, if only you truly live it. Nobody can live it other than you and nobody causes you to fall other than you. You must do it. It is not by talk, it is not by preaching, it is by reaching that which is already in you.

Then we are told in verse 78:35 that in that state, you do not hear any nonsense. The word *Laghw* refers to 'foolish, ineffectual, meaningless talk.'

Verse 78:35 means, 'no-nonsense and no lies.' Then verse 78:36 says, 'A reward from your Lord, a gift according to a reckoning,' meaning this is the reward of your Lord, this is what we aspire to. We aspire to hear the Lord's will. If your will is subservient to Allah's will then you will have constant victory. It means you want to reach that point of resonance between your mind, your will, your wish and Allah's perfect plot (*Qadhā' wa Qadr*). Whatever Allah has designed will take place, so we want to make our direction, hope, and will coincide with Allah's will so that we have perpetual joy.

Verse 78:37 says, 'The Lord of the heavens and the earth and what is between them, the All-Merciful, they are not able to address Him.' He is *Al-Rahmān*, the source of all mercy. On that day of reckoning, there is nothing we can do. We can make noise and lie, or we can speak the truth and practice disappearance in our prostration, but in that stage when the creation disappears, no action is possible.

What is generosity? A six month old child does not understand generosity but a child of seven or eight years old understands it. Give to your mummy, give to your daddy. We clap for them and encourage them. What are they doing? They are tapping into that zone of consciousness called generosity which is always there because it is an attribute of Allah. *Allah Azza wa Jal* is The Generous and for this reason, He is also called *Al-Karīm* (The Most Generous). You need to tap into that zone. That is why in *Sūrat al-Baqarah*, verse 2:138 says, 'take the colour of Allah's attributes.' Once you tap into that, enjoy it as a human being. Why? Because it is in our *fitrah* (the original nature of man, deeply imprinted within him and from which all diversity originates).

يَوْمَ يَقُومُ ٱلرُّوحُ وَٱلْمَلَٰٓئِكَةُ صَفًّا لَّا يَتَكَلَّمُونَ إِلَّا مَنْ أَذِنَ لَهُ ٱلرَّحْمَٰنُ وَقَالَ صَوَابًا ﴿٣٨﴾

The day on which the spirit and the angels shall stand in ranks; they shall not speak except he whom the Beneficent Allah permits and who speaks the right thing. (78:38)

ذَٰلِكَ ٱلْيَوْمُ ٱلْحَقُّ فَمَن شَآءَ ٱتَّخَذَ إِلَىٰ رَبِّهِۦ مَـَٔابًا ﴿٣٩﴾

That is the Day of Truth. So, whoever wishes to do so should take the path that leads to his Lord. (78:39)

إِنَّآ أَنذَرْنَٰكُمْ عَذَابًا قَرِيبًا يَوْمَ يَنظُرُ ٱلْمَرْءُ مَا قَدَّمَتْ يَدَاهُ وَيَقُولُ ٱلْكَافِرُ يَٰلَيْتَنِي كُنتُ تُرَٰبًا ﴿٤٠﴾

We have warned you of imminent torment, on the Day when every person will see what their own hands have sent ahead for them, when the disbeliever will say, 'If only I were dust!' (78:40)

This chapter is a warning. You now have a chance to redeem yourself from the lower self towards the higher self, which is your *rūh* (soul). The chapter ends with this reinforced warning that now you have the chance to do it. This is the *nabā*, the news: we all end up back where it all started, into our nothingness and the oneness of

Allah Azza wa Jal. Here I have a chance of practicing disappearance from my identity, my profile. Here I am this person, this doer and this generous being. If we don't practice neutrality, we become arrogant by our 'do-good' goodliness. This is the warning of this chapter. On that day of the end, there will be *Haqq*, which is the truth. The culmination is that we surrender that which is not ours. This means that the body goes back to where it came from, to the elements of this earth, and the soul returns to its source of *nūr* (light).

Consider verse 78:38: Here the word soul is singular but it means plural. All of the *arwāh* (souls) will be there because they are of the same origin, they are of the light. Consider *Surat al Isrā*, verse 17:85, which says, 'They ask you about the soul. Say: 'The soul belongs to the realm of my Lord.'

Verse 78:39 says that period is a perfect truth—there is no interference, no darkness, and it further reminds us that he who has willpower will find a way to his Lord. Verse 78:40 says, 'Surely We warn you of a punishment near at hand,' meaning we warned you of a chastisement (*'adhāb*). As I mentioned earlier, it is a purification zone which is close to us right now. If you and I choose to purify our intention and our actions, it is there for us.

Verse 78:40 continues to explain that whatever you have done is all there for you. We are the sum of our intentions and actions. The verse continues, saying even he who had denied this news, he who had denied the truth will see that there is none other than the One who wants us to recognise that *tawhīd* (Oneness), who brought us here into pluralities to practice. Allah is the Just and Justice belongs to *Allah Azza wa Jal.* You and I have to practice some semblance of justice, a bit of goodness, a bit of generosity so that we do not forget that life is based on balance. We are to return to that day, we know that is the *yawm al-haqq*, that is, absolute justice. Here it is relative justice. We are here practising that which will come later where we have no power at all. What better news than this? This is the *nabā* (news or announcement).

Chapter 12
SURAT AL-A'LA

I would like to share with you a brief interpretation of the inner meanings and the transformative maps that are given to us in this glorious chapter (87), *Sūrat al-A'lā*, which, according to many commentators was about the eighth chapter revealed in Makkah. It is immensely rich as a map of existence and it gives us the purpose of human beings on this earth and the direction that we need to constantly refer to. It is a brief chapter, and it is comprised of 19 verses with over 30 terms which to my mind constitute 5% to 7% of the key terms in the *Qur'an*. The *Qur'an* contains over 400 key Arabic terms. It is necessary to understand the roots of these terms to appreciate the different facets and reflections of these words. Accordingly, the best we can do is to provide an interpretation of the basic meaning, and from it we draw certain aspects of the culture, then the structure of the religion, and thereafter the spiritual parts which are transformative. It is a matter of information to transformation.

Qur'anic Verses

The Arabic text and the English translation of *Sūrat al-A'lā* follow immediately below. Thereafter I will focus my commentary on selected verses and words.

بِسْمِ ٱللَّهِ ٱلرَّحْمَٰنِ ٱلرَّحِيمِ

In the name of Allah, the Merciful to all, the Compassionate to each!

سَبِّحِ ٱسْمَ رَبِّكَ ٱلْأَعْلَى ﴿١﴾

1. *Glorify the name of your Lord, the Most High,*

ٱلَّذِى خَلَقَ فَسَوَّىٰ ﴿٢﴾

2. *Who creates, then makes complete,*

وَٱلَّذِى قَدَّرَ فَهَدَىٰ ﴿٣﴾

3. *Who determined and guided,*

وَٱلَّذِىٓ أَخْرَجَ ٱلْمَرْعَىٰ ﴿٤﴾

4. *Who brought forth the pasturage,*

فَجَعَلَهُۥ غُثَآءً أَحْوَىٰ ﴿٥﴾

5. *then made it dark debris.*

سَنُقْرِئُكَ فَلَا تَنسَىٰ ﴿٦﴾

6.   *We shall make you recite and you will not forget.*

إِلَّا مَا شَاءَ اللَّهُ إِنَّهُ يَعْلَمُ الْجَهْرَ وَمَا يَخْفَىٰ ﴿٧﴾

7.   *Save what Allah wills; surely, He knows what is spoken aloud and what is hidden.*

وَنُيَسِّرُكَ لِلْيُسْرَىٰ ﴿٨﴾

8.   *We shall show you the easy way.*

فَذَكِّرْ إِن نَّفَعَتِ الذِّكْرَىٰ ﴿٩﴾

9.   *So, remind, if reminding will help.*

سَيَذَّكَّرُ مَن يَخْشَىٰ ﴿١٠﴾

10.   *And he who fears shall remember,*

وَيَتَجَنَّبُهَا الْأَشْقَى ﴿١١﴾

11.   *but it will be ignored by the most wicked.*

ٱلَّذِى يَصْلَى ٱلنَّارَ ٱلْكُبْرَىٰ ﴿١٢﴾

12. *He who shall be scorched by the great Fire,*

ثُمَّ لَا يَمُوتُ فِيهَا وَلَا يَحْيَىٰ ﴿١٣﴾

13. *wherein he will neither die nor remain alive.*

قَدْ أَفْلَحَ مَن تَزَكَّىٰ ﴿١٤﴾

14. *He indeed shall be successful who purifies himself,*

وَذَكَرَ ٱسْمَ رَبِّهِ فَصَلَّىٰ ﴿١٥﴾

15. *and mentions the Name of his Lord, and prays.*

بَلْ تُؤْثِرُونَ ٱلْحَيَوٰةَ ٱلدُّنْيَا ﴿١٦﴾

16. *Yet you prefer the life of this world,*

وَٱلْأَخِرَةُ خَيْرٌ وَأَبْقَىٰ ﴿١٧﴾

17. *though the hereafter is better and more lasting.*

إِنَّ هَٰذَا لَفِى ٱلصُّحُفِ ٱلْأُولَىٰ ﴿١٨﴾

18. *All this is in the earlier scriptures,*

$$صُحُفِ إِبْرَٰهِيمَ وَمُوسَىٰ ﴿١٩﴾$$

19. the scriptures of Abraham and Moses.

Commentary on Selected Verses

$$سَبِّحِ ٱسْمَ رَبِّكَ ٱلْأَعْلَى ﴿١﴾$$

Glorify the name of your Lord, the Most High, (87:1)

$$ٱلَّذِى خَلَقَ فَسَوَّىٰ ﴿٢﴾$$

Who creates, then makes complete, (87:2)

$$وَٱلَّذِى قَدَّرَ فَهَدَىٰ ﴿٣﴾$$

Who determined and guided, (87:3)

$$وَٱلَّذِىٓ أَخْرَجَ ٱلْمَرْعَىٰ ﴿٤﴾$$

Who brought forth the pasturage, (87:4)

$$فَجَعَلَهُۥ غُثَآءً أَحْوَىٰ ﴿٥﴾$$

then made it dark debris. (87:5)

The word *sabbaha* is a key term made up of *seen, baa* and *haa*. The word *sabbaha* means to swim, let go, and float. All of it implies an expansive aspect of glorification. It implies something subtle. Consider *Sūrat al-Nūr*, verse 24:35, which says, 'Allah is the Light of the heavens and the earth,' which implies that *nūr* (light), from its subtle origin, appears eventually as light, as heat, and even as matter.

Sūrat al-'Alaq, verse 96:1 says, Recite, in the name of your Lord! He Who created! *Ism* (name) is used here as well as in the first verse of *Sūrat al-A'lā*. What is a name? If you say the name of something, it implies its meanings and uses. The names are attributes of Allah: for example, *Al-'Adhīm* (The Magnificent), *Al-Qawī* (The Most Strong) and *Al-Awwal* (The First). There are hundreds of attributes or qualities which are not included in the 99 names and qualities of Allah *(Asmā' al-husnā)*. For example, *Al-Sabbit* (The Ever Fixed, Ever Permanent, Ever Stable, Ever Constant).

Some of the names are beyond the realm of our worldly understanding of dualities. It is *Al-Wāhid* (The One), *Al-Ahad* (The Absolute One), *Al-Fard* (The Absolute Independent One) and *Al-Samad* (The Self Sufficient). For this reason, every *bismillah* is a key, to enter into that chapter. It gives you humble authority to enter. When we say *Bismillah ir-Rahman ir-Rahim*, we have invoked the ease of Allah's *rahma* (mercy). Then *Al-Hamdu*, all the praise, the *hamd*. Whatever you praise belongs to Allah, so you have entered into that treasure house.

Rabb, as it appears in verse 87, is most often translated as Lord. *Rubūbīyah* does not only mean Lord. *Rubūbīyah* is *tarbiyah*, it is to bring up, raise, or groom. It implies that it is giving you the doorway to the potential that you can rise to. Also, *Rabb Al-Bayt*, the Lord of the house; his job is to make sure the house is tidy, healthy, clean and orderly so that these different human beings can rest, recuperate, recollect and gather their higher and lower. *Al A'lā*, which is the definition of *Allah Azza wa Jal*, The Highest, The Ultimate, meaning that which is beyond measure, beyond mental capacity to fathom. *Fasawwa* in verse 87:2 means perfection. Allah brings everything to its fulfilment. Also consider *Sūrat al-Mulk*, verse 67:3, which says: then look again, can you see any disorder? Look again! And again! Even in chaos, there is order. People are quarrelling, people are unhappy, people are stealing from each other, and lying to each other, but if you look closer, it is because they are led by their desires.

They have a desire that is not in balance. They fail to consider *Al-'Adl* (The All-Just). They disregard fair play, so it results in chaos. Then, verse 87:3 is about *Qadhā' wa Qadr*. *Qadr* means everything is according to a measure; nothing is haphazard. Seek guidance from *Al-Hādī*. No one can guide you except the One. If somebody guides you, it serves as a means, a *wazīfa* (a duty, an assignment), but that duty reflects the *hidāyah* (guidance) that comes from *Allah Azza wa Jal*. Verse 87:4 then says, 'Who brings forth the herbage,' We are all in that state, desiring provision, health, wellness and ease of mind.

Verse 87:5 says, 'Then it turns it to rust brown stubble,' meaning that everything will pass; anything that is born will eventually die. It is interesting to consider the three verses where the words *sabbaha* and *yasbbahūna* appear. Firstly, in *Sūrat al-Yasin* verse 36:40, it says 'Neither is it allowable to the sun that it should overtake the moon nor can the night outstrip the day; and all float on in a sphere.' This verse brilliantly illustrates that everything in this existence moves within its sphere. The existence of everything—including you and I, the day and the night, man, woman, and all of creation—is based on phases, stages, and cycles.

Secondly, *Sūrat al-Hadid* verse 57:1 states, Everything in the heavens and earth glorifies Allah. It is in the past, *sabbah*, meaning they are already engaged in their glorification, following their programmed patterns according to their unique designs. The way the wasp does its *tasbīh* (glorification) differs from the lion, which is also distinct from how the oak tree glorifies.

Next we have the third verse from *Sūrat al-Jum'a*, verse 62:1, 'Whatever is in the heavens and whatever is in the earth declares the glory of Allah, the King, the Holy, the Mighty, the Wise.' It concludes in the same manner as *Sūrat al-Hadīd* verse 57:1, 'He is the Almighty, the Wise.' This is incredible. Allah is the most beloved, the most unique, the most verified, and the ultimate in wisdom and firmness. These three verses align perfectly, and then we have as wonderful verse from *Surah al-Isrā*, 17:47, 'There is nothing that does not sing His praise' meaning nothing is in existence unless it is transmitting its frequency. The storm does it, the atom does it. Everything expresses itself; it glorifies its nature. Allah has given it its light, its *rūh* (soul) and its earthiness. *Allahumma arana haqaiq al ashya kama* means that I want to see things as they truly are. I wish to see the scorpion as a scorpion, the lion as a lion and the beautiful bird singing as nothing but a bird.

Furthermore, *Sūrat al-Isrā* verse 17:44 states, 'There is nothing that does not sing His praise, but you do not understand their songs of praise' meaning that we don't comprehend their language. For instance when one of the ants said (27:18), 'Ants, enter your dwelling-places, lest Solomon and his hosts crush you, being unaware!' Suleyman (AS) heard, he understood. Did he understand that language? There are human beings who can often hear things that others cannot hear. It is not merely about hearing; it involves a certain transmission that can be received. We all have the potential for this receptivity, but we forgotten it. We have spent too many years and efforts on other matters. Thousands of years ago, human beings were far more intuitive; they could hear things from various parts of the world. However, we have lost this skill. In recent years we have invented the cell phone as part of our desire to be connected. Although we are now connected, we long for the experience of that connectivity with *Al-Khāliq* (the Creator). We are all the children of Adam.

Consider the beautiful verse from *Sūrat al-Ghāfir*, verse 40:55, 'and ask forgiveness for your sins, and glorify the praise of your Lord' meaning first ask for forgiveness, and recognise our mistakes and shortcomings, then 'Glorify your Lord with Praises' (see *Sūrat al-Nasr*, verse 110:3). That is why we say *astaghfiru'llāh* first, Allah first and then *Māshā' Allah*. This is how Allah has created it and as Imam Ali (RA) says: 'And if you don't like it, get out of this earth.' *Iqra'*, read it, see it, then as mentioned in *Sūrat al-Ghāfir*, verse 40:55, 'and glorify the praise of your Lord, at evening and dawn.' It means if you don't have that constant reference, you are not recharged. If you are not recharged then you are not energised and therefore you fail to realise your full potential as a human being.

$$\text{سَنُقْرِئُكَ فَلَا تَنسَىٰ ٦}$$

We shall make you recite and you will not forget. (87:6)

$$\text{إِلَّا مَا شَاءَ اللَّهُ إِنَّهُ يَعْلَمُ الْجَهْرَ وَمَا يَخْفَىٰ ٧}$$

Save what Allah wills; surely, He knows what is spoken aloud and what is hidden. (87:7)

$$\text{وَنُيَسِّرُكَ لِلْيُسْرَىٰ ٨}$$

We shall show you the easy way. (87:8)

$$\text{فَذَكِّرْ إِن نَّفَعَتِ الذِّكْرَىٰ ٩}$$

So, remind, if reminding will help. (87:9)

Verse 87:6 says, 'we make you read such that you will never forget what matters.' The important thing is that the heart or the *fitra* (the original nature of man, deeply imprinted within him and the source of all diversity), or your soul knows what matters most because the soul has already been exposed to the question, *alastu bi-Rabbikum* ("Am I not your Lord?"). The soul already carries the imprint of the *wujūd*, the presence of your Lord, *Allah Azza wa Jal*. Everything must be viewed with the recognition of *Wahdat al-Wujūd* (the Unity of Existence). Allah says, 'You will never forget that which matters.' Everything is *Māshā' Allah*, everything is in the hand of Allah and Allah can change and postpone. There are fixed destinies, such as the certainty that every living entity will die, but the precise date and circumstances may vary based on your intentions and actions.

Verse 87:8 reminds us, 'Allah knows what is obvious, what is allowed and what is hidden from man.' *Khāfiya* refers to the hidden. That is why the entire *Qur'an* is based on revelation from the unseen. Refer to *Sūrat al-Baqarah*, verse 2:3, which says, 'Who trust in the Unseen, and uphold the prayer.' It goes beyond trust. It entails knowing your dependence on the unseen. The unseen is vast, while the seen is small and limited. Consider *Sūrat al-Qiyāmah*, verse 75:18, which says, 'up to Us is its collection and recitation. When We recite it, follow its recitation.' Also ponder over *Sūrat al-Maryam*, verse 19:12, which says, 'take firm hold of the Book.' Once you have heard the truth, you can no longer waver. You know with certainty, *Lā ilāha illā Allāh*, and you know in truth the reflection of it is *Muhammadun Rasul Allah*. *Sūrat al-'Alaq*, verse 96:1, says, Recite, in the name of your Lord! He Who created! acknowledging the gift of language given to human beings by Allah. Language gives us a significant advantage. In verse 87:8, Allah promises the Prophet (S) and promises us as well that ease will come, but are we ready for it? Are we receptive to it? Are we going to see it? Or are we fixated on our own whims, expectations, dwelling in the past and being fearful of the future? Consequently, our presence is diminished.

That is why one of the main requirements of our *salāt* (prayers) is *Hudhur al qalb* (presence of heart), which means that after *wudhū'* (ritual ablution), we detach ourselves from the past and fully immerse ourselves in the present moment. The present moment is eternal, and by entering into it, we step into the realm of *azaliya*, the realm of permanence. The great teachings of the Prophet (S) remind us that Allah created us for *saadal abadiya*, everlasting joy, not just fleeting pleasure. As mentioned in verse 87:8 above, part of the promised ease is aligned with what we love and want, but it comes with conditions that need to be followed.

The conditions mentioned in verse 87:8 involve accepting and acknowledging the existence of an optimal way of living, an optimum way of conducting your intentions, actions, accountability, social responsibilities, and your readiness to let go of this world, rather than to be in a state of attachment.

Verse 87:9 says, 'So remind, for certainly, the reminder is of benefit.' Reminders are useful even if we don't immediately act upon them. There are dozens of beautiful verses with this word *dhikr* (remembrance, reflection, pronouncing, announcing). For instance, *Sūrat al-Kahf* verse 18:24, says, 'and mention your Lord, when you forget,' emphasising the need to remember Allah even in moments of forgetfulness, rush, illness, fear, or anxiety. Additionally, *Sūrat al-'Imrān*, verse 3:41 says, 'Remember your Lord frequently, and glorify Him each evening and dawn.'

The remembrance of Allah and the awareness of His presence hold great value for those who have certainty and security in their *Imān*. The term *amana yamino* signifies being secure. As mentioned in *Sūrat at-Tawbah*, verse 9:40, 'Do not grieve, for Allah is with us.' This assurance of Allah's presence provides a sense of security. Allah is already there, his *nūr* (light) resides in your heart, so what is there to be worried about?

Allah has no beginning and no end. If the loved one of someone has died, it is important to help them, to offer condolences and to give them time to grieve. Show empathy and compassion. However, this period of mourning should not extend indefinitely. Eventually, one must remember that *Allah* is *Al-Bāqī* (The Everlasting) and His light in your soul is also everlasting because the soul carries on.

$$سَيَذَّكَّرُ مَن يَخْشَىٰ ﴿١٠﴾$$

And he who fears shall remember, (87:10)

$$وَيَتَجَنَّبُهَا ٱلْأَشْقَى ﴿١١﴾$$

but it will be ignored by the most wicked. (87:11)

ٱلَّذِى يَصْلَى ٱلنَّارَ ٱلْكُبْرَىٰ ﴿١٢﴾

He who shall be scorched by the great Fire, (87:12)

ثُمَّ لَا يَمُوتُ فِيهَا وَلَا يَحْيَىٰ ﴿١٣﴾

wherein he will neither die nor remain alive. (87:13)

Allah reminds us that those who are in a state of cautious awareness always know that they are here to perfect their worship of Allah. They remember that they are by Allah, *Innā lillāhi wa-innaā 'ilayhi rāji'ūn*. When one says *Lā ilāha illā Allāh* it signifies a recognition that there is no problem or concern that cannot be resolved through the remembrance of Allah.

In verse 87:11 Allah uses the word *ashqā*. The word *shaqi* means he who is arrogant, he who is vain, he who avoids this reminder of their mortality. 'And the most unfortunate one will avoid it.' He who is a *shaqi* does not want to be reminded that he is from Allah to Allah, by Allah, to improve and increase his knowledge of Allah's ways.

Verse 87:12 provides a beautiful description of the big fire at the end and the implication is that there are smaller fires now, where people burn with jealousy, fear, and anxiety. These are the fires preparing us for the big fire.

On the other hand are those who constantly taste and smell *Janna* (paradise). They are like small gardens. The Prophet (S) once put his arm around Salman al Farsi, and mentioned that the garden is waiting for him even though he is not looking for it. You are preparing here for what you will receive later. How we live here will impact our destiny in the afterlife.

Verse 87:13 says, 'there it (Hellfire) is neither life as we experience it, nor the ease of finishing off on an end of death.' Instead, it is in between, it is turmoil that continues.

$$\text{قَدْ أَفْلَحَ مَن تَزَكَّىٰ} \quad ١٤$$

He indeed shall be successful who purifies himself, (87:14)

$$\text{وَذَكَرَ ٱسْمَ رَبِّهِ فَصَلَّىٰ} \quad ١٥$$

and mentions the Name of his Lord, and prays. (87:15)

$$\text{بَلْ تُؤْثِرُونَ ٱلْحَيَوٰةَ ٱلدُّنْيَا} \quad ١٦$$

Yet you prefer the life of this world, (87:16)

$$\text{وَٱلْأَخِرَةُ خَيْرٌ وَأَبْقَىٰ} \quad ١٧$$

though the hereafter is better and more lasting. (87:17)

You and I must humble ourselves, turning our ego upside down. Initially, we wanted certain things because we believed it was important, so by flipping our perspective, we no longer consider it important. When you are in full flight of health and wealth, you consider that a little more power is important. Think of yourself as being on the verge of death. At that moment, you are inclined to become more generous because worldly concerns no longer matter. Trivial matters lose their significance.

Falāh means success or succeeded, and it is derived from *Falaha* which means 'to turn, to change; to till, plough, split, cultivate.' One must be willing to turn the fertile soil of one's heart. The heart can then sustain growth that will eventually prove fruitful. *Hayya 'al al-Falāh*, an invitation to embrace success, beckons us. What is success? It lies in recognising that you are not who you think you are; you are a soul caught for a while in a body, therefore, honour the soul while tending to the needs of the body. This is rationality.

If rationality cannot lead you to spirituality, then see it as a halfway mark. The West heavily emphasises rationality and empirical knowledge. But what of love? What about unconditionality? What about generosity? This imbalance has pushed Western civilisation to the edge, of not just decadence but serious collapse. Of course you need to be rational, as a step, for you to be truly in your soul. But we must not stop there. We are both rational beings and spiritual souls.

The statement, 'He is successful who grows in purity', alludes to the importance of purifying the self, but not the lower self. *Sūrat an-Najm*, verse 53:32, says, 'So do not claim yourselves to be pure.' Do not say, 'I am all right.' Don't ever claim to be content with the self. *Sūrat al-Yusuf*, verse 12:53, says, 'the soul ever urges to evil' meaning it always misguides you. *Shaytān* (satan; ego-self) always lurks so it is important to be cautious. However, the soul remains inherently pure, making it necessary for unity. It is a matter of self-soul unison.

Once you have done that, then you have freed yourself from yourself. Verse 87:15, emphasises the importance of remembering the names of the Lord that are appropriate: *Al-Rahmān* (The All-Merciful), *Al-Rahīm* (The All-Compassionate), *Al-Awwal* (The First), *Al-Ākhir* (The Last), *Al-Dhāhir* (The Manifest), *Al-Bātin* (The Concealer), *Al-'Adhīm* (The Magnificent), *Al-Qawī* (The Most Strong), all of the great attributes, names and qualities of Allah. *Sūrat al-Ma'ārij*, verse 70:23 reminds us to be of 'Those who are constant in their prayer,' perpetually in a state of awareness and reflection.

Then *Allah Azza wa Jal* reminds us of our lower nature in verse 87:16, 'But no! You prefer the life of this world!'. It points out that we prioritise pursuits of this worldly life, falling into a survivalist mentality and behaving in ways that resemble animals. People often say, 'but let us be practical about this,' meaning let us be worldly and get at each other's throat, to see who can suffocate more. What is this miserable reality? The reality of this moment will change, and the reality of tomorrow will change, but the real capital which is the *nūr* (light) of Allah, remains constant. Are you referring to that reality? We do not deny small realities, such as caring for our body, and clarifying our minds, but we must also purify our heart. These are realities, but they become more constant by referring to the absolute reality, Allah's reality.

Earlier in this chapter, in verse 87:8 Allah reassures us saying, 'And We will ease your way to a state of ease.' Verse 87:17 says, 'although the Next World is better and most lasting.' That which comes later transcends the limits of time. Time will stop with our death. Upon our *qiyāmah* (resurrection) we will transition into another realm, beyond our current perception of space and time.

As-salāt ul Mi'rāj al mu'min (prayer is the ascension of the believer), holds significance in this context. By immersing ourselves fully into our *salāt (prayers)*, forgetting time and space and who we are, we touch upon that timeless zone. That is what also gives us the calibration and readiness to leave. Then you are ready to arrive; you are refreshed and recharged. It is transformation. *Islām* (submission) in its early days was transformative and experiential, that's why people came and were transformed. They became full of their humanity and divinity.

We all endured hundreds of years of not fully living our *dīn*. It is not solely the individual's fault, but a result of historical events that unfolded over time. It has taken nature hundreds of millions of years to bring us here. It will take another few hundred years to perfect the *dīn*. For this reason, we must be patient with others, recognising that their journey may be ongoing. But we must be impatient with ourselves. We often find ourselves impatient with others and patient with the ego-self. Take heed. A balanced approach allows for compassion towards others and a proactive attitude towards our own self-transformation.

إِنَّ هَٰذَا لَفِى ٱلصُّحُفِ ٱلْأُولَىٰ ﴿١٨﴾

All this is in the earlier scriptures, (87:18)

197

صُحُفِ إِبْرَٰهِيمَ وَمُوسَىٰ ﴿١٩﴾

the scriptures of Abraham and Moses. (87:19)

Verse 87:18 says the teachings and revelation (*wahy*) – this perfect unveiling – were already present in earlier scrolls and scriptures exactly as it came down to Ibrahim (AS) 4,000 years ago, and later on to Musa (AS). What we have the privilege of inheriting as Muslims culminated not only in the perfect book but also in the way of Muhammad (S) and the way of his family, of his close and great *Sahāba* (companions).

We have examples of people who have saved themselves from themselves, by Allah's *Rahma* (mercy). How? By putting themselves aside, as Prophet Muhammad (S) has said, readiness to leave worldly attachments allows them to truly live in the present.

I pray to Allah Azza wa Jal to make us worthy of our Dīn.

I pray to Allah Azza wa Jal to make us absorb and live our Qur'an.

I pray to Allah Azza wa Jal to make us worthy of Islām (submission), Imān (certainty and security that Allah knows and Allah sees), Ihsān (inner and outer excellence in thought and conduct).

Chapter 13

SURAT AL KAFIRUN, SURAT AL IKHLAS; SURAT AL FALAQ AND SURAT AN NAS

In this section, I will *share* four short chapters. Each begins with *'Qul'*: confess, admit, say, know! The *Qur'an* is a book of life that describes the seen and the unseen; what goes on earth and what is in the heavens and what we experience after death. The *Qur'an* is a book of *mithāls* (similitudes, parables), and all other types of teachings that reflect deeper meanings. It is the Book of signs. It is a book that describes events and describes the *nūr* (light), the power and the energy behind these events; Allah. It describes anything that anybody at any time is subjected to: the good and the bad, the up and the down. Many historical events are referred to in the *Qur'an*, but their patterns are repeated. There are also many instructions.

These four chapters are instructional. They were most likely revealed in Makkah. There are some opinions that two of these chapters are Madinan, but they are of a Makkan stance in that Makkah talks about the Absolute, the truth, the reality, and the story of humanity. These are short chapters, containing 22 verses in total.

Sūrat Al Kāfirūn

بِسۡمِ اللَّهِ الرَّحۡمَٰنِ الرَّحِيمِ

*In the name of Allah, the Merciful to all, the Compassionate to
each!*

قُلۡ يَٰٓأَيُّهَا الۡكَٰفِرُونَ ﴿١﴾

1. *Say: O unbelievers!*

لَآ أَعۡبُدُ مَا تَعۡبُدُونَ ﴿٢﴾

2. *I do not worship what you worship,*

وَلَآ أَنتُمۡ عَٰبِدُونَ مَآ أَعۡبُدُ ﴿٣﴾

3. *nor do you worship what I worship;*

وَلَآ أَنَا۠ عَابِدٌ مَّا عَبَدتُّمۡ ﴿٤﴾

4. *nor will I ever worship what you worship,*

وَلَآ أَنتُمۡ عَٰبِدُونَ مَآ أَعۡبُدُ ﴿٥﴾

5. *nor will you ever worship what I worship.*

$$\left(\text{٦}\right)\ \overline{}\ \text{لَكُمْ دِينُكُمْ وَلِيَ دِينِ}$$

6. You have your religion, and I have mine.

'Qul' (confess, admit, say, know!) is a command in the Qur'an. If I say something, it implies that I mean it. My mind, intention, and words should align. If there is a lack of connection, it can lead to internal fragmentation. The term 'Kaffara yakfuru' means to cover, deny, or fail to accept the truth. The truth is that every human being, regardless of strength, wealth or wellbeing, is in need. We need to submit to that inherent dependence as it is an aspect of Islām (submission). We rely on air. We need the complex faculties that go on without us being aware of them, including billions of neurons in our head and gut. We are always dependent, so admit it! If I deny this, I have fallen into a state of kufr (disbelief). I am denying the truth that I am a needy being and what I need is knowledge, admittance, submission, and obedience to the Glorious Creator, Allah.

'Abada means to adore, being passionately desirous of. As Muslims, we worship Allah and revere all His attributes. We are enamoured by the beauty, majesty, and all the great names and attributes of Allah. Who wouldn't yearn for knowledge? Allah is Al 'Alim (He who knows all), and we adore that attribute. Allah is Al-Jamāl, (The Most Beautiful), Al-Jamīl (The Beautiful, The Graceful), and Al-Karīm (The Most Generous). Allah is Al-'Adhīm (The Magnificent). Allah is Al Mālik al Mulk (The Master of the Kingdom).

Sūrat al-Baqara verse 2:255 says: 'Allah – there is no deity save Him, the Ever-Living, the Self-Subsistent Fount of All Being. Neither slumber overtakes Him, nor sleep. His is all that is in the heavens and all that is on earth. Who is there that could intercede with Him, unless it be by His leave? He knows all that lies open before men and all that is hidden from them, whereas they cannot attain to aught of His knowledge save that which He wills. His eternal power overspreads the heavens and the earth, and their upholding wearies Him not. And he alone is truly exalted, tremendous.'

When we admit that to Allah belongs whatever is seen and unseen in the heavens and the earth, then we embrace that we too belong to him. We are dependent but what a glorious dependency that is! We are dependent on the One; the only One from whom everything has emanated, by whose grace everything is sustained, and into His *Rahma* (mercy) everything is returned. We encounter problems when we incorrectly assume that we are independent. 'I can tackle it! Leave it to me, I will sort it out!' We react this way because we want power, glory and status. It helps to think of yourself in the grave. What is your status there? Ultimately, if you remember your dependency and are in a state of worship and adoration, then you will have *baraka* (grace). It will be flowing. It will not be constantly subjected to fight and flight. Creation is about worship. Worship implies perfecting that connection between the seen, the world of causality, the ups and the downs, and the unseen. They are never separate. It is only because we get preoccupied with what is in front of us that we forget that it was there before us and will remain after us. We are only a little spark which has come into life to recognise its original light, Allah.

The keyword here is *dīn* (way of life, a way that you transact with reality). Separation is an illusion. There is no separation, there is only the *nūr* (light) of Allah. From that light comes infinite levels and varieties of shadows. This chapter refers particularly to the Quraysh people who worshipped idols. Each idol signified an aspect of life. Even before the time of the Quraysh, people created the idea of a god of this or a god of that, or a god of fertility, or safety and so on. They implied certain aspects of lordship.

After Muhammad (S) declared his prophethood, the Quraysh people approached him saying, 'You talk about one God, yet we have so many. Let us worship ours for one year and yours for another. Whoever wins the next life, we will all win. Why not mix it all up?' These verses are a potent response. They say: 'I do not worship that which you are orientated towards.' In other words, I am in adoration of Allah. It is not the same as the symbolic idols that you have. Nor is my process of worshipping the same as yours.

How can you connect, unify, melt, and be energised by something that is your invention, your idol? In my case, I enter into a zone of grace, of *hudhur*, or presence as all of you experience, during times of intense and focused worship. Many people find that an hour or two of worship before *salāt al-maġhrib* helps them enter into realms of consciousness that are both discernible, limited, personal and touching upon that which is beyond—Infinite consciousness. We call it the *Ramadhān* moment. You do not know where you are, or who you are. Where are you when you fall into a deep sleep? Where are you when you are in dream consciousness? These levels of consciousness are all within the human potential.

Sūrat Al Ikhlās

بِسْمِ اللَّهِ الرَّحْمَنِ الرَّحِيمِ

In the name of Allah, the Merciful to all, the Compassionate to each!

قُلْ هُوَ اللَّهُ أَحَدٌ ۝

1. Say: 'He is Allah, Unique,

اللَّهُ الصَّمَدُ ۝

2. Allah, Self-sufficient.

لَمْ يَلِدْ وَلَمْ يُولَدْ ۝

3. Neither begetting nor begotten.

وَلَمْ يَكُن لَّهُ كُفُوًا أَحَدُۢ ﴿٤﴾

4. *And none can be His peer.*

Surah Ikhlas also begins with a declaration that calls upon us to admit, and to declare. To recite, read, and know Allah. Here we have a wonderful aspect of the *Qur'an* – a *mithāl* (similitude). We must understand that this is a unique form of comparison. You can relate to everything in some way, find examples or samples, but Allah is *'laysaka mathalisha'* (beyond comparison). That's it! He is a unique Reality, unique Truth, and unique Entity. As *Sūrat al-Nūr*, verse 24-35 says *Allāhu nūr al-samāwāti wa al-ard*, meaning, 'Allah is the light of the heavens and the earth.' He is the Light, from which all other lights cascade. From those lights, shadows come. We do not deny the shadow. We do not say that nothing exists in the realm of lower consciousness. On the contrary, they do exist.

The word *as-Samad* is exceptional. It is the only time it appears in the *Qur'an* and its origin (*Samadiyya*) holds over 40 different interpretations. It means that Allah is self-sustaining, self-supporting, and ever-effulgent on His own. No entity, be it a stone, animal or plant, exists in isolation. Everything has needs such as oxygen, water and so on. But Allah is beyond any of these needs. That is why we adore Allah, for each of us desires independence. However, we realise that our ultimate dependence is upon Allah. This understanding is also the essence of true *tawakkul*. The Prophet (S) had often said that if you truly embrace Allah's incomparability, then all other similarities become indicators towards Allah. They are all pointers, but the Truth is always the same.

Verse 112:4 says: 'And like Him there is none.' We have to transcend our limited understanding. If you truly want to have an understanding of the nature of the amazing Reality of Allah, then you have to have no thought and that is why all of our practices enable disappearance into no thought, especially in the case of *salāt* (prayers) and particularly the *sajdah* (devotional prostration in prayer) which is akin to *mi'raaj* (ascension). You must enter into another realm where you can't discern anything. The *Qur'an* repeatedly gives us examples that space and time are all relative. The classic example is the narration of the *Mi'raaj* (ascension). In a flash, the Prophet (S) went from one place to somewhere else entirely. A thousand years (as we calculate time) is like one day as far as Allah is concerned. Consider the people of *Kahf* (see Chapter 18, 'The Cave') who spent 309 years in a cave and assumed that only an afternoon had passed. Time and space are relative! We know it is relative because there is within us, a *rūh* (soul), *Min amri Rabbi* that instinctively knows the truth because it has embraced *Alastu birabbikum* (Am I not your Lord?) and the *Rabb* (Lordship) is not subject to time. You know within your own heart that there is something beyond speed that we can never imagine.

Sūrat Al Falaq

بِسْمِ ٱللَّهِ ٱلرَّحْمَٰنِ ٱلرَّحِيمِ

In the name of Allah, the Merciful to all, the Compassionate to each!

قُلْ أَعُوذُ بِرَبِّ ٱلْفَلَقِ ﴿١﴾

1. Say: 'I seek refuge in the Lord of the dawn,

مِن شَرِّ مَا خَلَقَ ﴿٢﴾

2. from the evil of what He has created,

205

وَمِن شَرِّ غَاسِقٍ إِذَا وَقَبَ ﴿٣﴾

3. *and from the evil of the utterly dark night when it comes,*

وَمِن شَرِّ ٱلنَّفَّـٰثَـٰتِ فِى ٱلْعُقَدِ ﴿٤﴾

4. *and from the evil of the blowers in knots.*

وَمِن شَرِّ حَاسِدٍ إِذَا حَسَدَ ﴿٥﴾

5. *from the evil of the envier when he envies.*

We have so many traditions that we have to know, recite, and read until we are unified with them. *Bismillah.* Say, admit, confess, announce! Admit, confess. To what? To our acceptance that we always need to take refuge! We always need to be in *istighfār*, always need to take cover, for Allah's *rahma* (mercy) to cover us, for Allah's generosity to cover our cruelty; for Allah's *'illm* (knowledge) to cover our ignorance.

Verse 113:2 says, 'From the evil of what He has created.' Sometimes we may think something is good for us. But in reality it may not be. For example, poverty may actually be better for us, but poverty encompasses outer and inner aspects. We need our outer wealth to decrease so that our inner richness can flourish. You can say 'No thank you. I don't need more. I am content with what I have, I am happy' instead of continuously chasing possessions. The pursuit of wealth doesn't end. Once we have a little, we want more. What a waste of life! Think about those moments when you experienced true inner, ecstatic joy – knowing that Allah is with you? *Sūrat at-Tawbah*, verse 9:40 says: 'Do not grieve, for Allah is with us.' And *Sūrat al-Yūnus*, verse 10:62 says, 'Surely, the friends of Allah, no fear shall fall upon them, nor shall they grieve.' The more issues we have, the more '*huzn*' (sadness, grief, sorrow, affliction) we will experience. When we observe the outer world, it's natural to feel sadness. We see wastage, unnecessary stupidity, enmity and animosity! However, these are not religious issues. They are more like animalistic tendencies within us. The animalistic part of us will want to find faults. We must rise above the animal.

Consider *Sūrat al-Ahzab*, verse 33:56: 'Allah and His angels bless the Prophet. O believers, bless him and greet him with the full greeting of peace.' Verse 33:43 reminds us, 'It is He Who blesses you' Realise that Allah wants us to be truly living the *Qul*, and the message of the *Qur'an*. Living the *Qur'an* requires a balance between knowledge (*'ilm*) and reason (*'aql*). What comes from the heart will also touch hearts, and this is what we need, a combination of head and heart. *Sūrat al-Mudathir*, verse 74:20 warns, 'And curse him again how he assessed.' We are calculating constantly! See *Sūrat al-Yūnus* verse 10:5: 'It is He who made the sun a radiance, and the moon a light, and determined it by stations, that you might know the number of the years and the reckoning.' However, beyond mere calculations you need to enter into the zone of your *rūh* (soul) which is within your *qalb* (heart, *qalb* is not a physical organ but an inner faculty). You need *qalb salīm* (pure heart) so that the *nūr* (light) of the soul within it shines, and so that you are guided. Consider *Sūrat al-Zumar*, verse 39:9, 'Are they equal – those who know and those who know not?' You know because you refer to the light, to the spark of Allah in your heart and you know you are accountable. We all need *hidāyah* (guidance) and call upon *Al-Hadi* (The Guide).

Hasad (envy) is a destructive emotion. It is destroyer of well-being and contentment. We should be grateful for what we have, recognising that someone else having more does not diminish our blessings.

Sūrat An Nās

بِسْمِ اللَّهِ الرَّحْمَنِ الرَّحِيمِ

In the name of Allah, the Merciful to all, the Compassionate to each!

قُلْ أَعُوذُ بِرَبِّ النَّاسِ ﴿١﴾

1. *Say: 'I seek refuge with the Lord of mankind,*

مَلِكِ النَّاسِ ﴿٢﴾

2. *King of mankind,*

إِلَهِ النَّاسِ ﴿٣﴾

3. *Allah of mankind,*

مِن شَرِّ الْوَسْوَاسِ الْخَنَّاسِ ﴿٤﴾

4. *against the harm of the slinking whisperer.*

الَّذِي يُوَسْوِسُ فِي صُدُورِ النَّاسِ ﴿٥﴾

5. *Who whispers in the hearts of mankind,*

208

مِنَ ٱلْجِنَّةِ وَٱلنَّاسِ ﴿٦﴾

6. of Jinn and mankind.

We will look at verse 114:4 which speaks of *waswās* (whispering, a *shaytān*ic negative energy that whispers doubt into the hearts and minds of men). The Arabic language is quite onomatopoeic. The sound itself conveys something. It means *shaytān* (satan; ego-self). One of our great imams was asked about *waswās* and he mentioned several rivers of *waswās*. One of them is greed. Another is having high or unreasonable expectations, or *amal*, expecting others to do things. Or according one's self status because we may know the *Qur'an*. Another 'river of *waswās*, is *shahawāt ad-dunyā* which is worldly desires, attachment, and lust. Love for *dunyā* (the world) is also a river of *waswās*,. The *dunyā* will not last. Acquisition or *tahsīl* is a further river of *waswās*,. 'I have more, come and see.'

In the end, we don't know what to do with our accumulated wealth, so it ends up in a museum. A fellow may spend ten billion pounds accumulating antiquities and now he doesn't know what to do with them. His *'hirs'* (covetousness or greed) is now going to be preserved forever in his name. Another river is *balā'* (affliction). 'Are they really against me? I heard them say something.' *Kibr*, which means pride is also a river of *waswās*,. Don't you want to be proud of yourself? Proud of what? Be proud of being one of the children of Adam. Another river is *tahqīr*, belittling others. Don't belittle the small things and say that I am a big man! Allah is Big! *Allāhu Akbar!* Allah is greater than we can ever imagine.

These are some of the poisonous rivers that bring about *shaytāniyyah* for us. That is why we are supposed to recite these verses. There are numerous traditions in this regard, and some of the classical commentators state that if you read them in the house a few times in the morning and at night, they will offer a safety and protection,

209

but ultimately it is your inner state that will be determinant. If your inner state expects the best from Allah and you are doing your best, then good energies will come. In truth, it is the goodness of Allah that is being harnessed if we ask for it, call upon it, desire it, and hope for it.

Chapter 14

SURAT AL-ZILZAL, SURAT AL 'ADIYAT, SURAT AL-QARI'AH

The *Qur'an* is the foundation and the authority of our *dīn*. As a general rule, it is advisable to defer to someone more knowledgeable on matters of health, governance, politics, and worldly affairs for guidance and as a source of authority until we develop our knowledge on the subject. In doing so, we hope to eventually access the higher authority within ourselves, which is wisdom.

A similar approach is required with the *Qur'an*. First, knowledge of the correct Arabic recitation and grammar is required. However, to access the higher, more subtle and deeper meanings, it is important to truly dive into the *Qur'an* and to *share* it. Of the over 200 classical *tafsīrs* (commentary on the *Qur'anic* verses), some specialise in the grammar, others specialise in the historical context in which the verses were revealed or the sequence in which some verses were complemented by or were overridden by verses which were revealed subsequently.

In the commentary of these three chapters, I hope to illustrate that the *Qur'an* has an outer, understandable, existential meaning as well as layers of inner meaning. There are numerous traditions and teachings on the inner meaning of the *Qur'an* that you may wish to access.

Sūrat al-'Adiyāt and *Sūrat al-Qāri'ah* are Makkan chapters. Makkan chapters address the higher aspects of creation, existence, the meaning of life, who we are, what happens after death and so on. *Sūrat al-Zilzāl* is thought to have been revealed in Madinah but in terms of its content, it may be described as a Makkan chapter.

Sūrat al-Zilzāl

Qur'anic Verses

The Arabic text and the English translation of the entire *Sūrat al-Zilzāl* follow immediately below. Thereafter I will focus my commentary on selected verses.

بِسۡـــمِ ٱللَّهِ ٱلرَّحۡمَٰنِ ٱلرَّحِيمِ

In the name of Allah, the Merciful to all, the Compassionate to each!

إِذَا زُلۡزِلَتِ ٱلۡأَرۡضُ زِلۡزَالَهَا ﴿١﴾

1. *When the earth is shaken violently in its quaking,*

وَأَخۡرَجَتِ ٱلۡأَرۡضُ أَثۡقَالَهَا ﴿٢﴾

2. *when the earth throws out its burdens,*

وَقَالَ ٱلۡإِنسَٰنُ مَا لَهَا ﴿٣﴾

3. *and man says: What ails it?*

يَوْمَئِذٍ تُحَدِّثُ أَخْبَارَهَا ﴿٤﴾

4. *That Day it shall tell its tales,*

بِأَنَّ رَبَّكَ أَوْحَىٰ لَهَا ﴿٥﴾

5. *for that her Lord has inspired her.*

يَوْمَئِذٍ يَصْدُرُ ٱلنَّاسُ أَشْتَاتًا لِّيُرَوْاْ أَعْمَالَهُمْ ﴿٦﴾

6. *On that Day, people will come forward in separate groups to be shown their deeds:*

فَمَن يَعْمَلْ مِثْقَالَ ذَرَّةٍ خَيْرًا يَرَهُ ﴿٧﴾

7. *So, he who has done an atoms weight of good shall see it*

وَمَن يَعْمَلْ مِثْقَالَ ذَرَّةٍ شَرًّا يَرَهُ ﴿٨﴾

8. *And he who has done an atoms weight of evil shall see it.*

Commentary on selected verses

This chapter has eight verses and it can be split into two sections. The first section urges us to observe the cataclysmic *Zilzāl* (earthquake) that will shake the earth. It describes a moment when the earth and all life on it will reach its end, as the cosmos begins to collapse. It is a time when the earth will bring out whatever is hidden in it (which may include solids, fluids, or precious stones). This chapter invites us to reflect on the power and significance of this event.

These verses convey the revealed truth that the millions of years that have passed were just a passing flash and that we will return to our origin, which the Prophet (S) described as *amaq*, meaning it cannot be seen. The earth and all life on it will return to its nothingness. 'Because your Lord has commanded it.'

Wahy is a beautiful word which means from a higher inspiration or that which is directly from Allah. It also means the pre-inspired design. The ordinary meaning of these verses relates to the *ākhira* (the Next Life) and the *zilzāl* (earthquake) but the inner meaning relates to our individual experience of *zilzāl* when we die. At that moment of death, all of the desires which we did not declare will be revealed because there will no longer be any hiding place. Therefore, just as the earth tells its news, so too will we!

The second section of this chapter completes the story of the cycle of life.

يَوْمَئِذٍ يَصْدُرُ ٱلنَّاسُ أَشْتَاتًا لِّيُرَوْاْ أَعْمَٰلَهُمْ ۝

On that Day, people will come forward in separate groups to be shown their deeds: (99:6)

Everything you do in this life (including your intentions) is recorded in every cell in your body, mind, and heart. You are the sum of your intentions and actions and on that day you will witness your actions. If your intentions and actions were uncertain and complex, then that is who you are. If they were clear, then that is who you are.

Each one of us wants goodness for ourselves and happiness that is durable and sustainable. If you want the same thing for everyone else, then your biography is clear. This earth is a testing ground for what comes after death, which heralds a time when we lose all power to act. During this lifetime we are given a portion of the ability to act, however, the ultimate source of that action is Allah. The energy comes from Allah, but we have been given a little leeway to do and change some things. Our lives on this earth are a nursery to allow us to practice the art of goodness (*al-a'māl al-sālihāt*). Many other verses in the *Qur'an* address this topic.

$$فَمَنْ يَعْمَلْ مِثْقَالَ ذَرَّةٍ خَيْرًا يَرَهُ ﴿٧﴾$$

So, he who has done an atoms weight of good shall see it. (99:7)

Mithqāl is a measure. It may refer to a measure of the weight of precious stones. If you do a tiny amount of good, you will experience it and if you have done *shar* (evil), you will experience that. Nothing is hidden! Allah sees all, Allah knows all.

Sūrat al 'Adiyāt

Qur'anic Verses

The Arabic text and the English translation of the entire *Sūrat al 'Adiyāt (100)* follow immediately below. Thereafter I will provide a general commentary on this *Sūrat*.

بِسْمِ ٱللَّهِ ٱلرَّحْمَٰنِ ٱلرَّحِيمِ

In the name of Allah, the Merciful to all, the Compassionate to each!

وَٱلْعَٰدِيَٰتِ ضَبْحًا ۝١

1. *By the charging stallions, panting.*

فَٱلْمُورِيَٰتِ قَدْحًا ۝٢

2. *With their hooves sparking!*

فَٱلْمُغِيرَٰتِ صُبْحًا ۝٣

3. *By raiders in the morning.*

فَأَثَرْنَ بِهِۦ نَقْعًا ۝٤

4. *Dust-raising.*

فَوَسَطْنَ بِهِۦ جَمْعًا ۝

5. *A midst an enemy troop appearing!*

إِنَّ ٱلْإِنسَـٰنَ لِرَبِّهِۦ لَكَنُودٌ ۝

6. *Man is an ingrate towards his Lord.*

وَإِنَّهُۥ عَلَىٰ ذَٰلِكَ لَشَهِيدٌ ۝

7. *Of this he himself is witness.*

وَإِنَّهُۥ لِحُبِّ ٱلْخَيْرِ لَشَدِيدٌ ۝

8. *For love of wealth, he is miserly to excess.*

۞ أَفَلَا يَعْلَمُ إِذَا بُعْثِرَ مَا فِى ٱلْقُبُورِ ۝

9. *Knows he not that when graves and their contents are strewn.*

وَحُصِّلَ مَا فِى ٱلصُّدُورِ ۝

10. *And that which is in the breasts is brought out –*

$$\text{إِنَّ رَبَّهُم بِهِمْ يَوْمَئِذٍ لَّخَبِيرٌ} \quad (١١)$$

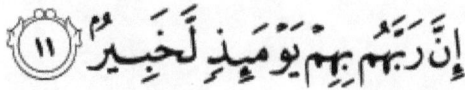

11. that their Lord that Day is All-Aware of them.

General commentary on this chapter

This chapter describes charging or galloping horses during the early part of the morning. Consider the wonderful tapestry the *Qur'an* is painting. It beautifully describes the speed, power and immense determination of these horses, but says they still end up in the centre of the disturbance of their own creation. And then the next part of this chapter reminds us that human beings are in a state of ingratitude and denial.

Reflect on the amazing shift in focus! How do you connect the two parts of this chapter? You are like one of those charging horses, rushing to your business until you suddenly find yourself in the middle of a crisis of debt, uncertainty and unfulfilled promises. This is an example of reading the *Qur'an* at various levels: the linguistic level, the historical level and the existential level. I am confident that future generations will reflect more on the impact of the choices they make, for fear of falling into the category of people which *Sūrat al-Fur'qān* (25:30) describes as follows: The Messenger shall say: 'My Lord, my people have decided to abandon this Qur'an.' This verse reminds us that we have become Muslims by name and we are not living the *Qur'an*. We have to live it and interact with it! With that interaction comes layer upon layer of subtler meaning, some of which can be discussed while others are so subtle that it is best to be quiet.

Consider verse 7 of this chapter, where Allah says 'Human beings are a witness to themselves'. If you do good you tell everyone about it, however, if the house collapses you run away and blame the architect! You know you want to show off and yet you claim to be modest. Why are you cheating? Who are you lying to? Be open, be honest.

Each one of us has numerous faults yet within us lies a *rūh* (soul) which is ever perfect. Outwardly, our actions and intentions go up and down. Ask to be forgiven. *Astaghfiru'llah, Astaghfiru'llah, Astaghfiru'llah!* Take cover in Allah's *rahma* (mercy) and you will find that your soul will be your authority and, therefore, in time you will truly live as a soul and not just as an ego. Reflect upon the day when all the graves will explode and that which you have kept in your heart will be revealed. Certainly, on that occasion, you will come to know that your Lord knew everything about you. He also knows it now. For this reason, it is important to have the presence of heart to benefit from your *'ibadah* (worship).

Concerning *salāt* (prayers), there are many preliminary matters to attend to, for example, to be in a state of *tahāra* (ritual purity), in *wudhū'* (ritual ablution), to know the direction for prayer, which prayer it is and how many *rak'a* (cycles of prayer) it is comprised of. The most important among these preliminary matters are *Hudhur al qalb*, which means the condition of your heart. If your heart is present then you will be thrilled and rejuvenated by your prayers.

As the Prophet (S) says, without presence of heart, there is nothing in *salāt* (prayers) other than tired knees. There is nothing in fasting other than hunger. Fasting is about restriction. Restriction of what? The first restriction of food is the most commonly referenced because we are all anxious about food, existence and survival. It is also about restricting your thoughts and restricting your heart so that you have nothing in it for the world. You will then discover the *nūr* (light).

Sūrat al-Qāri'ah

Qur'anic Verses

The Arabic text and the English translation of the entire *Sūrat al-Qāri'ah (101)* follow immediately below. Thereafter I will provide a general commentary on this *Sūrat*.

$$ بِسۡمِ ٱللَّهِ ٱلرَّحۡمَٰنِ ٱلرَّحِيمِ $$

In the name of Allah, the Merciful to all, the Compassionate to each!

$$ ٱلۡقَارِعَةُ ﴿١﴾ $$

1. *The Battering!*

$$ مَا ٱلۡقَارِعَةُ ﴿٢﴾ $$

2. *What is the Battering?*

$$ وَمَآ أَدۡرَىٰكَ مَا ٱلۡقَارِعَةُ ﴿٣﴾ $$

3. *How can you know what is the Battering?*

$$ يَوۡمَ يَكُونُ ٱلنَّاسُ كَٱلۡفَرَاشِ ٱلۡمَبۡثُوثِ ﴿٤﴾ $$

4. *A Day when mankind shall be like moths, scattered.*

وَتَكُونُ ٱلْجِبَالُ كَٱلْعِهْنِ ٱلْمَنفُوشِ ﴿٥﴾

5. When mountains shall be like tufts of wool, adrift.

فَأَمَّا مَن ثَقُلَتْ مَوَٰزِينُهُۥ ﴿٦﴾

6. And he whose scales are weighed down;

فَهُوَ فِى عِيشَةٍ رَّاضِيَةٍ ﴿٧﴾

7. he shall have a life of joy.

وَأَمَّا مَنْ خَفَّتْ مَوَٰزِينُهُۥ ﴿٨﴾

8. But he whose scales are light;

فَأُمُّهُۥ هَاوِيَةٌ ﴿٩﴾

9. his matron shall be the Pit.

وَمَآ أَدْرَىٰكَ مَا هِيَهْ ﴿١٠﴾

10. But how can you know what that is?

نَارٌ حَامِيَةٌ ﴿١١﴾

11. A red-hot Fire!

Qara'a is to knock or hit and it is often translated as a calamity. *Al-Qāri'ah* refers to the ultimate, immense bang! On that occasion, human beings will scatter like moths not knowing where to go.

A man once told the Prophet (S) about his wish to die. The Prophet responded, 'You are not sensible, and you are not respectful if you wish to die.' The man said, 'I have seen it all. I have done it all.' To this, the Prophet (S) retorted, 'Then help others! Take the opportunity to serve others! Be content with the will of Allah.' Verse 101:5 reminds us that mountains will become like discarded wool. *Manfūsh* means puffed up. *Sūrat al-Naml* verse 27:88 similarly reminds us that mountains will pass like clouds.

As *Sūrat ar-Rahmān* (55:27) reminds us, the only absolute is Allah's *nūr* (light) and everything else will disintegrate.

The more you refer to the Ultimate, the more you find that your earthly challenges and experiences are insignificant. Your actions will be of no use if you do not care for that which matters most, which is remembrance of Allah and the knowledge and acceptance that you cannot do anything without Allah having willed it. His will supersedes your will. The *Qur'an* tells us further that if actions are taken with no intention other than *Fī sabīl Allāh* (in the path of Allah, for the sake of Allah), then it will touch hearts.

The second section of this chapter (verses 101:6 and 101:7) reminds us that 'he whose actions & intentions have been weighty in this life, certainly, that being is in a very agreeable way of life.' In *Sūrah al-Muzzammil*, verse 73:5, Allah says, 'Behold, We shall cast upon thee a weighty word' Anything that is described in the *Qur'an* as 'heavy' is an important and good thing in the eye of Allah. The *nafs*, the lower self, and the ego want ease. We often tell ourselves 'Never mind! Let's laugh a bit, let's enjoy more silly leisurely moments and activities.' On the contrary, the truth is heavy. Allah says that the mountains and the earth could not accept this *amanah* (trust), yet human beings accepted it. What is this *amanah*? It is the weight and the truth that you do not exist. The so-called you is only a *rūh* (soul) which is *min amri Rabbi* (by Allah's command) and the rest is only a shadow.

Your purpose is to acknowledge Allah's presence, Allah's dominance, Allah's *rahma*, Allah's mercy and Allah's greatness so that you perfect your worship. For this reason, we have wonderful occasions like the month of *Ramadhān*, which is the month of abstention. What is the ultimate worship? The Prophet (S) describes the *salāt* (prayers) as *mi'rāj al mu'min* (the ascension of the believer). What is *mi'rāj* (ascension)? It is flying into a realm where you do not know how high or how far you have transcended. In an instant, at a speed beyond the speed of light, the Prophet (S) transcended and travelled from where he was to Jerusalem! Is that what happens to you when you are in *sajdah* (devotional prostration in prayer)? You need to work at perfecting your worship. Practice, practice, practice, until you are perpetually in a state of transcendence. The light in you is by Allah's command. So what else is there? If you have accepted the heavy truth that there is none other than the One and only One then you would be happy forever. Outwardly, you deal with the outer comings and goings, but it does not turn you upside down. You recognise an unhappy event (for example, you recognise that people are suffering) but it should not overwhelm you. You deal with it as best you can but it does not enter and blacken your heart. This is the mark of a being whose weight is heavy. Verse 101:8 reminds us that if you accept this amazing decree of Allah, that you are here only to worship Him, then your weight is light.

Verse 101:9 refers to *Umm*, which means mother or the womb, and it also reminds you that you will be wrapped around in that which will fall. *Hawa'* means desires. Why not do this? Why not that? It's the *nafs*! This is the stupidity of the human ego. I say 'No' to my ego. Enough is enough! *Astaghfiru'llah* (take cover in Allah)! Then you will find the *nūr* (light) of Allah is the only Light. Everything else is a shadow.

'He certainly is in an abyss. And what do you know about that abyss?' We have all experienced some aspects of disturbance, turmoil, bad companionship, bad business and misunderstandings. These are small fires. In *Sūrat al-A'lā* verse 87:12, Allah describes *Jahannam* as 'the great fire.' The chapter concludes with the description 'Raging, glowing fire,' meaning there is no stability and anything in the fire goes back to its original state of decomposed molecules and atoms.

In conclusion, these three magnificent chapters are meaningful for anybody who is seeking inner, deeper, subtler, and timeless meaning. It is a manual to not only exist but to move from the constant worry of survival into the glorious stage of arrival. Many commentators such as Ibn Arabi and Ahmed bin Ajiba have commented that verses and chapters that were once considered to have a limited meaning are also subtle and have a timeless impact. Ahmed bin Ajiba reserves a section in his *tafsīr* (commentary on the *Qur'an*) for such timeless verses and he calls the section *ishāra*, meaning signs. The *Qur'an* is not something to be recited and then to be placed on a bookshelf. We should handle this with urgency. How do we know how long we will live for? If we wake up to the truth right now, then at least we will have connected to a level of consciousness that will also help us during illness and in any other difficult situation.

I can only express my gratitude to Allah for *Islām* (submission). I can only express my gratitude to Allah for the *Qur'an*. I am grateful for being amongst decent human beings and Muslims.

Chapter 15

SURAT AL-BAQARAH -
VERSES 153-157

يَـٰٓأَيُّهَا ٱلَّذِينَ ءَامَنُوا۟ ٱسْتَعِينُوا۟ بِٱلصَّبْرِ وَٱلصَّلَوٰةِ إِنَّ ٱللَّهَ مَعَ ٱلصَّـٰبِرِينَ ﴿١٥٣﴾

*O believers, seek help in patience and prayer; Allah stands with
those who are patient. (2:153)*

وَلَا تَقُولُوا۟ لِمَن يُقْتَلُ فِى سَبِيلِ ٱللَّهِ أَمْوَٰتٌۢ بَلْ أَحْيَآءٌ وَلَـٰكِن لَّا تَشْعُرُونَ ﴿١٥٤﴾

*Do not say that those who are killed in Allah's cause are dead;
they are alive, though you do not perceive it. (2:154)*

وَلَنَبْلُوَنَّكُم بِشَىْءٍ مِّنَ ٱلْخَوْفِ وَٱلْجُوعِ وَنَقْصٍ مِّنَ ٱلْأَمْوَٰلِ وَٱلْأَنفُسِ وَٱلثَّمَرَٰتِ وَبَشِّرِ
ٱلصَّـٰبِرِينَ ﴿١٥٥﴾

*We shall be testing you with some fear and famine, with loss
of wealth, lives and crops: But give glad tidings to the patient.
(2:155)*

الَّذِينَ إِذَآ أَصَٰبَتْهُم مُّصِيبَةٌ قَالُوٓاْ إِنَّا لِلَّهِ وَإِنَّآ إِلَيْهِ رَٰجِعُونَ ﴿١٥٦﴾

Those who say, when afflicted with a calamity, 'We belong to Allah and to Him we shall return. (2:156)

أُوْلَٰٓئِكَ عَلَيْهِمْ صَلَوَٰتٌ مِّن رَّبِّهِمْ وَرَحْمَةٌ وَأُوْلَٰٓئِكَ هُمُ ٱلْمُهْتَدُونَ ﴿١٥٧﴾

These will be given blessings and mercy from their Lord, and it is they who are rightly guided. (2:157)

In this chapter, I would like to share reminders of what celebration and joyfulness are about. We all want to be joyful at all times, not just joyful one day and suffering thereafter. Suffering is due to ignorance, wrongdoing, injustice, and lack of wisdom. We need, therefore, to be modest, courageous, and wise at all times.

When you are free from blaming and accusing others then you will grow in courage, justice, and wisdom. You will ultimately realise that the perfect Light of the creator is ever there. You will constantly be challenged by duality; the good and the bad and the ups and the downs. However, every restriction has its equivalent expansion. When you go to sleep, you are restricted in your normal worldly activities and you enter into another zone where you replenish and relax and where body, mind, and heart are in equilibrium.

The month of fasting has its outer restrictions. You restrict your diet, what you look at, what you say, and your activities, in the hope that you have greater expansion regarding insight, meaning, lights, and delights.

In this section, I will share five verses from *Sūrat al-Baqarah*, verses 153 to 157. These verses sum up the same story but from a different angle. The story is that no human being will ever be spared the opportunity of being given difficulties, restrictions, and constrictions but some will come out of these challenges victorious, and others will come out of them smashed.

What is the way? What is the map? Verse 2:153 says: 'All those of you, who have taken refuge in and have trust and reliance upon *Allah Azza wa Jal* trust that there is perfection behind what appears, rely upon patience and *salāt* (prayers). Surely Allah is with those, who are patient.' *As-Sabūr* (The Patient) is one of Allah's names referenced in the list of ninety-nine names. Here we are advised to rely upon patience and stop time.

What are a few 100 years? Where was the world 10,000 years ago? The passing of time is inconsequential. *Islām* came to us 1,400 years ago yet look at the state of many so-called Muslims.

Having patience does not mean that you are lazy. On the contrary, do what you can but also understand that there are situations when you cannot speed up matters. If you have an unhealthy diet and are experiencing ill health as a result of your diet, your health is not going to improve overnight. It will take some time for your metabolism, your hormones, and similar things to change. You need to be at it, but with patience and perseverance, knowing that you are on a proper programme and that you will ultimately emerge from it in a state of equilibrium of mind, body, and heart.

In this verse Allah says: 'Seek help through patience and prayer.' Don't assume that those who have left this world, whether they have died in battle defending their homes, their *dīn*, or those who have strived in the way of Allah are dead. They are certainly alive.

In verse 2:154, Allah says, don't ever think that those who have gone before us truly doing their utmost to know more of Allah's attributes, to serve in the way of Allah, to serve their community, whether it is an outer, or inner jihad, don't ever think they are dead. They are ever alive. This implies that the *rūh* (soul) of those who have gone with that clarity is already in the upper heavens. The word *sabr* (patience) is mentioned more than 70 times in the *Qur'an*. Many verses emphasise that those who are patient will be given their reward (see for example verse 39:10).

Our great teachers classified patience into four categories. The first is when one is faced with affliction and difficulty. For example, you are out of work, you have no money, people have deserted you, or your wife is angry with you, and there is nothing you can do about it. This is called *balā* (affliction). You should be patient. Do not antagonise your opponent, take revenge, or answer back. Be patient and the affliction will pass much like the clouds do.

The second category relates to goodness, wealth, and power. Many of us mess up our own lives when we are wealthy. I personally know more people who have suffered because of wealth, than because of a lack of it. This is because with wealth everything comes to you, everybody wants to be associated with you. As the Prophet (S) and Imam Ali (RA) said: 'True wealth is about you feeling content in your heart that no one can give you more or take away from you unless it is by Allah's design. Trust in Allah's design and you will always be content and centred. Nobody can give you more or less than that which is appropriate for you.' Allah says in *Sūrat al-Qamr* verse 54:49: 'Everything in existence is created according to a measure.' For example, your actions have resulted in you experiencing dreadful difficulty so you have to admit you were wrong, and be patient and your difficulties will eventually end.

The third category is obedience. Obedience of turning away from your ego. Don't you know who I am? I am a *hafiz al Qur'an* (one who has memorised the *Qur'an*). I have made donations to 10 mosques. This is not how we should live. Be wary of anyone who proclaims they are doing something *Fī sabīl Allāh* (in the path of Allah, for the sake of Allah) because often their true intention is to gain greater authority through serving others or being generous. *Allah Azza wa Jal* tells us if we do good, it is for ourselves, so don't brag (see *Sūrat al-Isrā* verse 17:7). The Prophet (S) never said I fear upon my people, other than when he said: 'I fear upon my people with misguided so-called *'ulamā* (scholars of *Islāmic* religious law) because they want power.' Everybody loves power but the wise person loves the All-Powerful and the Light of the All-Powerful illuminates their heart.

Those with visible power, no matter who they are, will be disempowered. Think of them as dead. That is why the great ones, when they were under threat by the rulers, said: 'May Allah forgive us and forgive you.' You cannot do anything for me other than what

Allah has written for me and I am in Allah's hand and *innā lillāhi wa-innaā 'ilayhi rāji'ūn*, which means: 'We are for Allah, from Allah and to Allah we return.' You can avail yourself of this level of protection through knowledge, wisdom, and tuning your heart to the Ultimate, but you have to be honest regarding your state. If you fear another human being then you need to work on yourself to transcend from your ego state (your lower self) to your heart state (your higher self). When you have done so, then you are already in the garden.

The fourth aspect of patience relates to the mistakes we make. When you make a mistake, turn it around and say: May Allah's *khayr* (goodness) remind me, may you remind me, let us be reminders to each other so that I don't suffer further.

Patience is one of the most wonderful qualities that Allah has designed. It is a field of energy. Once you tap into it you will find it is wonderful because you stop time.

Allah does not need your help; your *du`a* (an act of supplicating to Allah), *salāt* (prayers), patience and fasting are for you. Why? Because for the first 20, 30 or 40 years of your life you identified with your ego, and your personality, and you will suffer as a result of that until you realise that this so-called self is only a shadow of the real self, which is your *rūh*.

Why are you not aware of that light? It is because your heart is darkened. It is darkened because of your cruelty, arrogance, fears, anxieties, and lust. These things can be cured. If you want more lust, then go for it but you will pay for it. Be open about it and be correct. If you want more wealth, give your *zakāt* (purity tax), but say it is Allah who has given it to me for a while and it may also be taken away from me at any time.

Remember that the air that you inhale may not come out. Be aware that the only capital you have is time. Wake up. Are you ready to continue to the next realm? What are the conditions for that continuation? The conditions are that your mind is clear and your heart is pure. Allah says watch out, *Sūrat al-An'ām* verse 6:123: but they scheme only against themselves, without realizing it. Allah says: I am the ultimate designer. You think you are a designer of something, you are a plotter of something, you are a schemer of something? I have allowed you to scheme because all of the so-called schemes are secondary to my original scheme.

See verse 2:255, *Ayat al Kursī*: 'To Allah belongs whatever is in the heavens and earth.' So what do you and I have? At best we are guardians. In *Sūrat ale-'Imrān* (3:92) Allah defines the ultimate path of salvation: 'Give that which you want to keep.' So watch what you are hiding! If you do this you will find that you are truly Allah's guest. Wait as a courteous guest would and you will find that what you need will be given to you. The ultimate path and level is for you to have only one need, which is to pray that you do not think that you have needs. What an incredible state of freedom it is to know that you have no needs and Allah will provide whatever you need.

As the great Prophets have said: 'He who created me will guide me.' Fear of provision is a very important issue to be mindful of. If you have been fending for yourself such that it has become a habit, you will eventually learn that, in truth, you are Allah's guest and that all that you are doing is borrowing energy and transferring it into action. Ever-increasing difficulty in life is an indicator that you are identified by your ego-self which is a sickness. The key remedy is to say: 'Allah has done it. I was the agent but don't thank me, thank Allah. I happened to be there.'

When I was growing up in Iraq I was told this story: A fellow was crossing a bridge in Baghdad, and he spotted somebody drowning so he jumped into deep water. It was winter and the winds were strong. The river Tigris can have an exceptionally high volume of water flow and it is muddy. After struggling for some time he was able to rescue the drowning man. People who had gathered at the side of the river noticed he was an *'Ālim* (scholar) because his turban was floating in the water. They started reciting *'Allāhu Akbar, Allāhu Akbar,* (Allah is greater) what a great man, you saved somebody.' He was an honest fellow. He came out of the water and said: 'Who was the bastard who pushed me off the bridge and into the water?' At best you are a means or an instrument. Thank Allah for enabling you to do something for others because in truth there is no otherness. We are all the same at heart. As the Prophet (S) said, 'The difference between our people is a mercy.' I am not the same as I was an hour ago. You are not the same as you will be in two minutes. All of it changes but there is one eternal source of life and light that does not change and it is in our hearts.

Then the third verse continues magnificently. It says, 'Certainly, all of you (human beings), all of humanity will be afflicted, tried and tested by some fear.' Who has no fear? The man fears the wife and the wife fears the man and the children are mixed up in-between. We experience anxiety and insecurity. Where will my provision come from?

One of the greatest masters in history was named Ibn 'Atā Allāh al-Iskandarī. He passed away in 1309 in Cairo and there is a large mosque and a shrine to honour him in one of the main cemeteries in the city. In one of his teachings, The Book of Wisdom, he says: 'Appeal to no one but Him to relieve you of a pressing need that He Himself has brought upon you.' He says nobody but Him can relieve you in that state of ultimate desperation. It is '*Īd* for those who are enlightened because you know you cannot turn to anyone. '*Īd* means that which returns. A day in which you are constantly aware of Allah's presence with you is an '*Īd*. So every instant can be an '*Īd*, meaning a return to the original state that we aspire to. Thank Allah that you cannot turn to anyone except to Allah who has always been there.

Allah assures you that He will always give you some shortage (see verse 2:155), meaning you will have a shortage of parents, friends, sisters, brothers, extended family and so on. They will all die. Do you know anyone who is in their 40s or 50s that has not experienced cycles in his or her life when they felt insecure about their welfare, money, their jobs? Everybody will experience this, and you must recognise it as a form of Allah's *rahma* (mercy).

Verse 2:155 reminds you that you will be tested by the fruits that you were expecting. Everybody goes into business expecting more money. Why do you want more? You say it will help you build more mosques. Why do you want to build more mosques? Allah says in the *Qur'an*: 'Give good news to those who are patient,' meaning those who can switch off desires – for money, status and so on. I have known people who were exceptionally successful in this life and I would ask them, so what do you want? They said: I just want to have five days to myself with no connection or communication. But they cannot do it because they are scared.

As the Shah was leaving Iran over 40 years ago, the last thing he said at the airport was: 'How can they live without me?' The poor fellow was destitute for the last few years of his life. Nobody wanted him. Consider the increasing number of tycoons who have billions yet they don't know where to turn to switch off. There are a few lucky ones who begin to give away their wealth before it is too late. So it is as simple as that. Give of your time and give of your wealth. Some people only give of their wealth while others give of their time and keep their wealth. The balance is to give both your time and your wealth because your true wealth is your time and you will then find you have all the time in the world and Allah will give you that vastness of *sabr* (patience).

We are reminded of the concept of *balā* (affliction). Consider beautiful verses in the *Qur'an* such *Sūrat as-Sajdah* verse 32:21 and *Sūrat al-A'rāf* verse 7:168. In these verses (and similar verses in other chapters) Allah says, 'We make you taste part of what you were doing, you begin to taste the dreadfulness, the bitterness of your cleverness so that you return.'

But what does it mean to return? It means to turn back and read the map. The map exists within us. There is *shaytān* (satan; ego-self) in me, my lower self and there is *Rahmān* (mercy) in me, the *nūr* (light) of Allah is my *rūh* (soul). It reminds us of the importance of *Iqra'*, the first command revealed in the *Qur'an*.

The Prophet (S) often used to make the *du'ā'* (an act of supplicating to Allah): 'O my Lord, O Allah, O my *Rabb*, let me see things as they are.' You must consider: is it your ego speaking or are you speaking from your heart out of joy just as a bird that sings? There is a difference between what is from the heart and will touch hearts to what is from the head and will only reach heads. What is real will always be real, and the *Qur'an* is full of examples, such as (addressing the Prophet (S), He says: 'Give them the good news that you are truly here to be in ecstatic joyfulness knowing Allah's way and if you don't do it you will suffer.' Like a bird, sing what is in your heart.

The word *'adhāb* is often incorrectly translated as affliction or punishment. The correct translation is restriction, constriction, and leaving behind. If you leave this world without having discovered the light of eternal joy in your heart you will be in *'adhāb*. This means you are restricted from it. Here, you can access the truth, by turning away from falsehood. You can access the soul, the higher self, by turning away from the lower self. After death, you have no power. You will be in *'adhāb* because you are not fully clear that Allah is guiding you, Allah is in you, Allah is before you, Allah is after you. So Allah reminds us in the *Qur'an*: 'Where do you run to? So you have cornered yourself by yourself'. Allah's magnificent gift to you is your soul. When you live with the earth under your foot and not the *dunyā* (world) on your head crushing you, you are truly *'abd Allah'*, meaning you are complete.

Verse 2:156 is about those who, when they are afflicted with difficulty choose to confess, admit, and declare, 'We are for Allah to discover Allah; we are from Allah and we return to Allah.' You are only a shadow. Turn away from the shadow and you will enter the meadow of the ever-present garden. Note, the garden is not a place. *Sūrat al-Hadīd* verse 57:21 says that the width of the garden is that of the heavens and the earth. When this verse was revealed, the Prophet (S) was asked if the width of the garden is that of the heavens and the earth then where is fire? He replied: 'But where is the night when the day comes?' When you begin to discover the joy of the garden in your heart, you will not be lusting after a little more property here.

The last verse says Allah blesses those who constantly see His mercy and who know that they are from Allah to Allah by Allah, and have patience even though they are in difficulty, meaning they admit they are in difficulty, they understand why it happened and they see the *rahma* (mercy) in the perfect cause and effect.

The verse continues: 'They are the people, who are well-guided.' Here is the ultimate good news: 'He who declares the truth and who trusts in and is reliant upon Allah, who is never absent, we will give them a most sweet way of life and they will get their reward, better than what they were doing' (see *Sūrat al-Nahl* verse 16:96).

In your own way, do something for others until you discover there is no otherness, there is only Oneness, there was only One, there is only One, and there will only ever be One. Talk about One, have integrity, say what is in your heart and your head, and unify them, so you will be one person. If there is no unity of heart and head then that hypocrisy will shatter you. This is the path to redeeming oneself from oneself to becoming truly alive by the *rūh* (soul).

Then comes the verse that sums it up: They are the people whose Light leads them like a torch because of their *Imān* (certainty and security that Allah knows and Allah sees); due to their faith and trust that Allah is with them, Allah will guide them, Allah will show them how best to redeem themselves from their own mistakes. Such people are constantly attuned to the *nūr* (light) of Allah, which is the most perfect guide, the most perfect power, ever-present.

Chapter 16

SURAT AL-QADR

It is said that everything in existence is an attempt at imbibing one of the attributes of Allah. Why do people feel joyful before and after breaking the fast? It relates to one of the attributes which we all want to emulate, yet emulation is impossible because it is one of the unique attributes, like *As-Samad* (The Self Sufficient). Allah does not need anything or anyone. He announces His glory and once you are caught in it you are on the path of *tawhīd* (Oneness), meaning you are in the precinct of that One light.

Qur'anic Verses

The Arabic text and the English translation of the entire *Sūrat al-Qadr (97)* follow immediately below. Thereafter I will provide a general commentary on this *Sūrat*.

بِسْمِ اللهِ الرَّحْمَٰنِ الرَّحِيمِ

In the name of Allah, the Merciful to all, the Compassionate to each!

إِنَّا أَنزَلْنَٰهُ فِى لَيْلَةِ ٱلْقَدْرِ ﴿١﴾

1. We sent it down in the Night of Determination.

وَمَآ أَدْرَىٰكَ مَا لَيْلَةُ ٱلْقَدْرِ ﴿٢﴾

2. *But how can you know what is the Night of determination?*

لَيْلَةُ ٱلْقَدْرِ خَيْرٌ مِّنْ أَلْفِ شَهْرٍ ﴿٣﴾

3. *The Night of determination is better than a thousand months.*

تَنَزَّلُ ٱلْمَلَـٰٓئِكَةُ وَٱلرُّوحُ فِيهَا بِإِذْنِ رَبِّهِم مِّن كُلِّ أَمْرٍ ﴿٤﴾

4. *In it the angels and the Spirit are sent down, by their Lord's leave, attending to every command.*

سَلَـٰمٌ هِىَ حَتَّىٰ مَطْلَعِ ٱلْفَجْرِ ﴿٥﴾

5. *Peace it is, till the rising of dawn.*

Allah Azza wa Jal declares to us that there is the *'Alam al-Qadr* (the Realm of Order) or the pattern of commands which are all in the unseen. This relates to the higher realms of *Lahut, Hāhūt, Jabarut,* and *Malakūt.* Then in *'Alam al Mulk* (The Realm of the Sovereignty of Allah), we have *qadr,* measure, discernible relationships in the realm of the seen.

Laylat al-Qadr, meaning, after the darkness of the unseen you come into the day.

You then have the realm of *'aql,* discrimination, earthly rationality, and reasoning to contain emotion. The realm of the higher in you, which is your soul, is the realm of intuition, insight, and unveiling. Both realms are essential. Without willingness and ability, nothing will happen. You may be capable of understanding, but if you are not ready for it then it is of no use. In other words, you may have the capability but not the readiness. Accordingly, growth in maturity, capability, discernment, and clarity of mind will lead to purity of heart.

All religions and all paths which relate to human evolution focus on the alignment of the head and heart. In the first 20 to 40 years of life head and ego prevail, and thereafter it transitions smoothly to the heart, which is the zone of intuition and joy. You transition from pleasure, which can also give you displeasure, to joy, which is endless. Once that begins to set in you can tolerate the high voltage of what may be revealed to you. I have known people who knew exactly which month and day they would die. It takes a real *rūhani* (spiritual) being to know that without being upset about it.

Laylat al-Qadr is when the two zones, the unseen and the seen, completely meet and recharge. That is why everything in life is subject to movements or cycles which have their frequencies. This includes amazing events when the unseen and the seen connect. The annual event which we celebrate is *Laylat al-Qadr*. Look at the perfection of the path of Muhammad (S). Nobody knows exactly when *Laylat al-Qadr* is. It could be any time during the last 10 nights of *Ramadhān* (probably the 21st, 23rd, 25th or 27th night). It is, therefore, always advisable, during the last 10 days of the month of *Ramadhān* to close yourself in a bit, step out of the self and you might reach a point (provided you are diligent and vigilant) where you truly have given up voluntarily. You realise you are bankrupt. What did you arrive with? What will you have to take away? Do so and you will be exposed to the ultimate treasure.

The Prophet (S) describes the universe thus: 'It is like a tiny ring at the edge of a desert that has no end.' So when you suddenly become angry and begin behaving like a donkey then think of yourself as dead at that minute. What are you angry about? It does not matter! If there is something that you can do about it, then do it, if there is nothing you can do, then have *sabr*, switch off, stop time and you will be amazed that years later nothing is the same. So what does it matter? What are a few million years after all? Be geological in your timing. A few million years here and there does not matter!

Be aware! We were born yesterday, we will die tomorrow and in between, we experience nonsense at the hand of human beings. Don't be in a rush. It does not matter. Do your work, enjoy it, live your *dīn*, constantly, go into the unfathomable bliss and have a few friends. Who are you to change the world?

Nabi Allah Ibrahim (AS) could read hearts and wherever he saw the heart to be criminal he would cut the person's head off. Allah said to him 'What are you doing? If I wanted to have only a perfect thing I would have it and I already have billions of worlds of perfection. This is an experiment for the sons of Adam, who by will, want to come back to the garden, which is also already there.' The garden is not somewhere else; it is not subject to space or time. When the *Kun* (Be!) came (*Kun fayakun* means 'Be! And it is'), this amazing miracle of the crack of space and time occurred. Therefore, the fabric of life is woven by space and time and they are inseparable.

The advent of technology and global connectivity will result in an increasing number of people who want to be present now. For this reason, spirituality is on the ascent and religiosity is on the descent. Who wants religious paraphernalia and strange people in funny coats and hats? It was important 700 years ago for people to have a sheet on their heads because it had many uses (for example, it could be used to shield from the heat of the sun or as clothing).

I will never forget a story about an experience my father once had. He was sailing on the Black Sea and a fellow traveller, who was a Russian man, pointed to my father's turban and asked him 'What is this?' In response, my father pointed to his hat and asked: 'What is this? It is only useful for transporting water but my turban has 55 uses.' It was a pre-*Islāmic* garment because it was useful at that time. Who needs a sheet on his head in this day and age? We respect it because it was worn by *Rasul Allah* (S). It was perfect for his time but not so now.

Scholars such as Imam Ghazali even questioned the usefulness of marriage. He lived in Baghdad and during the best time of his life (which was the latter 10 years or so) he moved to Khorasan. *Insh'allah* we will visit this place one day. He was of the view that the pattern of people having more and more children needed to be addressed because the area was already overpopulated. For this reason, he issued a fatwa: Don't get married! At that time there were thousands of *'ulamā* (scholars of *Islāmic* religious law) in Iraq but he was the chief so they did not dare to create a fuss, but some people asked him 'Are you going against *Rasul Allah* (S)?' He denied that he was. *Rasul Allah* (S) said the perfect thing. Marry and bear children. But that was in his time. However, if you do so today, it will be more difficult to perfect your *'ibadah* (worship) because the level of materialism is very high so there is more distraction in marriage. If you are serious about discovering the Creator, then stop being distracted. Therefore, everything has a specific context.

Laylat al-Qadr is the night in which the seen and the unseen are inseparable. You don't know whether you are in the heavens or on earth. You are nowhere. There is no you. It is insufficient for you to have that unity of the seen and the unseen, meaning *Laylat al-Qadr*, in you. As Imam Ali (RA) says, 'if you are not able and willing to truly enter into that ecstatic state of *'Īd* every day, then there is no *'Īd* for you.' *'Īd* means return. Return to what? To realise that you exist by courtesy of the Maker of it all, who is the true source of all creation. Then you are in the true state of *adab* (courtesy), reverence, and joyfulness. The pattern of creation has already been designed, but we have to finish it off by will. That is the meaning of Adam because the angels have no will. (Adam has been given this will to use it to consciously re-plug into the One and Only inner power that there is-Allah.) That is the meaning of *alum Adam al asma*. What is it? It is all the things that we love. Who doesn't love well-being? Who doesn't love the continuity of wholesomeness? These are Allah's qualities. Who doesn't want to be independent of anyone? Who doesn't want to be the seer, to see the past and future? He is the Seer, He is the hearer!

So *Laylat al-Qadr* is the night when it is easier because you have, over the course of the month of *Ramadhān*, been withdrawing a bit more and you have been observing abstention from the outer which increases attention to the inner and saying 'no' to disturbance and 'yes' to harmony! It is as simple as that. This is the formula. Give yourself space. How? Change your mind. How? Be willing to change, in every way. Change your attitude. How? Be willing to die and be joyful about it. The Prophet (S) was once asked how much time is required for a person to wake up to the knowledge of Allah before he dies so that he goes straight to the garden. The Prophet (S) said: 'If it comes a year before he dies then he is saved. Then he said no, a year is too long. It can be a month, a week, a day, an hour, a minute or a blink of an eye.' Such a person has gone into the zone of pre-consciousness, pre-conditioned consciousness of the "I", the "me", pre-reason into the zone of infinite consciousness, divine consciousness, and supreme consciousness, and in so doing has caught a glimpse of *Laylat al-Qadr*. It is the moment or the state that you must be in at all times and in your *sajdah* (devotional prostration in prayer).

We have the package but it has not been unwrapped yet. Some of us were brought up in an ambience of genuine awareness of the Divine Presence. When I was a child, whenever a poor man would come knocking at the door with great ferocity and shouting 'wealth belongs to Allah and whoever considers himself generous is the lover of Allah,' then as children we were trained to love running up to offer our plate of food. So we were immersed in constant awareness that at any minute you may die so what have you done? In those days there was no theft, abusiveness, or divorce. All conflict was kept quiet because it was considered shameful. We have a wonderful saying in Arabic: 'If you do not have *hayā'* (meaning shame) then do what you want.' Shame in this context means that Allah sees you, Allah knows all, so watch out. The end of distance brings the beginning of presence.

The whole world wants to improve on this idea of awareness. That is why Eastern philosophies, especially Taoism, Buddhism, and Confucianism, are growing so rapidly in the West. Muslims want to compete but we are not living our *dīn* so how can we compete with these systems? We have the package but we have not opened the ribbon. Be courteous, visualise *Rasul Allah* (S) at all times, be his friend, and live his way and then you will see wonder upon wonder! Do not fall for personalities. Instead, follow the light in your heart and thank whoever helps you in that direction because therein lies the Light. What is stopping you? It is your own self-made shadow.

You have designed your cocoon and every cocoon is different. You have been influenced by your parents, genetic background, your DNA, environment, culture, and many other things. You cannot deny the shadows; instead, you have to somehow slip through the shadows, by the mercy of the Light that is in you which is the Divine Presence. If anybody helps, thank them and move on. You have come alone, you go alone, and there is no loneliness at all because Allah has been the energy behind it, from beginning to end. Therefore, we say *Lā ilāha illā Allāh*, which means liberation from everything, from yourself, as well as from your family and everybody else. That is the path. Once you realise that in truth, there is no otherness and that everybody is the same as you, then you will understand that it is truly Divine Love that glues everything together.

Insh'allah we will have nothing other than the nights of *qadr* (power). Every night is *qadr* and every day is *'Īd*. There are easier times and cycles, so *insh'allah* during these last 10 nights of *Ramadhān*, I pray for you, as I pray for myself, that you go into such an era of sensitivity and lightness that you will realise that you have been created to live on that waveband. I pray for you to have the best of health, the best of contentment, the best of tolerance, and the best of everything, and for you to *share* with others that are less fortunate than you, no matter who they are.

Chapter 17

SURAT AS-SHAMS

By all accounts, this chapter is one of the earliest ones. Most of the very layered and highly revealing chapters, especially the early Makkan chapters, encompass a wide range of human and worldly activities. It was likely to have been revealed immediately after *Sūrat al-Qadr*, and like many early Makkan chapters, it connects the seen and the unseen, the heavens and earth, and this world and the next. It is a potent chapter.

Qur'anic Verses

The Arabic text and the English translation of the entire *Sūrat as-Shams (91)* follow immediately below. Thereafter I will focus my commentary on selected verses.

بِسْمِ اللَّهِ الرَّحْمَنِ الرَّحِيمِ

In the name of Allah, the Merciful to all, the Compassionate to each!

وَالشَّمْسِ وَضُحَاهَا ﴿١﴾

1. By the sun and its morning glow!

وَٱلْقَمَرِ إِذَا تَلَٰهَا ﴿٢﴾

2.   *And by the moon as it follows it.*

وَٱلنَّهَارِ إِذَا جَلَّٰهَا ﴿٣﴾

3.   *By the day, when it burnishes it!*

وَٱلَّيْلِ إِذَا يَغْشَٰهَا ﴿٤﴾

4.   *And the night when it draws a veil over it,*

وَٱلسَّمَآءِ وَمَا بَنَٰهَا ﴿٥﴾

5.   *by the sky and how He built it.*

وَٱلْأَرْضِ وَمَا طَحَٰهَا ﴿٦﴾

6.   *And the earth and Him Who extended it,*

وَنَفْسٍ وَمَا سَوَّٰهَا ﴿٧﴾

7.   *by the self and how He formed it,*

فَأَلْهَمَهَا فُجُورَهَا وَتَقْوَىٰهَا ۝

8. and inspired it to its rebellion and piety!

قَدْ أَفْلَحَ مَن زَكَّىٰهَا ۝

9. He will indeed be successful who purifies it,

وَقَدْ خَابَ مَن دَسَّىٰهَا ۝

10. and he will indeed fail who corrupts it.

كَذَّبَتْ ثَمُودُ بِطَغْوَىٰهَا ۝

11. In their arrogant cruelty, the people of Thamud denied,

إِذِ ٱنۢبَعَثَ أَشْقَىٰهَا ۝

12. when the most wicked among them rose.

فَقَالَ لَهُمْ رَسُولُ ٱللَّهِ نَاقَةَ ٱللَّهِ وَسُقْيَىٰهَا ۝

13. The messenger of Allah said to them, leave Allah's camel to
drink,

فَكَذَّبُوهُ فَعَقَرُوهَا

فَدَمْدَمَ عَلَيْهِمْ رَبُّهُم بِذَنبِهِمْ فَسَوَّىٰهَا ﴿١٤﴾

14. *but they called him a liar and slaughtered her, therefore their Lord crushed them for their misdeed and levelled them.*

وَلَا يَخَافُ عُقْبَهَا ﴿١٥﴾

15. *And He fears not its consequence.*

Commentary on selected verses

وَٱلشَّمْسِ وَضُحَىٰهَا ﴿١﴾

By the sun and its morning glow! (91:1)

وَٱلْقَمَرِ إِذَا تَلَىٰهَا ﴿٢﴾

And by the moon as it follows it. (91:2)

وَٱلنَّهَارِ إِذَا جَلَّىٰهَا ﴿٣﴾

By the day, when it burnishes it! (91:3)

وَٱلَّيۡلِ إِذَا يَغۡشَىٰهَا ﴿٤﴾

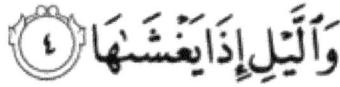

And the night when it draws a veil over it, (91:4)

Contemplate the day and the effulgence so you can understand the meaning of cause and effect. In the daylight, we want to know: what can we do; what can we plant; how can we eat; how can we transact? We witness the outcomes of our actions. Then the night comes with its tranquillity and serenity providing you with some respite from the effects of cause and effect, from the ups and the downs of life.

Shams, which means sun, had a different connotation in early Arabic heritage and until recently in Lebanon and Syria, where it was associated with the term priest. The connection stems from our dependency on the sun as it is the fundamental source of life on earth. Interestingly, the *Qur'an* gives us the whole cosmology of the universe including how the stars and galaxies drifted away from each other. Allah uses the word *farq,* which means the breaking of a seam, implying that the stars and galaxies were once gathered and they drifted apart, in dispersion. *Farq* also means distinguishing left from right or dividing or segregating.

On the other hand, *jamā'* is to connect or gather. In our hearts, we resonate with both concepts, *jam'a* and *farq.* We like to be gathered with those we favour. It echoes the original state of togetherness as well as the ultimate gathering that will be repeated at the end of time. This chapter tells us that it all began at a certain time (with a beginning) and it will end at a certain time, with *Allah Azza wa Jal* being the ultimate gatherer, the provider of energy, patterns, and designs that permeate it all.

Allah says, 'Consider the greatness by the effulgence of the Sun in its fullness, *duhā.'* Elsewhere in the *Qur'an,* we are also told to contemplate with wonder the enormity of the cosmos. There are billions of stars and millions of galaxies. Allah is trying to make us reach a point of exhaustion, of giving up. See *Sūrat al-Najm* verse

53:42 which says, 'and to your Lord, it ends.' Where is the beginning and where is the end? So as we realise the greatness of this creation we are humbled, and we realise that the loss of the little we have on this earth is not the end of the world.

When the Prophet (S) described the whole cosmos he said: 'All of your world, all of our world, as far as Allah's creation is concerned, is like a little ring thrown at the edge of a desert that has no end.' It puts things into perspective. Humanity's entire journey is to expand our consciousness and to realise that worldly acquisition should not be your life's mission. It is more important for you to know who you are, the meaning of death, and the qualities and attributes of your Creator, *Allah Azza wa Jal*. For this reason, Allah warns us that we are fragile creatures and Allah describes us thus: We created you weak and dependent. Don't be arrogant and think that you control the Earth. Many other verses in the *Qur'an* refer to this message.

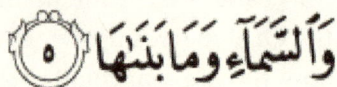

$$\text{وَٱلسَّمَآءِ وَمَا بَنَـٰهَا ﴿٥﴾}$$

by the sky and how He built it. (91:5)

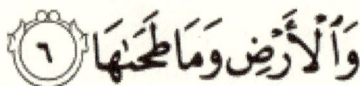

$$\text{وَٱلْأَرْضِ وَمَا طَحَـٰهَا ﴿٦﴾}$$

And the earth and Him Who extended it, (91:6)

Contemplate these pluralities. The first 10 verses of this chapter describe pluralities: man and woman, day and night. Here, Allah wants us to contemplate the heavens. Its vastness is beyond our ability to measure. Some galaxies have disappeared and many stars disappeared millions of years ago. Within the Adamic heart lays a precious design which contains within it the story of creation. There are several theories of how this cosmos came about, the most prevalent and the most accepted is called the Big Bang, meaning that it occurred in one instant and the first nanosecond was the most important because everything thereafter followed this pattern. The cosmos is ever receding in a Big Bang. As Allah's creation, we experience the same pattern. From the moment you were conceived, everything is receding from you. Consider the past five years or the past year of your life. Everything is going away from you including your family. Receding from where? Where is the centre of it? This chapter, especially the verses which have to do with heaven and earth, are a challenge to who you are. Oh, human being who are you? You are the centre of your Universe and within you lies the Light that has created all the Universes. The sacredness of Allah's light in the human heart presents a huge responsibility. If you do not realise that there is the sacred Light in you, you will not truly respect other human beings. All human beings are composed of the Light of *Allah Azza wa Jal* which is the highest possible gift.

Ard is earth. We have in the *Qur'an* often repeated descriptions of both *ard* and *dunyā*. *Dunyā* is when you have an attachment or love for an earthly thing.

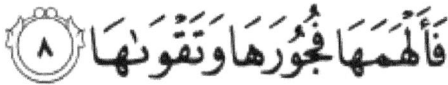

$$\text{فَأَلْهَمَهَا فُجُورَهَا وَتَقْوَىٰهَا ﴿٨﴾}$$

and inspired it to its rebellion and piety! (91:8)

Allah turns our attention from the cosmos, from this amazing challenge, and says: 'But look at your *nafs*. Who are you, the so-called person?' Each of us is made up of two parts; one is discordant and is not following its proper rhythm, while the other side is in a state of *taqwā*, is cautious and wants what is durable. The best path is to tune in to your *rūh* (soul), because your soul is forever and it is *Min amri Rabbi* (a mercy to the worlds), and to strive for your personality to be in unison in your heart, with your soul.

قَدْ أَفْلَحَ مَن زَكَّهَا ٩

He will indeed be successful who purifies it, (91:9)

He who has managed to do this has purified the outer. Purifying the outer does not mean that I will not make a mistake. I am both a body that is decaying and a *rūh* (soul) that is ongoing and the relationship between the *rūh* (soul) and my body is my *nafs* (ego-self). It is my *nafs* (ego-self) that enables my body to carry on and have some discipline about diet and health so that I interact with the world as best as I can. The purpose of this life is to purify my attachments, my desires, and my waywardness with age. Each one of us has both of these sides in us, the higher and the lower. At the moment of death, you will no longer care for that which you considered important during your lifetime. Why not remember death at every moment? Put things in perspective. You thought it was very important for you to get the contract but you were unsuccessful. Don't be depressed about it and become another victim of the pharmaceutical industry by taking anti-depressants. You tried your best and Allah wanted something better for you. It does not matter!

These verses remind us that he who has managed to groom the self, by making the self subservient to the soul, has won. Consider these words in the call to prayer: *Hayya'alal-Falāh*, meaning plough and turn so you are renewed. All of us want renewal. You want every breath you take to be fresh, yet the light that is in your heart is beyond time. You are in the middle of an unending cosmos and a short-lived life but within it is the secret of life, your soul, your perpetuity. We don't know what Allah's programmes are. We are like little bats trying to find our way through the darkness.

The *Qur'an* has revealed knowledge. Accordingly, it says, purify and groom the self because the *nafs* is *amara bi su*, meaning it is always wayward and restless and the resting point is the *qalb*, the soul which is forever constant. The more you refer to your soul, the greater your experience of constancy, but you also accept the changes and the oscillations presented by life experience. Nothing is in existence unless it oscillates. Everything in existence resonates at a certain frequency. For example, the frequency of your breathing and the frequency of your heartbeat all end up creating your human frequency. Like a star, each one of us has our pulsation.

$$وَقَدْ خَابَ مَن دَسَّىٰهَا ﴿١٠﴾$$

And he will indeed fail who corrupts it. (91:10)

He who always blames others is lost. *Dassa* means to scheme or conceal. The first ten verses tell you to look at the cosmos and at your cosmology. Who are you? You are the centre of your cosmos. The last five verses address the social side of our life.

$$كَذَّبَتْ ثَمُودُ بِطَغْوَىٰهَآ ﴿١١﴾$$

In their arrogant cruelty, the people of Thamud denied, (91:11)

The people of *Thamud* denied that the purpose of this life is to see the perfection of the Creator.

$$إِذِ ٱنۢبَعَثَ أَشْقَىٰهَا ﴿١٢﴾$$

when the most wicked among them rose. (91:12)

And the worst amongst them, who were their leaders, denied it all.

فَقَالَ لَهُمْ رَسُولُ اللَّهِ نَاقَةَ اللَّهِ وَسُقْيَٰهَا (١٣)

The messenger of Allah said to them, leave Allah's camel to drink! (91:13)

To understand this verse, refer to *Sūrat Ash-Shu`ara*, verse 26:142 in which the story of the *Thamud* is told to us. They denied whoever Allah sent to them, the messengers and especially their Prophet Saleh (A.S). The rest of the story is revealed in *Sūrat al-A'raf*, verse 7:73, where He says: 'And then we sent to them Saleh but they told him to give us a sign, give us a proof, so he said, "There will come a she-camel from this cave but do not deny the she-camel water [at the time water was in short supply] and Allah will give you a sign, but watch out because if you deny this sign you will be destroyed."'

فَكَذَّبُوهُ فَعَقَرُوهَا

فَدَمْدَمَ عَلَيْهِمْ رَبُّهُم بِذَنبِهِمْ فَسَوَّىٰهَا (١٤)

but they called him a liar and slaughtered her, therefore their Lord crushed them for their misdeed and levelled them. (91:14).

They denied the sign and killed the she-camel because they forgot. How many of us have been in a situation where we didn't know where to turn? Allah's mercy is upon all of us. He puts us in a situation – a worldly situation or a human relationship – where we don't know where to turn. We have all had difficulties but we forget them.

This brings to mind a story. The Arabs had a habit of allocating a portion of their fortune to Allah, or to charity, especially during times of great difficulty or strife. There is a story of a fellow crossing a river in Iraq where the water flow was quite strong. Halfway through he began sinking and was forced to contemplate the possibility of his own death because he could not swim. So he said: 'I give half of my camels to the cause of Allah.' However, as he got closer to the shore, and closer to the certainty of his survival, he began bargaining with Allah. He said: 'But Allah does not need my camels, He is the creator of all camels.' We forget, but Allah tells us in the *Qur'an* you cannot forget things that matter and that you have to live with.

Are you unified? If you are not one, how can you talk about the One? Our entire *dīn* is based on *tawhīd*, the One. If you are lying and deceiving others by having five different bank accounts (one for yourself, one for your partner and one for your income tax) then you are already shattered and do not ever think you can talk about the One. Realise constantly that this is a short period in life for us to discover the qualities and attributes of *Allah Azza wa Jal*.

After the people of *Thamud* killed the she-camel, what *Nabi* Saleh (A.S) had warned them about indeed came to pass. As a result of their action, they experienced Allah's natural consequence. So, you are not punished because of your wrongdoing, you are punished by your wrongdoing. Your action itself will do it to you. Allah does not mete out punishment. Instead, Allah has designed it perfectly. If you follow perfection, you only see perfection upon perfection. Even at the moment of your death, you are in joyful perfection. You know that now the shadows in this world are no longer possible; there is only the light of the Hereafter.

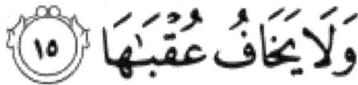

$$ \text{وَلَا يَخَافُ عُقْبَهَا} \quad (١٥) $$

And He fears not its consequence. (91:15)

'Uq'bāhā is what comes after. Allah has designed it perfectly. The Prophet (S) says: 'Allah has designed some people for the garden, nor is He going to be concerned and others are for the fire, nor is He going to be concerned.' This means that Allah is not part of this interaction yet He has designed it. Allah is the Creator of these multiple patterns and designs and He has given us the *'aql* and the suffering so that we take His offering. His offering is to see the perfections of *Al-Qādir* (The Most Able), *Al-Awwal* (The First), *Al-Dhahir* (The Manifest), *Al-Bātin* (The Concealed), and all of the great attributes.

If you do not follow the patterns then you experience shaded *al-Arqam* (The Companion), by your transgression. Allah does not want you to transgress. He wants you to choose the right thing, which is a connection between the *nafs* (ego-self), the body, the *'aql* (mind), the feelings, the emotions, and the *rūh* (soul). Our access to Allah is through our *rūh*. This access to the soul is through the *nūr* (light) of what we have.

Allah's consciousness is above all consciousness, but you and I have limited consciousness. This limited consciousness expands by referring to the higher consciousness in us which is a reflection of the divine supreme consciousness. That is why we say, *ruduhul illalah*, meaning if you don't know something, turn it back to Allah, meaning, return to the supreme consciousness and say I don't know. Allah knows and maybe Allah will let me know, or not, but I trust that whatever He has given me is always the best for me. Sometimes the best for me is constriction, abstention, and fasting, but I will ultimately realise it was the best for me. Whatever knowledge I have, Allah's knowledge is higher and I trust that Allah has created me for me to progress, not regress.

To progress from being a tiny cell into what he designed to be above angels because Allah said: 'I told the angels to prostrate to Adam.' To prostrate meaning to be subservient to this incredible entity that is part heavenly and part earthly. Therefore, take responsibility by being ready to give up that which is not yours, which is your soul. Accept that your lower self will make mistakes but your higher self is always there to guide you if you refer to it.

This is the *dīn*. It is that which you and I live by, meaning we are accountable to ourselves, between ourselves and to our Creator. We are always trying to correct our mistakes, to be tolerant and generous, and to take on the *sibghat'Allah*. *Sibghat* is colour. What are the colours of Allah? They are His qualities. His generosity. Allah is ever forgiving but do we ever forgive? We have to take on these qualities. Allah is forgiving, so the least you can do is to try and forgive. Once you have a store of emotion (for example, your response is 'they did not love me, they did not honour me'), then you are in trouble because Allah has honoured you and has created you as a human being and that is sufficient. It is also a huge responsibility. He has given you the potential of the highest consciousness and the way to it is to recognise the lower, deal with it, put it right and then you will become like the Sun and like the Moon. Incidentally, many *tafsīrs* (commentaries on the *Qur'anic* verses) say the Moon is like the Prophet, reflecting the light of Allah, which is the Sun. Put things in perspective and then you will realise what an amazing gift Allah has given you as a human being. But you need to treasure it, you need to respect it and you need to realise that the next day may never come. There is urgency in life to discover the pure source of light in your heart, and our *dīn* does it. There is an urgency to discover the right time to pray, to stop, to be honest, and to be aware of what you are saying and to whom you are saying it. That is why the tongue is locked between two layers; your teeth and your lips. So guard it! Once you have said something you cannot take it back. There are many other human beings like you and I, wanting the best for themselves but they may not know that the best for themselves is disappearance in *sajdah* (devotional prostration in prayer). That is why we have to practice it constantly and *insh'allah* we will practice it collectively as well as individually until we are constantly aware that *in'Allaha ma'ana!* (Do not worry. Allah is certainly with us) (see *Sūrat at-Tawbah* verse 9:40).

Chapter 18

SURAT AL-QIYAMAH

*S*ūrat al-Qiyāmah, *Sūrat al-Insān, Sūrat al-Mulk, Sūrat al-Waqi'ah, Sūrat al-Kahf, and Sūrat an-Nūr* were revealed in the first few years (following the first revelation) and they focus primarily on truth (*haqīqah*) and patterns. These chapters contain everything known and unknown and therefore, they are for all of humanity. They represent a manual on how to be aware, how to survive and whom to refer to so that by our stupidity, we do not cause ourselves irreparable damage.

Qur'anic Verses

The Arabic text and the English translation of the entire *Sūrat al-Qiyāmah (75)* follow immediately below. Thereafter I will focus my commentary on selected verses and words.

بِسۡـــمِ ٱللَّهِ ٱلرَّحۡمَٰنِ ٱلرَّحِيمِ

In the name of Allah, the Merciful to all, the Compassionate to each!

لَآ أُقۡسِمُ بِيَوۡمِ ٱلۡقِيَٰمَةِ ﴿١﴾

1. Yes indeed! I swear by the Day of Resurrection!

وَلَآ أُقْسِمُ بِٱلنَّفْسِ ٱللَّوَّامَةِ ٢

2.   Nay! I swear by the self-accusing soul.

أَيَحْسَبُ ٱلْإِنسَنُ أَلَّن نَّجْمَعَ عِظَامَهُۥ ٣

3.   Does man imagine We shall not reassemble his bones?

بَلَىٰ قَدِرِينَ عَلَىٰ أَن نُّسَوِّيَ بَنَانَهُۥ ٤

4.   Yea! We are able to make complete his very fingertips.

بَلْ يُرِيدُ ٱلْإِنسَنُ لِيَفْجُرَ أَمَامَهُۥ ٥

5.   But man wishes to persist in his debauchery.

يَسْئَلُ أَيَّانَ يَوْمُ ٱلْقِيَمَةِ ٦

6.   He asks when the Day of Resurrection shall come.

فَإِذَا بَرِقَ ٱلْبَصَرُ ٧

7.   But when the sight is dazed,

$$\text{وَخَسَفَ ٱلْقَمَرُ ﴿٨﴾}$$

8. *and the moon is eclipsed,*

$$\text{وَجُمِعَ ٱلشَّمْسُ وَٱلْقَمَرُ ﴿٩﴾}$$

9. *And the sun and the moon are brought together,*

$$\text{يَقُولُ ٱلْإِنسَـٰنُ يَوْمَئِذٍ أَيْنَ ٱلْمَفَرُّ ﴿١٠﴾}$$

10. *on that Day man will say, 'Where can I escape?'*

$$\text{كَلَّا لَا وَزَرَ ﴿١١﴾}$$

11. *Truly, there is no refuge.*

$$\text{إِلَىٰ رَبِّكَ يَوْمَئِذٍ ٱلْمُسْتَقَرُّ ﴿١٢﴾}$$

12. *With your Lord alone shall on that day be the place of rest.*

$$\text{يُنَبَّؤُا۟ ٱلْإِنسَـٰنُ يَوْمَئِذٍ بِمَا قَدَّمَ وَأَخَّرَ ﴿١٣﴾}$$

13. *Man shall on that day be informed of what he sent before and what he put off,*

بَلِ ٱلْإِنسَـٰنُ عَلَىٰ نَفْسِهِۦ بَصِيرَةٌ ﴿١٤﴾

14. *but man is a clear witness against himself,*

وَلَوْ أَلْقَىٰ مَعَاذِيرَهُۥ ﴿١٥﴾

15. *even though he offers his excuses.*

لَا تُحَرِّكْ بِهِۦ لِسَانَكَ لِتَعْجَلَ بِهِۦٓ ﴿١٦﴾

16. *Move not your tongue with it, seeking to hasten it along.*

إِنَّ عَلَيْنَا جَمْعَهُۥ وَقُرْءَانَهُۥ ﴿١٧﴾

17. *Up to Us is its collection and recitation.*

فَإِذَا قَرَأْنَـٰهُ فَٱتَّبِعْ قُرْءَانَهُۥ ﴿١٨﴾

18. *When We recite it, follow its recitation,*

ثُمَّ إِنَّ عَلَيْنَا بَيَانَهُۥ ﴿١٩﴾

19. *Then it is up to Us to expound it.*

كَلَّا بَلْ تُحِبُّونَ ٱلْعَاجِلَةَ ﴿٢٠﴾

20. *No indeed; but you love the hasty world,*

وَتَذَرُونَ ٱلْأَخِرَةَ ﴿٢١﴾

21. *and neglect the hereafter.*

وُجُوهٌ يَوْمَئِذٍ نَّاضِرَةٌ ﴿٢٢﴾

22. *Upon that day faces shall be radiant.*

إِلَىٰ رَبِّهَا نَاظِرَةٌ ﴿٢٣﴾

23. *To their Lord their eyes are lifted*

وَوُجُوهٌ يَوْمَئِذٍ بَاسِرَةٌ ﴿٢٤﴾

24. *and on that Day there will be the sad and despairing faces,*

تَظُنُّ أَن يُفْعَلَ بِهَا فَاقِرَةٌ ﴿٢٥﴾

25. *Knowing a back-breaker shall befall them.*

كَلَّا إِذَا بَلَغَتِ ٱلتَّرَاقِيَ ﴿٢٦﴾

26. *No indeed; when it reaches the clavicles*

وَقِيلَ مَنْ رَاقٍ ﴿٢٧﴾

27. *and it is said, 'Who is an enchanter,*

وَظَنَّ أَنَّهُ ٱلْفِرَاقُ ﴿٢٨﴾

28. *and he thinks that it is the parting,*

وَٱلْتَفَّتِ ٱلسَّاقُ بِٱلسَّاقِ ﴿٢٩﴾

29. *and affliction is combined with affliction;*

إِلَىٰ رَبِّكَ يَوْمَئِذٍ ٱلْمَسَاقُ ﴿٣٠﴾

30. *on that day he will be driven towards your Lord.*

فَلَا صَدَّقَ وَلَا صَلَّىٰ ﴿٣١﴾

31. *But he neither believed nor prayed.*

وَلَٰكِن كَذَّبَ وَتَوَلَّىٰ ﴿٣٢﴾

32. *Instead, he cried lies and departed,*

ثُمَّ ذَهَبَ إِلَىٰ أَهْلِهِ يَتَمَطَّىٰ ﴿٣٣﴾

33. *walking back to his people with a conceited swagger.*

أَوْلَىٰ لَكَ فَأَوْلَىٰ ﴿٣٤﴾

34. *Closer and closer it comes to you.*

ثُمَّ أَوْلَىٰ لَكَ فَأَوْلَىٰ ﴿٣٥﴾

35. Closer and closer still.

أَيَحْسَبُ ٱلْإِنسَـٰنُ أَن يُتْرَكَ سُدًى ﴿٣٦﴾

36. Does man think he shall be abandoned to futility?

أَلَمْ يَكُ نُطْفَةً مِّن مَّنِيٍّ يُمْنَىٰ ﴿٣٧﴾

37. Was he not a sperm drop to be discharged?

ثُمَّ كَانَ عَلَقَةً فَخَلَقَ فَسَوَّىٰ ﴿٣٨﴾

38. Then he was a clinging clot, that He created and formed,

فَجَعَلَ مِنْهُ ٱلزَّوْجَيْنِ ٱلذَّكَرَ وَٱلْأُنثَىٰ ﴿٣٩﴾

39. And made from it a pair, male and female?

أَلَيْسَ ذَٰلِكَ بِقَـٰدِرٍ عَلَىٰ أَن يُحْىِۦَ ٱلْمَوْتَىٰ ﴿٤٠﴾

40. Is not He, then, able to bring the dead back to life?

Commentary on Selected Verses

لَآ أُقۡسِمُ بِيَوۡمِ ٱلۡقِيَٰمَةِ ۝١

Yes indeed! I swear by the Day of Resurrection! (75:1)

وَلَآ أُقۡسِمُ بِٱلنَّفۡسِ ٱللَّوَّامَةِ ۝٢

Nay! I swear by the self-accusing soul. (75:2)

Lā means 'no', however, in this instance, it is used to emphasise the first sentence of this chapter. So, it is certain this is a testimony, that this is sacred and a reminder that there is a *yawm*. *Yawm* is translated as day, but it specifically refers to 'the day of resurrection'. Similarly, other terms in the *Qur'an* refer to the day of reckoning, the day of gathering, and the day of *yawm ud-dīn* (the day of resurrection). All of these terms are used in the *Qur'an* to remind us that a final event will take place and that there are three major phases concerning this event.

The first phase is in the unseen before embodiment in the womb, followed by the second phase which is the first two to three years of human life when memories begin to form, and the final phase is the phase after death. The more you are mindful of the day of reckoning, the more likely you are to review your actions in this life. You ought to question whether what you are doing is helpful to you in the long run, or if it is just a short, pleasurable experience which will ultimately result in displeasure.

The *nafs* (ego-self) and its mapping have been very well elaborated in our traditions, especially by the people of *'Irfān* (knowledge, wisdom gnosis) or *tasawwuf* (Sufism). There are many perspectives regarding the ego-self.

The most classical teaching is that there are seven layers of the self. The first layer is *an-nafs al-ammārah*, meaning 'the commanding self'

264

in the egotistic sense. This layer is analogous to the personality of a toddler, meaning whatever you say the commanding self disagrees. The second layer is *an-nafs al-lawwāmah*, meaning 'the reproachful self' or 'the blaming self'. The third layer is *an-nafs al-mulhamah*, meaning 'the inspired self'. The fourth layer is *an-nafs al-mutma'innah*, meaning 'the certain self'. The fifth layer is *an-nafs ar-rādiyah*, meaning 'the contented self'. The sixth layer is *an-nafs al-mardhiyah*, meaning 'the self with which everything is contented'. Finally, the seventh layer is *an-nafs al-kāmilah*, meaning 'the completed self', which is epitomised by the Prophet (S). Complete in what way? The completed and perfected person lives the middle path in this world. The term *ummatan wasatan* means a balanced nation.

In verse 75:2 Allah refers to *an-nafs al-lawwāmah* and asks 'how is it that we blame ourselves?' In other words, how is it that when we reflect on our interactions we can contemplate whether we could have been more generous, patient, forgiving, compassionate, or rational? How do we know that we have the potential to display such attributes? It is because Allah has put the seeds of those traits in us and they are accessible to us through our *rūh* (soul). So He says, 'by that which is in you, you feel guilty; it is because of what I have given you out of My Generosity, which is your *rūh* (soul).'

$$\text{أَيَحْسَبُ ٱلْإِنسَٰنُ أَلَّن نَّجْمَعَ عِظَامَهُۥ ﴿٣﴾}$$

Does man imagine We shall not reassemble his bones? (75:3)

$$\text{بَلَىٰ قَٰدِرِينَ عَلَىٰٓ أَن نُّسَوِّىَ بَنَانَهُۥ ﴿٤﴾}$$

Yea! We are able to make complete his very fingertips (75:4)

There are two important words in these verses. The first is *jamā*. Nothing in existence comes about in isolation. Instead, it is always part of two. In other words, everything in existence is signified by duality. There is always an opposite which complements it. *jamā* and *farq* complement each other. *Jamā'* is gatheredness and *farq* is dispersion. Before we were created, before existence and the universe, everything was gathered in singularity and there was only Absolute Light. When creation occurred, there was dispersion. Allah is reminding us that after you die everything will again disperse. The different aspects of the human being will return to their different levels. In other words, the body will return to its earthly level and the soul will return to its origin in the unseen.

We are challenged in this verse: Don't you think it can again be returned? We like to be gathered with our family and friends because everyone remembers the original togetherness and the lack of separation from Allah, but we have been brought into separation to yearn for the gathering. We have descended from the garden to yearn to return to the garden.

The second important word is *banānahu*, which means the fingertips and is a reference to individuality. Each person has a unique fingerprint. A related point is that a baby is born with almost no fingerprints and people of advanced age often lose their fingerprints. The implication is that you lose your ego and identity as you age. You are born without an ego but as you grow you develop an ego, which causes you to believe that life is all about you and that you are in control. However, you reach a point when you realise that there is only One in control, and if you allow your control to be aligned with that then you have unified your will with Allah's will. Then there will be no regrets and you become more aware of the meaning behind the form and the essence.

بَلْ يُرِيدُ ٱلْإِنسَـٰنُ لِيَفْجُرَ أَمَامَهُۥ ﴿٥﴾

But man wishes to persist in his debauchery; (75:5)

266

$$\text{يَسْتَلُ أَيَّانَ يَوْمُ الْقِيَمَةِ} \; \textcircled{\scriptsize ٦}$$

He asks when the Day of Resurrection shall come. (75:6)

$$\text{فَإِذَا بَرِقَ الْبَصَرُ} \; \textcircled{\scriptsize ٧}$$

But when the sight is dazed (75:7)

$$\text{وَخَسَفَ الْقَمَرُ} \; \textcircled{\scriptsize ٨}$$

and the moon is eclipsed, (75:8)

$$\text{وَجُمِعَ الشَّمْسُ وَالْقَمَرُ} \; \textcircled{\scriptsize ٩}$$

And the sun and the moon are brought together, (75:9)

It is difficult to translate verse 75:7. *Bariq* is a root word for 'lightning'. There are no longer any shadows from the moment we die and we ultimately revert to the Original Light from that point onwards. We are lifeless as far as the body is concerned, and the *rūh* (soul) which is Pure Light carries on.

There are three important astronomical entities. The sun is a source of energy and heat and it generates filtered light for us on earth. The second is the earth and third is the moon. These three entities exemplify the balance of light, life, and the awareness and consciousness of things including pure consciousness.

Verse 75:9 refers to the event when the whole universe will collapse and revert to its original state. Allah reminds us in the *Qur'an* repeatedly that whatever has a beginning will also have an end. In other words, it came into being from that original command and it will reach maturity and ultimately come to an end. There are no less than 40 verses in the *Qur'an* on this topic.

$$يَقُولُ ٱلْإِنسَٰنُ يَوْمَئِذٍ أَيْنَ ٱلْمَفَرُّ ﴿١٠﴾$$

on that Day man will say, 'Where can I escape?' (75:10)

The term 'day' in the *Qur'an* should be read as a 'period of time' because there are several other verses which say that a day with Allah is like 1,000 years, or 50,000 years, as we calculate time. As you have probably experienced, sometimes half an hour feels like days or five minutes feels like a very long and exhausting time. The important point is that time is relative.

$$كَلَّا لَا وَزَرَ ﴿١١﴾$$

Truly, there is no refuge (75:11)

$$إِلَىٰ رَبِّكَ يَوْمَئِذٍ ٱلْمُسْتَقَرُّ ﴿١٢﴾$$

With your Lord alone shall on that day be the place of rest.
(75:12)

Verse 75:11 tells us not to blame anybody else. We experience ourselves in terms of our intention and our conduct. Somebody who is content and happy may be constantly referring to higher consciousness and someone who is constantly complaining and blaming everybody else may be in *shaytān's* (satan; ego-self) den. Every atom announces itself, every tree announces itself, every scorpion announces itself and every human being also announces himself or herself. The purpose of this laboratory called Earth is for us to move from sight to insight.

Mustaqarr is an important word denoting the ultimate state of rest or conclusion. *Mustaqarr* means foundation, so the implication is that our *'ibādah*, our acts of worship, are for us to constantly refer to *Allah Azza wa Jal*. Every day in our life is an opportunity for us to practice *yawm al-qiyāmah* (the day of resurrection). It means 'flee to Allah' and 'return it to Allah'. Dozens of verses in the *Qur'an* teach us to refer to the higher to see if an action will align us with the higher. On the other hand, if an action is aligned with the lower it will destroy and confuse us in every way.

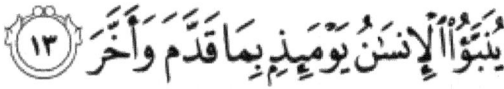

$$ يُنَبَّؤُاْ ٱلْإِنسَٰنُ يَوْمَئِذٍ بِمَا قَدَّمَ وَأَخَّرَ ﴿١٣﴾ $$

Man shall on that day be informed of what he sent before and what he put off. (75:13)

This verse reminds us that time will stop, and we will move from space and time or this capsule on this Earth into a realm where the past, present, and future are all the same.

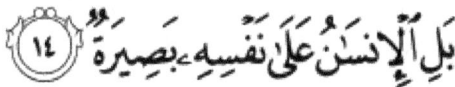

$$ بَلِ ٱلْإِنسَٰنُ عَلَىٰ نَفْسِهِۦ بَصِيرَةٌ ﴿١٤﴾ $$

but man is a clear witness against himself, (75:14)

This statement connects all periods of our life. He said what about *an-nafs al-lawwāma* (the blaming self)? There is something within you that can be *basīrah* (witness) upon you. You know within yourself if you are lying or if you are hesitant, fearful, anxious or insecure. You know because within you exists a realm that knows. The more you refer to that realm, the closer you move towards being unified with *Al-'Alim, Allah Azza wa Jal*.

$$وَلَوْ أَلْقَىٰ مَعَاذِيرَهُۥ ﴿١٥﴾$$

even though he offer his excuses. (75:15)

Ma'aadheer is an excuse or blame. We find it easy to apportion blame. I am right and everybody else is wrong. Everybody wants to play God not realising that God's *nūr* (light) is in you, witnessing you. Where do you escape to? What are you going to occupy? You are already occupied by Divine Light. Once you accept that occupation then you are in *Islām* (submission). Come to see the blessedness of that path of acceptance then you will have *Imān*.

$$لَا تُحَرِّكْ بِهِۦ لِسَانَكَ لِتَعْجَلَ بِهِۦٓ ﴿١٦﴾$$

Move not your tongue with it, seeking to hasten it along (75:16)

This verse addresses the Prophet (S) and it also addresses us as the followers of the Prophet (S). It says, 'Do not rush with the news of the *Qur'an*,' meaning it will come to you at the right time. Do not be afraid.

$$إِنَّ عَلَيْنَا جَمْعَهُۥ وَقُرْءَانَهُۥ ﴿١٧﴾$$

Up to Us is its collection and recitation, (75:17)

$$فَإِذَا قَرَأْنَٰهُ فَٱتَّبِعْ قُرْءَانَهُۥ ﴿١٨﴾$$

when We recite it, follow its recitation (75:18)

When it has come to you, then 'announce it', meaning follow it. Your experience in this regard is like that of a person who is in the depths of the ocean. When he surfaces he first notices the horizon, and only then does he see the trees and birds. Similarly, concerning the Qur'an, you may not get the whole picture in one go. You need time to make sense of it or to describe it. Many Qur'anic verses were revealed in the context of historical events. It often took time for the revelation to demonstrate the truth of the event or the reason, and when it does, the sharī'a (event) and haqīqah (revelation) are united.

ثُمَّ إِنَّ عَلَيْنَا بَيَانَهُۥ ﴿١٩﴾

Then it is up to Us to expound it (75:19)

كَلَّا بَلْ تُحِبُّونَ ٱلْعَاجِلَةَ ﴿٢٠﴾

No indeed; but you love the hasty world, (75:20)

وَتَذَرُونَ ٱلْأَخِرَةَ ﴿٢١﴾

And neglect the hereafter (75:21)

In these verses, Allah describes our lower nature. We expect answers immediately because we are impatient. Allah knows that and so He constantly advises us to be patient and that is one of His names, *Al-Sabūr* (The Patient). The Prophet (S) shared dozens of reminders that running after short-term pleasures will destroy you because pleasure also brings displeasure. It is part of the law of duality. Whenever you remember *ākhira* (the Next Life) you remember your death, which may cause you to postpone the immediate desire for short-term pleasure. In doing so you are seeking the truth and the light of truth in your heart which is forever. That is the meaning of *sabr* (patience).

Life began two billion years ago and at least five extinctions which we know of have taken place since then, which resulted in almost all life on earth disappearing for certain periods. That is why the Prophet (S) reminds us there were many Adams in the past and not only on this earth or only in this form of life. Be geological in your time calculations, be patient and do not be disappointed. How can you know what Allah's timing is? Do what you can. Be joyful in your knowledge that Allah is here and He is with you. Are you with Him or are you with your whims, fantasies, thoughts, illusions, and lusts?

وُجُوهٌ يَوْمَئِذٍ نَّاضِرَةٌ ﴿٢٢﴾

Upon that day faces shall be radiant. (75:22)

إِلَىٰ رَبِّهَا نَاظِرَةٌ ﴿٢٣﴾

To their Lord, their eyes are lifted, (75:23)

وَوُجُوهٌ يَوْمَئِذٍ بَاسِرَةٌ ﴿٢٤﴾

and on that Day there will be the sad and despairing faces (75:24)

تَظُنُّ أَن يُفْعَلَ بِهَا فَاقِرَةٌ ﴿٢٥﴾

Knowing a back-breaker shall befall them. (75:25)

كَلَّا إِذَا بَلَغَتِ ٱلتَّرَاقِيَ ﴿٢٦﴾

No indeed; when it reaches the clavicles (75:26)

These verses are a magnificent reminder that the soul is a prisoner here for a while to connect the seen and the unseen, and that the ultimate magic and miracle takes place when it is about to leave this realm. It is at that point that the soul suddenly connects with the eternal, unifying light.

وَقِيلَ مَنْ رَاقٍ ﴿٢٧﴾

and it is said, 'Who is an enchanter, (75:27)

The *rūh* (soul) is loyal to its Creator because it has accepted Allah's command: 'Am I not your Lord?' It will not look up to bankers and other wizards because nothing else exists. When people are close to the point of death they are at ease because there is nothing of this world which is occupying them and they are about to move into another realm.

وَظَنَّ أَنَّهُ ٱلْفِرَاقُ ﴿٢٨﴾

and he thinks that it is the parting. (75:28)

If you have identified with the body then you will fear your departure. However, if you have practised having connectivity between the head and heart, between the self and soul, then you know death is not something to fear. *Firaq* is a departure that is considered the most natural. It is a union rather than a departure because there is no longer the illusion that you are this body. Every day you are closer to departure, which is when the soul is united with its origin.

وَٱلْتَفَّتِ ٱلسَّاقُ بِٱلسَّاقِ ﴿٢٩﴾

And affliction is combined with affliction; (75:29)

إِلَىٰ رَبِّكَ يَوْمَئِذٍ ٱلْمَسَاقُ ﴿٣٠﴾

on that day he will be driven towards your Lord (75:30)

فَلَا صَدَّقَ وَلَا صَلَّىٰ ﴿٣١﴾

But he neither believed nor prayed. (75:31)

During that period, everybody will be driven towards their Lord. No longer will you have free will or power. Are you ready to abandon your free will and power? Have you practised enough abandonment of them? Have you practised your *sajdah* such that when you go into it you do not know if you will come out of it? If you have practised it genuinely, then it is the completion of the journey and a joyful return from whence you came. The descent of Adam (AS) is his ascent! You have come into this world to realise the Maker of it all. This is the most joyful news. No longer will you have to deal with the ups and downs, shadows and lights, good news or bad news. There is only the *nūr* (light) of the Creator by whose courtesy and generosity you and I have come about and by whose courtesy and generosity we will return. At that point of return, this affliction of being in the *dunyā* (this world) will be over and a new chapter will begin. What better news is there than that?

وَلَٰكِن كَذَّبَ وَتَوَلَّىٰ ﴿٣٢﴾

Instead, he cried lies and departed; (75:32)

274

But you never reminded yourself of or confirmed the truth. Instead, you always denied it.

$$\text{ثُمَّ ذَهَبَ إِلَىٰ أَهْلِهِ يَتَمَطَّىٰ ﴿٣٣﴾}$$

walking back to his people with a conceited swagger. (75:33)

This verse implies that recognising your habits will highlight what you have identified as important in this life, meaning money, spouses, homes, cars and so on. In the end, what use are such attachments?

$$\text{أَوْلَىٰ لَكَ فَأَوْلَىٰ ﴿٣٤﴾}$$

Closer and closer it comes to you. (75:34)

$$\text{ثُمَّ أَوْلَىٰ لَكَ فَأَوْلَىٰ ﴿٣٥﴾}$$

Closer and closer still. (75:35)

Allah is closer to you than closeness. The light in you, your heart, your soul, is closer to you, meaning it is your source of life. However, if you have not practised that remembrance and awareness, then you are in trouble.

$$\text{أَيَحْسَبُ الْإِنسَانُ أَن يُتْرَكَ سُدًى ﴿٣٦﴾}$$

Does man think he shall be abandoned to futility? (75:36)

$$\text{أَلَمْ يَكُ نُطْفَةً مِن مَّنِيٍّ يُمْنَىٰ} \quad ٣٧$$

Was he not a sperm drop, to be discharged (75:37)

$$\text{ثُمَّ كَانَ عَلَقَةً فَخَلَقَ فَسَوَّىٰ} \quad ٣٨$$

Then he was a clinging clot, that He created and formed, (75:38)

Allah shaped us by giving us a physical form which began as a little thing and which grew into a fully developed human being.

$$\text{فَجَعَلَ مِنْهُ الزَّوْجَيْنِ الذَّكَرَ وَالْأُنثَىٰ} \quad ٣٩$$

And made from it a pair, male and female? (75:39)

This verse refers to the plurality of male and female. The genders are complementary and they want to unify into one because the origin is the One and the return is to the One.

$$\text{أَلَيْسَ ذَٰلِكَ بِقَادِرٍ عَلَىٰ أَن يُحْيِيَ الْمَوْتَىٰ} \quad ٤٠$$

Is not He, then; able to bring the dead back to life? (75:40)

Allah Azza wa Jal reminds us repeatedly that the entire *Qur'an* is founded on this view: You have come from nothingness, from the unseen, into life on this Earth to complete your knowledge and understanding of the light of the universe or cosmos and you will return to that after death. There will be a day of reckoning, and it will have two phases. During the first phase, everything will be destroyed by the first blow of the trumpet and after the second blow of the trumpet, everything returns to see itself as it had completed or did not complete itself. The completion of the self means self-abandonment, honesty, and sincerity that there was only One Creator. There is only that, which is based on *Lā ilāha illā Allāh* (and the news that has come to us is the echo of that *Muhammadun Rasul Allah*).

Chapter 19

SURAT AL-FATIR

Sūrat al-Fātir is chapter 35 in the *Qur'an*. During the first 200 years after the departure of the Prophet (S) the names of the chapters were formalised. Chapters were given names based on the most prominent issue the chapter addressed. In this case, *fātir* refers to *Fitrah* which is the original nature of man, deeply imprinted within him and from which all diversity originates. It is also a reference to the original, primal crack; creation began after that mysterious event of *kun fa-yakūn*, which produced this amazing plethora of everything from nothingness. The most prevalent name of this chapter is *fātir*, but equally, in some of the earlier publications of the *Qur'an*, it is called *Sūrat al-Malā'ika*, because the word *malā'ika* (angels) appears in it. *Fitra* is more appropriate because this chapter is about this initial event from which the universe emerged from the unseen and Adam (AS) arose together with all that we as human beings need to thrive. This chapter consists of 45 verses. I will summarise a few of the topics raised and you will notice that each issue is repeated at least twice in this chapter.

Qur'anic Verses

The Arabic text and the English translation of the entire *Sūrat al-Fātir* follow immediately below. Thereafter I will focus my commentary on selected verses and words.

بِسْمِ اللَّهِ الرَّحْمَنِ الرَّحِيمِ

In the name of Allah, the Merciful to all, the Compassionate to each!

ٱلْحَمْدُ لِلَّهِ فَاطِرِ ٱلسَّمَٰوَٰتِ وَٱلْأَرْضِ جَاعِلِ ٱلْمَلَٰٓئِكَةِ رُسُلًا أُولِىٓ أَجْنِحَةٍ مَّثْنَىٰ وَثُلَٰثَ وَرُبَٰعَ يَزِيدُ فِى ٱلْخَلْقِ مَا يَشَآءُ إِنَّ ٱللَّهَ عَلَىٰ كُلِّ شَىْءٍ قَدِيرٌ ﴿١﴾

1. *Praise be to Allah, Originator of the heavens and earth! It is He Who appoints the angels as envoys, having two, three, four wings – He adds to His creation what He wills. Allah has power over all things.*

مَّا يَفْتَحِ ٱللَّهُ لِلنَّاسِ مِن رَّحْمَةٍ فَلَا مُمْسِكَ لَهَا وَمَا يُمْسِكْ فَلَا مُرْسِلَ لَهُۥ مِنۢ بَعْدِهِۦ وَهُوَ ٱلْعَزِيزُ ٱلْحَكِيمُ ﴿٢﴾

2. *Whatever mercy Allah opens to people, none can hold back; Whatever He holds back, none can confer after Him. He is Almighty, All-Wise.*

يَٰٓأَيُّهَا ٱلنَّاسُ ٱذْكُرُوا۟ نِعْمَتَ ٱللَّهِ عَلَيْكُمْ هَلْ مِنْ خَٰلِقٍ غَيْرُ ٱللَّهِ يَرْزُقُكُم مِّنَ ٱلسَّمَآءِ وَٱلْأَرْضِ لَآ إِلَٰهَ إِلَّا هُوَ فَأَنَّىٰ تُؤْفَكُونَ ﴿٣﴾

3. *O people, remember the grace of Allah upon you. Is there any other creator save Allah who provides for you from heaven and earth? There is no Allah but He, so how can you be so deceived?*

وَإِن يُكَذِّبُوكَ فَقَدْ كُذِّبَتْ رُسُلٌ مِّن قَبْلِكَ وَإِلَى اللَّهِ تُرْجَعُ الْأُمُورُ ﴿٤﴾

4.   If they call you a liar, messengers before you were called
liars, and to Allah all matters revert.

يَـٰٓأَيُّهَا النَّاسُ إِنَّ وَعْدَ اللَّهِ حَقٌّ فَلَا تَغُرَّنَّكُمُ الْحَيَوٰةُ الدُّنْيَا وَلَا يَغُرَّنَّكُم بِاللَّهِ الْغَرُورُ ﴿٥﴾

5.   O people, Allah's promise is true, so let not this present life
seduce you, and let not the Tempter tempt you away from Allah.

إِنَّ الشَّيْطَـٰنَ لَكُمْ عَدُوٌّ فَاتَّخِذُوهُ عَدُوًّا إِنَّمَا يَدْعُواْ حِزْبَهُۥ لِيَكُونُواْ مِنْ أَصْحَـٰبِ السَّعِيرِ ﴿٦﴾

6.   Satan is your enemy, so treat him as an enemy. He merely
invites his gang of followers to be denizens of the raging Flame!

الَّذِينَ كَفَرُواْ لَهُمْ عَذَابٌ شَدِيدٌ وَالَّذِينَ ءَامَنُواْ وَعَمِلُواْ الصَّـٰلِحَـٰتِ لَهُم مَّغْفِرَةٌ وَأَجْرٌ كَبِيرٌ ﴿٧﴾

7.   Those who disbelieve – there awaits them a terrible
chastisement; but those who believe, and do deeds of
righteousness – theirs shall be forgiveness and a great wage.

أَفَمَن زُيِّنَ لَهُۥ سُوٓءُ عَمَلِهِۦ فَرَءَاهُ حَسَنًا فَإِنَّ ٱللَّهَ يُضِلُّ مَن يَشَآءُ وَيَهْدِى مَن يَشَآءُ فَلَا تَذْهَبْ نَفْسُكَ عَلَيْهِمْ حَسَرَٰتٍ إِنَّ ٱللَّهَ عَلِيمٌۢ بِمَا يَصْنَعُونَ ٨

8. *Consider a person whose evil deed is made attractive to him, and he regards it as good. Allah leads astray whomever He pleases and guides whomever He pleases. So let not your soul perish with grief over them: Allah knows full well what they do.*

وَٱللَّهُ ٱلَّذِىٓ أَرْسَلَ ٱلرِّيَٰحَ فَتُثِيرُ سَحَابًا فَسُقْنَٰهُ إِلَىٰ بَلَدٍ مَّيِّتٍ فَأَحْيَيْنَا بِهِ ٱلْأَرْضَ بَعْدَ مَوْتِهَا كَذَٰلِكَ ٱلنُّشُورُ ٩

9. *Allah it is Who sends forth the winds, agitating clouds, which We drive forth to a parched land, and thereby revive the ground after it has died. Likewise is the resurrection.*

مَن كَانَ يُرِيدُ ٱلْعِزَّةَ فَلِلَّهِ ٱلْعِزَّةُ جَمِيعًا إِلَيْهِ يَصْعَدُ ٱلْكَلِمُ ٱلطَّيِّبُ وَٱلْعَمَلُ ٱلصَّٰلِحُ يَرْفَعُهُۥ وَٱلَّذِينَ يَمْكُرُونَ ٱلسَّيِّـَٔاتِ لَهُمْ عَذَابٌ شَدِيدٌ وَمَكْرُ أُو۟لَٰٓئِكَ هُوَ يَبُورُ ١٠

10. *Whoso desires grandeur, all grandeur belongs to Allah. To Him ascends speech that is pure, and righteous deeds He elevates. As for those who contrive evil, terrible punishment awaits them, and their contriving itself shall be in vain.*

وَٱللَّهُ خَلَقَكُم مِّن تُرَابٍ ثُمَّ مِن نُّطْفَةٍ ثُمَّ جَعَلَكُمْ أَزْوَٰجًا وَمَا تَحْمِلُ مِنْ أُنثَىٰ وَلَا تَضَعُ إِلَّا

بِعِلْمِهِ وَمَا يُعَمَّرُ مِن مُّعَمَّرٍ وَلَا يُنقَصُ مِنْ عُمُرِهِ إِلَّا فِى كِتَٰبٍ إِنَّ ذَٰلِكَ عَلَى ٱللَّهِ يَسِيرٌ ﴿١١﴾

11. *It is Allah who created you from dust and later from a drop*
of fluid; then He made you into two sexes; no female conceives
or gives birth without His knowledge; no person grows old or
has his life cut short, except in accordance with a Record: all
this is easy for God.

وَمَا يَسْتَوِى ٱلْبَحْرَانِ هَٰذَا عَذْبٌ فُرَاتٌ سَآئِغٌ شَرَابُهُ وَهَٰذَا مِلْحٌ أُجَاجٌ وَمِن كُلٍّ

تَأْكُلُونَ لَحْمًا طَرِيًّا وَتَسْتَخْرِجُونَ حِلْيَةً تَلْبَسُونَهَا وَتَرَى ٱلْفُلْكَ فِيهِ مَوَاخِرَ

لِتَبْتَغُوا۟ مِن فَضْلِهِ وَلَعَلَّكُمْ تَشْكُرُونَ ﴿١٢﴾

12. *The two seas are not alike: this one is fresh and sweet water,*
tasty to drink, that one salty and bitter. From both you eat flesh
that is soft, and you extract jewellery to wear. Therein you can
see ships ploughing through the waves, that you may seek of
His bounty — perchance you will give thanks.

يُولِجُ ٱلَّيۡلَ فِى ٱلنَّهَارِ وَيُولِجُ ٱلنَّهَارَ فِى ٱلَّيۡلِ وَسَخَّرَ ٱلشَّمۡسَ وَٱلۡقَمَرَ كُلٌّ يَجۡرِى لِأَجَلٍ مُّسَمًّى ذَٰلِكُمُ ٱللَّهُ رَبُّكُمۡ لَهُ ٱلۡمُلۡكُ وَٱلَّذِينَ تَدۡعُونَ مِن دُونِهِۦ مَا يَمۡلِكُونَ مِن قِطۡمِيرٍ ۝

13. *He makes the night to enter into the day and makes the day to enter into the night, and He has subjected the sun and the moon, each of them running to a stated term. That is Allah, your Lord; to Him belongs the Kingdom; and those you call upon, apart from Him, possess not so much as the skin of a date-stone.*

إِن تَدۡعُوهُمۡ لَا يَسۡمَعُوا۟ دُعَآءَكُمۡ وَلَوۡ سَمِعُوا۟ مَا ٱسۡتَجَابُوا۟ لَكُمۡ وَيَوۡمَ ٱلۡقِيَٰمَةِ يَكۡفُرُونَ بِشِرۡكِكُمۡ وَلَا يُنَبِّئُكَ مِثۡلُ خَبِيرٍ ۝

14. *if you call them they cannot hear you; if they could hear, they could not answer you; on the Day of Resurrection they will disown your idolatry. None can inform you [Prophet] like the One who is all aware.*

يَٰٓأَيُّهَا ٱلنَّاسُ أَنتُمُ ٱلۡفُقَرَآءُ إِلَى ٱللَّهِ وَٱللَّهُ هُوَ ٱلۡغَنِىُّ ٱلۡحَمِيدُ ۝

15. *O humankind, it is you who stand in need of Allah — Allah is All-Sufficient, All-Praiseworthy;*

إِن يَشَأۡ يُذۡهِبۡكُمۡ وَيَأۡتِ بِخَلۡقٍ جَدِيدٍ ۝

16. *if He wills, He can do away with you and bring in a new creation,*

284

وَمَا ذَلِكَ عَلَى ٱللَّهِ بِعَزِيزٍ ۝

17. *that is not difficult for Allah.*

وَلَا تَزِرُ وَازِرَةٌ وِزْرَ أُخْرَىٰ وَإِن تَدْعُ مُثْقَلَةٌ إِلَىٰ حِمْلِهَا لَا يُحْمَلْ مِنْهُ شَيْءٌ وَلَوْ كَانَ ذَا
قُرْبَىٰ إِنَّمَا تُنذِرُ ٱلَّذِينَ يَخْشَوْنَ رَبَّهُم بِٱلْغَيْبِ وَأَقَامُوا ٱلصَّلَوٰةَ وَمَن تَزَكَّىٰ فَإِنَّمَا
يَتَزَكَّىٰ لِنَفْسِهِ وَإِلَى ٱللَّهِ ٱلْمَصِيرُ ۝

18. *No soul burdened can carry the burden of another. If a soul heavy-laden calls for help with its load, not a speck of it shall be carried, not even by a relative. You are to warn those who fear their Lord in the realm of the unseen, and who perform the prayer. Whoso is pure in soul, his purity rebounds to his own benefit, and to Allah is the final destination.*

وَمَا يَسْتَوِي ٱلْأَعْمَىٰ وَٱلْبَصِيرُ ۝

19. *Unequal are the blind and those who see;*

وَلَا ٱلظُّلُمَٰتُ وَلَا ٱلنُّورُ ۝

20. *Nor the darkness and the light,*

وَلَا ٱلظِّلُّ وَلَا ٱلْحَرُورُ ۝

21. *nor the [cooling] shade and the scorching heat.*

وَمَا يَسْتَوِى ٱلْأَحْيَآءُ وَلَا ٱلْأَمْوَاتُ إِنَّ ٱللَّهَ يُسْمِعُ مَن يَشَآءُ وَمَآ أَنتَ بِمُسْمِعٍ مَّن فِى ٱلْقُبُورِ ﴿٢٢﴾

22. *Unequal are the living and the dead. Allah hears whom He pleases, but you cannot make them hear, those who are in their graves.*

إِنْ أَنتَ إِلَّا نَذِيرٌ ﴿٢٣﴾

23. *You are but a warner.*

إِنَّآ أَرْسَلْنَاكَ بِٱلْحَقِّ بَشِيرًا وَنَذِيرًا وَإِن مِّنْ أُمَّةٍ إِلَّا خَلَا فِيهَا نَذِيرٌ ﴿٢٤﴾

24. *We sent you with the Truth, a herald of glad tidings and a warner, and there is no nation but a warner had passed it by.*

وَإِن يُكَذِّبُوكَ فَقَدْ كَذَّبَ ٱلَّذِينَ مِن قَبْلِهِمْ جَآءَتْهُمْ رُسُلُهُم بِٱلْبَيِّنَاتِ وَبِٱلزُّبُرِ وَبِٱلْكِتَابِ ٱلْمُنِيرِ ﴿٢٥﴾

25. *If they call you a liar, so too did those who came before them cry lies; their messengers had come to them with wonders, with the Psalms and the Luminous Book,*

ثُمَّ أَخَذْتُ ٱلَّذِينَ كَفَرُوا۟ فَكَيْفَ كَانَ نَكِيرِ ﴿٢٦﴾

26. *Then I seized the unbelievers – behold how I reversed their fortunes!*

أَلَمْ تَرَ أَنَّ ٱللَّهَ أَنزَلَ مِنَ ٱلسَّمَآءِ مَآءً فَأَخْرَجْنَا بِهِۦ ثَمَرَٰتٍ مُّخْتَلِفًا أَلْوَٰنُهَا وَمِنَ ٱلْجِبَالِ جُدَدٌ بِيضٌ وَحُمْرٌ مُّخْتَلِفٌ أَلْوَٰنُهَا وَغَرَابِيبُ سُودٌ ۝

27. *Have you not seen how Allah causes water to descend from the sky with which We bring forth fruits diverse in colours? And mountain-tracks, white and red, diverse in colours, and other pathways, dark and obscure?*

وَمِنَ ٱلنَّاسِ وَٱلدَّوَآبِّ وَٱلْأَنْعَٰمِ مُخْتَلِفٌ أَلْوَٰنُهُۥ كَذَٰلِكَ إِنَّمَا يَخْشَى ٱللَّهَ مِنْ عِبَادِهِ ٱلْعُلَمَٰٓؤُا۟ إِنَّ ٱللَّهَ عَزِيزٌ غَفُورٌ ۝

28. *So also humans, beasts of burden and cattle of diverse colours? From among His worshippers, only the learned fear Allah. Allah is Almighty, All-Forgiving.*

إِنَّ ٱلَّذِينَ يَتْلُونَ كِتَٰبَ ٱللَّهِ وَأَقَامُوا۟ ٱلصَّلَوٰةَ وَأَنفَقُوا۟ مِمَّا رَزَقْنَٰهُمْ سِرًّا وَعَلَانِيَةً يَرْجُونَ تِجَٰرَةً لَّن تَبُورَ ۝

29. *Those who recite Allah's scripture, keep up the prayer, give secretly and openly from what We have provided for them, may hope for a trade that will never decline,*

لِيُوَفِّيَهُمْ أُجُورَهُمْ وَيَزِيدَهُم مِّن فَضْلِهِۦٓ إِنَّهُۥ غَفُورٌ شَكُورٌ ۝

30. *that He may pay them in full their wages and enrich them of His bounty; surely He is All-forgiving, All-thankful.*

وَٱلَّذِىٓ أَوۡحَيۡنَآ إِلَيۡكَ مِنَ ٱلۡكِتَٰبِ هُوَ ٱلۡحَقُّ مُصَدِّقًا لِّمَا بَيۡنَ يَدَيۡهِ إِنَّ ٱللَّهَ بِعِبَادِهِۦ لَخَبِيرٌۢ بَصِيرٌ ﴿٣١﴾

31. What We inspired you with from the Book is the Truth,
confirming what came before. Regarding His servants, Allah is
All-Experienced, All-Seeing.

ثُمَّ أَوۡرَثۡنَا ٱلۡكِتَٰبَ ٱلَّذِينَ ٱصۡطَفَيۡنَا مِنۡ عِبَادِنَا فَمِنۡهُمۡ ظَالِمٌ لِّنَفۡسِهِۦ وَمِنۡهُم مُّقۡتَصِدٌ وَمِنۡهُمۡ سَابِقٌۢ بِٱلۡخَيۡرَٰتِ بِإِذۡنِ ٱللَّهِ ذَٰلِكَ هُوَ ٱلۡفَضۡلُ ٱلۡكَبِيرُ ﴿٣٢﴾

32. Then We bequeathed the Book to those of Our servants
whom We chose: some wronged themselves, some mixed good
with evil, and some were quick to do righteous deeds, by Allah's
leave. And that is the greatest of favours.

جَنَّٰتُ عَدۡنٍ يَدۡخُلُونَهَا يُحَلَّوۡنَ فِيهَا مِنۡ أَسَاوِرَ مِن ذَهَبٍ وَلُؤۡلُؤًا وَلِبَاسُهُمۡ فِيهَا حَرِيرٌ ﴿٣٣﴾

33. They will enter lasting Gardens where they will be adorned
with bracelets of gold and pearls, where they will wear silk
garments.

وَقَالُوا ٱلۡحَمۡدُ لِلَّهِ ٱلَّذِىٓ أَذۡهَبَ عَنَّا ٱلۡحَزَنَ إِنَّ رَبَّنَا لَغَفُورٌ شَكُورٌ ﴿٣٤﴾

34. And they shall say, 'Praise belongs to Allah who has put
away all sorrow from us. Surely our Lord is All-Forgiving, All-
Thankful,

ٱلَّذِىٓ أَحَلَّنَا دَارَ ٱلْمُقَامَةِ مِن فَضْلِهِۦ لَا يَمَسُّنَا فِيهَا نَصَبٌ وَلَا يَمَسُّنَا فِيهَا لُغُوبٌ ﴿٣٥﴾

35. *who of His bounty has made us to dwell in the abode of everlasting life wherein no weariness assails us neither fatigue.'*

وَٱلَّذِينَ كَفَرُوا۟ لَهُمْ نَارُ جَهَنَّمَ لَا يُقْضَىٰ عَلَيْهِمْ فَيَمُوتُوا۟ وَلَا يُخَفَّفُ عَنْهُم مِّنْ عَذَابِهَا كَذَٰلِكَ نَجْزِى كُلَّ كَفُورٍ ﴿٣٦﴾

36. *As for the unbelievers, theirs is the fire of hell. They shall not be judged and thus die, nor shall they be spared any of its torment. Thus do We reward every single unbeliever.*

وَهُمْ يَصْطَرِخُونَ فِيهَا رَبَّنَآ أَخْرِجْنَا نَعْمَلْ صَٰلِحًا غَيْرَ ٱلَّذِى كُنَّا نَعْمَلُ أَوَلَمْ نُعَمِّرْكُم مَّا يَتَذَكَّرُ فِيهِ مَن تَذَكَّرَ وَجَآءَكُمُ ٱلنَّذِيرُ فَذُوقُوا۟ فَمَا لِلظَّٰلِمِينَ مِن نَّصِيرٍ ﴿٣٧﴾

37. *In it they shall scream: 'Our Lord, take us out and we will act righteously, other than what we used to do!' Did We not grant you span of life enough for one who remembers to have remembered? The warner came to you, so taste your torment. The wrongdoers shall have none to support them.*

إِنَّ ٱللَّهَ عَٰلِمُ غَيْبِ ٱلسَّمَٰوَٰتِ وَٱلْأَرْضِ إِنَّهُۥ عَلِيمٌۢ بِذَاتِ ٱلصُّدُورِ ﴿٣٨﴾

38. *Allah is knower of the unseen in the heavens and earth, He knows full well what lies within breasts.*

هُوَ ٱلَّذِى جَعَلَكُمْ خَلَـٰٓئِفَ فِى ٱلْأَرْضِ فَمَن كَفَرَ فَعَلَيْهِ كُفْرُهُۥ وَلَا يَزِيدُ ٱلْكَـٰفِرِينَ كُفْرُهُمْ عِندَ
رَبِّهِمْ إِلَّا مَقْتًا وَلَا يَزِيدُ ٱلْكَـٰفِرِينَ كُفْرُهُمْ إِلَّا خَسَارًا ۝

39. *It is He who appointed you viceroys in the earth. So
whosoever disbelieves, his unbelief shall be charged against
him; their unbelief increases the disbelievers only in hate in
Allah's sight; their unbelief increases the disbelievers only in
loss.*

قُلْ أَرَءَيْتُمْ شُرَكَآءَكُمُ ٱلَّذِينَ تَدْعُونَ مِن دُونِ ٱللَّهِ أَرُونِى مَاذَا خَلَقُوا مِنَ ٱلْأَرْضِ أَمْ لَهُمْ شِرْكٌ فِى
ٱلسَّمَـٰوَٰتِ أَمْ ءَاتَيْنَـٰهُمْ كِتَـٰبًا فَهُمْ عَلَىٰ بَيِّنَتٍ مِّنْهُ بَلْ إِن يَعِدُ ٱلظَّـٰلِمُونَ بَعْضُهُم بَعْضًا إِلَّا
غُرُورًا ۝

40. *Say: 'Have you considered your associates on whom you
call, apart from Allah? Show me what they have created in the
earth; or have they a partnership in the heavens?' Or have We
given them a Book, so that they are upon a clear sign from it?
Nay, but the evildoers promise one another naught but delusion.*

۞ إِنَّ ٱللَّهَ يُمْسِكُ ٱلسَّمَـٰوَٰتِ وَٱلْأَرْضَ أَن تَزُولَا وَلَئِن زَالَتَا إِنْ أَمْسَكَهُمَا مِنْ أَحَدٍ مِّنۢ
بَعْدِهِۦ إِنَّهُۥ كَانَ حَلِيمًا غَفُورًا ۝

41. *Allah holds the heavens and the earth, lest they remove; did
they remove, none would hold them after Him. Surely He is All-
Clement, All-Forgiving.*

وَأَقْسَمُوا بِاللَّهِ جَهْدَ أَيْمَـٰنِهِمْ لَئِن جَآءَهُمْ نَذِيرٌ لَّيَكُونُنَّ أَهْدَىٰ مِنْ إِحْدَى ٱلْأُمَمِ فَلَمَّا جَآءَهُمْ نَذِيرٌ مَّا زَادَهُمْ إِلَّا نُفُورًا ﴿٤٢﴾

42. *They swore by Allah a mighty oath that if a warner would
come to them, they would be more rightly guided than any
nation. But when a warner did come to them, this merely
increased them in aversion,*

ٱسْتِكْبَارًا فِى ٱلْأَرْضِ وَمَكْرَ ٱلسَّيِّئِ وَلَا يَحِيقُ ٱلْمَكْرُ ٱلسَّيِّئُ إِلَّا بِأَهْلِهِ فَهَلْ يَنظُرُونَ إِلَّا سُنَّتَ ٱلْأَوَّلِينَ فَلَن تَجِدَ لِسُنَّتِ ٱللَّهِ تَبْدِيلًا وَلَن تَجِدَ لِسُنَّتِ ٱللَّهِ تَحْوِيلًا ﴿٤٣﴾

43. *(In) behaving proudly in the land and in planning evil; and
the evil plans shall not beset any save the authors of it. Then
should they wait for aught except the way of the former people?
For you shall not find any alteration in the course of Allah; and
you shall not find any change in the course of Allah.*

أَوَلَمْ يَسِيرُوا فِى ٱلْأَرْضِ فَيَنظُرُوا كَيْفَ كَانَ عَـٰقِبَةُ ٱلَّذِينَ مِن قَبْلِهِمْ وَكَانُوٓا أَشَدَّ مِنْهُمْ قُوَّةً وَمَا كَانَ ٱللَّهُ لِيُعْجِزَهُۥ مِن شَىْءٍ فِى ٱلسَّمَـٰوَٰتِ وَلَا فِى ٱلْأَرْضِ إِنَّهُۥ كَانَ عَلِيمًا قَدِيرًا ﴿٤٤﴾

44. *Have they not travelled in the land and seen how those
before them met their end, although they were superior to them
in strength? God is not to be frustrated by anything in the
heavens or on the earth: He is all-Knowing, all-Powerful.*

وَلَوْ يُؤَاخِذُ اللَّهُ النَّاسَ بِمَا كَسَبُواْ مَا تَرَكَ عَلَى ظَهْرِهَا مِن دَآبَّةٍ وَلَـٰكِن يُؤَخِّرُهُمْ إِلَىٰ أَجَلٍ مُّسَمًّى فَإِذَا جَاءَ أَجَلُهُمْ فَإِنَّ اللَّهَ كَانَ بِعِبَادِهِ بَصِيرًا ﴿٤٥﴾

45. Had Allah taken people to task for what they earned, He would not have left a crawling creature on the face of the earth. Instead, He postpones them to a stated term. When their final end arrives, Allah, in regard to His servants, is All-Seeing.

Commentary on selected verses

ٱلْحَمْدُ لِلَّهِ فَاطِرِ ٱلسَّمَوَٰتِ وَٱلْأَرْضِ جَاعِلِ ٱلْمَلَـٰٓئِكَةِ رُسُلًا أُوْلِىٓ أَجْنِحَةٍ مَّثْنَىٰ وَثُلَـٰثَ وَرُبَـٰعَ

يَزِيدُ فِى ٱلْخَلْقِ مَا يَشَآءُ إِنَّ ٱللَّهَ عَلَىٰ كُلِّ شَىْءٍ قَدِيرٌ ﴿١﴾

Praise be to Allah, Originator of the heavens and earth! It is He Who appoints the angels as envoys, having two, three, four wings – He adds to His creation what He wills. Allah has power over all things. (35:1)

Malā'ika is mentioned in the very first verse of this chapter. Its root is *malak* which is connected with control. Angels are controlled entities in the unseen. They are controlled by Allah and this verse tells us that they have many wings which is a reference to power. The Prophet (S) said that during the *mi'rāj* (ascension), he saw Jibrā'īl (Angel Gabriel) with 600 wings which implies a greater power in terms of speed and the ability to move within space. Our mind is an instrument that connects us to material issues, to earthly matters, to causalities, the up and the down, the good and the bad. It is an important faculty which enables us to survive and live in this world. However, we also have the *rūh* (soul) which is from another world, *'Ālam al-Ghayb* (the Realm of the unseen) and which is exposed to far greater horizons than the mind is exposed to. For this reason, if we do not refer to our soul, we feel inadequate, incomplete, empty, and unfulfilled.

مَّا يَفْتَحِ ٱللَّهُ لِلنَّاسِ مِن رَّحْمَةٍ فَلَا مُمْسِكَ لَهَا وَمَا يُمْسِكْ فَلَا مُرْسِلَ لَهُۥ مِنۢ بَعْدِهِۦ وَهُوَ ٱلْعَزِيزُ

ٱلْحَكِيمُ ﴿٢﴾

Whatever mercy Allah opens to people, none can hold back; Whatever He holds back, none can confer after Him. He is Almighty, All-Wise. (35:2)

This is a beautiful verse which reminds us that *rahma* (which is grace, mercy or goodness), has to be opened, for us to be connected to this field of energy of goodness and generosity. It is a field of energy but that does not mean that our connection to it is constant. This verse tells us that when Allah opens it for you, nothing will close it and if it is not opened for you by Allah, nothing can open it. It reinforces our dependence on the highest energy source in creation.

$$\text{يَـٰٓأَيُّهَا ٱلنَّاسُ ٱذْكُرُوا۟ نِعْمَتَ ٱللَّهِ عَلَيْكُمْ هَلْ مِنْ خَـٰلِقٍ غَيْرُ ٱللَّهِ يَرْزُقُكُم مِّنَ ٱلسَّمَآءِ وَٱلْأَرْضِ}$$
$$\text{لَآ إِلَـٰهَ إِلَّا هُوَ فَأَنَّىٰ تُؤْفَكُونَ} \; (٣)$$

O people, remember the grace of Allah upon you. Is there any
other creator save Allah who provides for you from heaven and
earth? There is no Allah but He, so how can you be so deceived?
(35:3)

Is there any other creation than the One? Your *rizq* (provision) will come from the heavens and the earth. *Rizq* from the earth relates to our material sustenance, encompassing what we consume from the plant and animal kingdom. However, there is also provision from the unseen, which includes matters of the heart, emotions, relationships and connections. These aspects of our existence are from the unseen and from the *sama'ah*, which means that which is high. *Islām* (submission) is based on trusting in this map of the seen (in which we can relate to each other through our senses, our mind and our memory) and the unseen (which is far, far greater).

An analogy can be drawn from contemplating our sphere of existence in the universe. Our existence on Earth is a tiny part of the larger cosmic system. The Milky Way contains countless stars, each with its own planetary system. This verse invites us to reflect on what comes to us from the unseen.

On a deeper level, our cells, the human body and the earth are made from cosmic dust. However, in terms of *nūr* (light), there is a divine element that is beyond our comprehension. It is *min amri Rabbi*, meaning (we don't know what it is. Each human being has a divine spark and for this reason) the *Qur'an* (5:32) says: 'If you kill one person it is as though you have killed all of creation, and if you have brought to life one person you have brought to life all of creation.'

Allah is One, and we all have within us that rope of Oneness which is our *rūh*. This verse emphasises remembrance of the *ni'mah* of Allah, (reminding us of our existence in the womb and the inevitability of death). By that remembrance, our minds align with the ultimate truth, resonating with divine presence. The more frequently and the more deeply we remember, the more fully present we become, free from concerns of the past or worries about the future. This state of presence provides us with energy and vitality.

The verse also highlights a recurring theme in the *Qur'an* – the role of the Prophets. Prophets were sent to guide humanity out of darkness and ignorance. Their teachings offered illumination to those in need.

وَإِن يُكَذِّبُوكَ فَقَدْ كُذِّبَتْ رُسُلٌ مِّن قَبْلِكَ وَإِلَى اللَّهِ تُرْجَعُ الْأُمُورُ ﴿٤﴾

If they call you a liar, messengers before you were called liars, and to Allah all matters revert. (35:4).

Allah's message here is simple: if they deny you, if they refuse you as they did with our glorious Prophet, then do not be saddened with such people, as you are in good company.

يَٰٓأَيُّهَا ٱلنَّاسُ إِنَّ وَعْدَ ٱللَّهِ حَقٌّ فَلَا تَغُرَّنَّكُمُ ٱلْحَيَوٰةُ ٱلدُّنْيَا وَلَا يَغُرَّنَّكُم بِٱللَّهِ ٱلْغَرُورُ ﴿٥﴾

O people, Allah's promise is true, so let not this present life seduce you, and let not the Tempter tempt you away from Allah.
(35:5)

This verse delivers a key message: Do not become arrogant about what you have in this world. You have come here to improve your way of worship, your way of connectedness and this will not change. Do not be distracted. Use the *dunyā* (this world), do not deprive yourself, but know that you are the highest of creation. Experience joy and goodness, but these should be stepping stones to ultimate, continuous, and sustained goodness in your heart. Having friends, a family, an extended family or a clan is helpful to give you a bit of earthly security and status. But it is your focus on heavenly security and heavenly confidence that determine the extent to which you dive into your own heart and dwell with that *nūr* (light) given to you by *Allah Azza wa Jal*. The soul is an aspect of *Allah Azza wa Jal*. If we become forgetful and deviate, we leave room for *shaytān* (satan; ego-self).

إِنَّ ٱلشَّيْطَٰنَ لَكُمْ عَدُوٌّ فَٱتَّخِذُوهُ عَدُوًّا إِنَّمَا يَدْعُواْ حِزْبَهُۥ لِيَكُونُواْ مِنْ أَصْحَٰبِ ٱلسَّعِيرِ ﴿٦﴾

Satan is your enemy, so treat him as an enemy. He merely invites his gang of followers to be denizens of the raging Flame! (35:6)

Shaytān here refers to that which obstructs the human from rising to the point from which Adam (AS) descended. Adam, you and I, our soul and our *nafs* (ego-self), were designed in the garden. We are designed to seek out the eternal garden and that is why we love gardens in this world and we love places of peace and tranquillity. This is why humans inherently feel insecure in this world; we know it will not last. *Shaytān* (satan; ego-self) is that which distracts us from climbing back to that garden.

Adam, by his questioning, descended into this world of duality and no longer remained in inner ecstasy in his garden. Our purpose then is to return or ascend back up that ladder through worship, not questioning. What is that ladder other than our *'ibādah*? All *'ibādah* leads us to a single focus so that the soul illumines us. We do not only listen to reason and wisdom, we also have inspiration. Watch out for distractions on your path of return to your inner garden, in readiness for the garden in the Hereafter.

$$\text{ٱلَّذِينَ كَفَرُواْ لَهُمْ عَذَابٌ شَدِيدٌ وَٱلَّذِينَ ءَامَنُواْ وَعَمِلُواْ ٱلصَّٰلِحَٰتِ لَهُم مَّغْفِرَةٌ وَأَجْرٌ كَبِيرٌ}$$

۝

Those who disbelieve – there awaits them a terrible chastisement;
but those who believe, and do deeds of righteousness – theirs shall
be forgiveness and a great wage. (35:7)

This verse refers to both *kufr* (denial, ingratitude) and *Imān* (certainty and security that Allah knows and Allah sees) which is a further example of duality. From the One, from the same light, comes darkness; good and bad, up and down. This verse reminds us to not consider what we are doing as the ultimate pursuit.

$$\text{أَفَمَن زُيِّنَ لَهُۥ سُوٓءُ عَمَلِهِۦ فَرَءَاهُ حَسَنًا فَإِنَّ ٱللَّهَ يُضِلُّ مَن يَشَآءُ وَيَهْدِى مَن يَشَآءُ فَلَا}$$
$$\text{تَذْهَبْ نَفْسُكَ عَلَيْهِمْ حَسَرَٰتٍ إِنَّ ٱللَّهَ عَلِيمٌۢ بِمَا يَصْنَعُونَ}$$ ۝

Consider a person whose evil deed is made attractive to him, and
he regards it as good. Allah leads astray whomever He pleases
and guides whomever He pleases. So let not your soul perish with
grief over them: Allah knows full well what they do. (35:8)

This verse relates to those who think that whatever they do is good. For example, you like to make more money so that you may give more to your family or to charity, but who is to say that is the right balance? Who said it is not enough for you now?

Are you ready to leave this world joyfully? Are you constantly serving others? Serving others begins in childhood. The child loves the attention of their mother because they see their mother as the ultimate God. Gradually, they have relationships with other people as an extension of that relationship until they discover that all connections have emerged from the One and only Giver, from the One and only Light from which infinite lights and shadows have emanated. This is the beginning of the awakening. Do not deny worldly situations, but more than that you should realise where they came from.

وَٱللَّهُ ٱلَّذِىٓ أَرْسَلَ ٱلرِّيَٰحَ فَتُثِيرُ سَحَابًا فَسُقْنَٰهُ إِلَىٰ بَلَدٍ مَّيِّتٍ فَأَحْيَيْنَا بِهِ ٱلْأَرْضَ بَعْدَ مَوْتِهَا ۚ كَذَٰلِكَ ٱلنُّشُورُ ۝

Allah it is Who sends forth the winds, agitating clouds, which We drive forth to a parched land, and thereby revive the ground after it has died. Likewise is the resurrection (35:9)

This is a very descriptive verse about winds which bring clouds, and rains which bring the dead earth back to life. Just as the dead earth is revived, so will we in terms of our resurrection. Look at this incredible *mithāl* (similitude). This is the map of *Islām, Imān* and *Ihsān* (inner and outer excellence in thought and conduct). You are only half alive because of your excessive involvement with material issues, and you should be mindful that whatever you have earned in this earthly existence (meaning the extent to which you have purified yourself from your lower self) is the state in which you will come to life in the afterlife.

مَن كَانَ يُرِيدُ ٱلْعِزَّةَ فَلِلَّهِ ٱلْعِزَّةُ جَمِيعًا ۚ إِلَيْهِ يَصْعَدُ ٱلْكَلِمُ ٱلطَّيِّبُ وَٱلْعَمَلُ ٱلصَّٰلِحُ يَرْفَعُهُ ۚ وَٱلَّذِينَ يَمْكُرُونَ ٱلسَّيِّئَاتِ لَهُمْ عَذَابٌ شَدِيدٌ ۖ وَمَكْرُ أُوْلَٰٓئِكَ هُوَ يَبُورُ ۝

Whosoever desires grandeur, all grandeur belongs to Allah. To Him ascends speech that is pure, and righteous deeds He elevates. As for those who contrive evil, terrible punishment awaits them, and their contriving itself shall be in vain. (35:10)

Do not ask for status in this life. Allah is status, Allah is the Glorious. If you want status, you are competing with Him. We need to live our lives sensibly in terms of serving, helping and doing. Do your bit, be sensible, serve, help and creation will recognise that. The whole of humanity is essentially the same. Each person has a *rūh* and a *nafs* and each person likes to acknowledge those who are more *rūhani*, meaning those who are living according to the light of their souls.

وَٱللَّهُ خَلَقَكُم مِّن تُرَابٍ ثُمَّ مِن نُّطْفَةٍ ثُمَّ جَعَلَكُمْ أَزْوَٰجًا وَمَا تَحْمِلُ مِنْ أُنثَىٰ وَلَا تَضَعُ إِلَّا بِعِلْمِهِۦ وَمَا يُعَمَّرُ مِن مُّعَمَّرٍ وَلَا يُنقَصُ مِنْ عُمُرِهِۦ إِلَّا فِى كِتَٰبٍ إِنَّ ذَٰلِكَ عَلَى ٱللَّهِ يَسِيرٌ ﴿١١﴾

It is Allah who created you from dust and later from a drop of fluid; then He made you into two sexes; no female conceives or gives birth without His knowledge; no person grows old or has his life cut short, except in accordance with a Record: all this is easy for Allah. (35:11)

This verse relates to the question of decree and destiny out of duality. It says Allah created you from dust; and from the womb began two genders, male and female. All that we experience in this life reflects the duality and is already part of the design, decree, and destiny. We are reminded that Allah's ways of creation are according to infinite varieties of designs and patterns. We are given a minor role in this regard. Are you free or is it predestined? This is a subject of much debate. The truth of it is that the designs have been ordained and we have a degree of involvement in the process. For example, if you put your foot in the wrong place, you may slip into a bad destiny and the end of it is according to your *niyyah* (intention). The Prophetic teaching is that you will be given provision according to your intention. Allah's design is perfect, beyond our ability to control, and is comprised of phase after phase and spheres within spheres. However, you and I are also accountable. Ask yourself: what is my intention in going there? Is it to help someone in need? Is this somebody who has less than me in ability, energy, or knowledge? In other words, if you are truly walking in the way of Allah to gain more knowledge, to serve yourself and others, then, as the Prophet (S) said, if you die in that state you are a *shahīd* (martyr). Although ultimately Allah is the Doer and the Giver, you have the opportunity to continuously improve yourself, to live more as a soul.

وَمَا يَسْتَوِى ٱلْبَحْرَانِ هَٰذَا عَذْبٌ فُرَاتٌ سَآئِغٌ شَرَابُهُۥ وَهَٰذَا مِلْحٌ أُجَاجٌ وَمِن كُلٍّ تَأْكُلُونَ لَحْمًا طَرِيًّا وَتَسْتَخْرِجُونَ حِلْيَةً تَلْبَسُونَهَا وَتَرَى ٱلْفُلْكَ فِيهِ مَوَاخِرَ لِتَبْتَغُوا۟ مِن فَضْلِهِۦ وَلَعَلَّكُمْ تَشْكُرُونَ ﴿١٢﴾

The two seas are not alike: this one is fresh and sweet water, tasty to drink, that one salty and bitter. From both you eat flesh that is soft, and you extract jewellery to wear. Therein you can see ships ploughing through the waves, that you may seek of His bounty — perchance you will give thanks. (35:12)

These verses again emphasise duality. He says, and from both of the seas, one of them is salty so you cannot quench your thirst and the other one is sweet water from which you can, and from both, you extract food. You can also extract items to decorate yourself. Look at Allah's incredible wisdom here. He says we love to decorate ourselves with turbans and gold jewellery because we love status, and we love status because of the soul which is of such a high status that the ego-self mistakes itself as having high status and as a result, we identify with our silly biographies.

Then we have the beautiful repetitive word *tashkurūn*, meaning that all of this has been provided so that we are in a state of gratitude and so that we can remember the origin. By constantly being in gratitude for what we have instead of constantly taking, we remember to put things into context, and this enables our minds to be open to both causality and creativity.

$$يُولِجُ ٱلَّيْلَ فِى ٱلنَّهَارِ وَيُولِجُ ٱلنَّهَارَ فِى ٱلَّيْلِ وَسَخَّرَ ٱلشَّمْسَ وَٱلْقَمَرَ كُلٌّ$$
$$يَجْرِى لِأَجَلٍ مُّسَمًّى ذَٰلِكُمُ ٱللَّهُ رَبُّكُمْ لَهُ ٱلْمُلْكُ وَٱلَّذِينَ تَدْعُونَ مِن دُونِهِ$$
$$مَا يَمْلِكُونَ مِن قِطْمِيرٍ ۝١٣$$

He makes the night to enter into the day and makes the day to enter into the night, and He has subjected the sun and the moon, each of them running to a stated term. That is Allah, your Lord; to Him belongs the Kingdom; and those you call upon, apart from Him, possess not so much as the skin of a date-stone. (35:13)

This is the key message of this chapter: the night culminates in the day and the day culminates in the night, in a pattern that repeats itself. Those who imagine that something other than Allah is the cause of it all, do not even control a husk. What is inside a husk? Some say the atom. What is inside the atom? In the last 30 years, science has reached a point of impasse, and the more we probe to determine the building block of creation, the more we realise that we simply do not know. Allah reminds us that we are middle people, *ummatan wasatan*. We are between the astrophysical magnificence and the subatomic unseen, infinite world. And we have all of it within us.

$$إِن تَدْعُوهُمْ لَا يَسْمَعُوا دُعَاءَكُمْ وَلَوْ سَمِعُوا مَا ٱسْتَجَابُوا لَكُمْ وَيَوْمَ ٱلْقِيَٰمَةِ يَكْفُرُونَ$$
$$بِشِرْكِكُمْ وَلَا يُنَبِّئُكَ مِثْلُ خَبِيرٍ ۝١٤$$

If you call them they cannot hear you; if they could hear, they could not answer you; on the Day of Resurrection they will disown your idolatry. None can inform you [Prophet] like the One who is all aware. (35:14)

This verse says that those who claim that they have something or some knowledge, if you call them, they will not hear. The issue of readiness to hear is very important. There are three levels. Those who are deaf cannot hear. Secondly, most people can hear, see, and touch, but are they ready to receive the message? The third level is one of not only receiving the message, but also of responding to it. For every action, there should be a reaction. When the message is shared, are they ready to understand it and are they willing to respond? If not, then do not waste your time. Do not disturb others unless it is going to be good for them and unless they will respond to the message.

يَٰٓأَيُّهَا ٱلنَّاسُ أَنتُمُ ٱلۡفُقَرَآءُ إِلَى ٱللَّهِ وَٱللَّهُ هُوَ ٱلۡغَنِيُّ ٱلۡحَمِيدُ ١٥

O humankind, it is you who stand in need of Allah — Allah is All-Sufficient, All-Praiseworthy. (35:15)

All human beings need something to overcome the limitations of consciousness and for growth, development, and evolution. The verse says all of us are needy, including the greatest ones, meaning the Prophets. So what were the Prophet's needs? Did they want more glory and more money like we do? At that level, the ultimate need is to truly be in *tawakkul* (reliance upon Allah) and to have no visible need. However, the need to have no need is a need in itself. Therefore, Allah declares that all of us are needy.

إِن يَشَأۡ يُذۡهِبۡكُمۡ وَيَأۡتِ بِخَلۡقٍ جَدِيدٍ ١٦

if He wills, He can do away with you and bring in a new creation, (35:16)

If we do not follow the decreed patterns that Allah designed, He will bring new people. The Prophet (S) has said that there were other

Adamic beings, however, we do not know if this was on this earth or elsewhere. We know there could be cycles and also we know there are multi-universes—universes within universes.

$$\text{وَمَا ذَٰلِكَ عَلَى ٱللَّهِ بِعَزِيزٍ ﴿١٧﴾}$$

that is not difficult for God. (35:17)

Allah has created an overflow of His *rahma* (mercy), but He is not going to be affected if we do not worship Him. We only hurt and demean ourselves, and the gifts that we are given by Allah, if we do not worship Him properly.

$$\text{وَلَا تَزِرُ وَازِرَةٌ وِزْرَ أُخْرَىٰ ۚ وَإِن تَدْعُ مُثْقَلَةٌ إِلَىٰ حِمْلِهَا لَا يُحْمَلْ مِنْهُ شَيْءٌ وَلَوْ كَانَ ذَا}$$
$$\text{قُرْبَىٰٓ ۗ إِنَّمَا تُنذِرُ ٱلَّذِينَ يَخْشَوْنَ رَبَّهُم بِٱلْغَيْبِ وَأَقَامُوا۟ ٱلصَّلَوٰةَ ۚ وَمَن تَزَكَّىٰ فَإِنَّمَا}$$
$$\text{يَتَزَكَّىٰ لِنَفْسِهِ ۚ وَإِلَى ٱللَّهِ ٱلْمَصِيرُ ﴿١٨﴾}$$

No soul burdened can carry the burden of another. If a soul heavy-laden calls for help with its load, not a speck of it shall be carried, not even by a relative. You are to warn those who fear their Lord in the realm of the unseen, and who perform the prayer. Whoso is pure in soul, his purity rebounds to his own benefit, and to God is the final destination. (35:18)

Do not blame others for what they have done.

$$\text{وَمَا يَسْتَوِى ٱلْأَعْمَىٰ وَٱلْبَصِيرُ ﴿١٩﴾}$$

Unequal are the blind and those who see; (35:19)

He who is blind is not the same as he who sees. He who is a fool is not the same as he who is wise.

$$وَلَا ٱلظُّلُمَٰتُ وَلَا ٱلنُّورُ ﴿٢٠﴾$$

Nor the darkness and the light, (35:20)

Darkness is not the same as light.

$$وَلَا ٱلظِّلُّ وَلَا ٱلْحَرُورُ ﴿٢١﴾$$

nor the [cooling] shade and the scorching heat (35:21)

This verse emphasises the importance of knowing how to differentiate and the need to use our *'aql* (intellect). We need to be able to differentiate between the right time and place. In this regard, refer also to *Sūrat al-Furqān* (chapter 25).

$$وَمَا يَسْتَوِي ٱلْأَحْيَاءُ وَلَا ٱلْأَمْوَٰتُ إِنَّ ٱللَّهَ يُسْمِعُ مَن يَشَآءُ وَمَآ أَنتَ بِمُسْمِعٍ مَّن فِي ٱلْقُبُورِ ﴿٢٢﴾$$

Unequal are the living and the dead. Allah hears whom He pleases, but you cannot make them hear, those who are in their graves. (35:22)

This brilliant verse together with verse 14, of this chapter, summarises the subject. One can only warn those who are truly cautious about the presence of the divine *rahma*. It reminds us that those who are dead (which could also refer to those who are dead at heart) are different from those who are living. Humans tend to focus on the seen and measurable, but we do not take the middle path which also considers the unseen. Allah granted us an *'aql* (intellect) but we deceive ourselves. The middle path exists when you have unified the self and the soul. The question of how one walks the middle path is a key aspect of our *dīn* and the answer is to have caution in the unseen. We spend so much time concerned with the seen, the bottom line, the numbers, and the measurement, but what about that which is immeasurable? That is where a constant and consistent deficiency exists in human beings, which is why thousands of messengers have been sent to us. We have intellect and fantastic memories, yet we can also be exceptionally deceptive. Unless we have unified the self and the soul by being aware that Allah knows all, we may be caught. Why not render our account now? Allah knows all, so we need to be accountable in every way and be free of the burden we have put upon ourselves. The verse continues: 'you cannot make those who are in the graves hear.' Those who are in the grave do not imagine that those who are on two legs are alive. Half of the capacity of the mind is concerned about the past and failures, and the other half is fearful of the future. What about the heart?

$$ \text{إِنْ أَنتَ إِلَّا نَذِيرٌ ﴿٢٣﴾} $$

You are but a warner. (35:23)

$$ \text{إِنَّا أَرْسَلْنَاكَ بِالْحَقِّ بَشِيرًا وَنَذِيرًا وَإِن مِّنْ أُمَّةٍ إِلَّا خَلَا فِيهَا نَذِيرٌ ﴿٢٤﴾} $$

We sent you with the Truth, a herald of glad tidings and a warner, and there is no nation but a warner had passed it by. (35:24)

These are beautiful descriptions of the Prophet (S). *Nadheer* (warner) and *mubashir* (glad tidings) are usually used together in the *Qur'an*. The Prophet (S) gave people the good news that we have in us the *nūr* (light) of Allah and that if we fail to refer to the unseen and remember the unseen, then we are lost. We cannot blame anybody else.

Verse 24 confirms that the truth was revealed that we are heavenly beings having an earthly experience. This means we are in exile here on earth and need to be awakened to realise that our bodies are only a little universe that we need to take care of for a while. We need not be overly anxious or concerned about it, but know that it is our vehicle. Then we begin to discover the truth that what is in us is richer than all earthly wealth. This is the *rahma* (mercy) of Allah.

$$\text{وَإِن يُكَذِّبُوكَ فَقَدْ كَذَّبَ ٱلَّذِينَ مِن قَبْلِهِمْ جَآءَتْهُمْ رُسُلُهُم بِٱلْبَيِّنَٰتِ وَبِٱلزُّبُرِ وَبِٱلْكِتَٰبِ ٱلْمُنِيرِ ﴿٢٥﴾}$$

If they call you a liar, so too did those who came before them cry lies; their messengers had come to them with wonders, with the Psalms and the Luminous Book. (35:25)

This verse repeats an earlier point: if they deny you and they don't listen to you, remember that those who came before you as messengers were also denied and those messengers came with evidence. Their evidence reminds us of our eventual deaths and questions our readiness for death. It also requires us to reflect on our inner state. Are you ready for death? Are you happy about it? What is your inner state? All of the messengers came with evidence through the different books (such as the Bible and the Torah) and the illumined book, the *Qur'an*.

$$\text{ثُمَّ أَخَذْتُ ٱلَّذِينَ كَفَرُواْ فَكَيْفَ كَانَ نَكِيرِ ﴿٢٦﴾}$$

Then I seized the unbelievers – behold how I reversed their fortunes! (35:26)

Those who are in denial will reach the conclusion that they have wronged themselves. This verse introduces a few different issues: the diversity of creation, duality in unity, and generosity of provision. We are reminded of the arrogance of those who deny the Messenger (S) and his message. That arrogance is akin to *shaytān* (satan; ego-self) and *kufr* (denial, ingratitude). We remember how rain raises life from the dead and in the same way we remember Allah's *rahma* during the resurrection. Similarly, we consider the cycles of poverty and wealth and learn to differentiate the levels of connections including sublime connections.

Even one chapter in the *Qur'an* suffices as a manual for survival, success, and victory, because you will know who the Ever Victorious is. Then you identify with that *nūr* (light) and all is well. Then you will enjoy the shadows.

Chapter 20

SURAT YA SIN

In this chapter, I will share commentary that is especially relevant to us today. *Sūrat al-Yā Sīn (36)* is considered by many to have been revealed in Makkah, although some believe a few verses were revealed in Madinah. It is often referred to as the *'Heart of Qur'an'*, *'Qalb ul-Qur'an'*. A 'heart' means that which contains the entire story of the being. If the heart is well (meaning both the physical heart as well as the metaphorical heart) then you are cheerful.

There are numerous prophetic traditions about the *Qur'an*, and many are specific to *Sūrat al-Yā Sīn*. For example, if it is recited during a person's death, it is believed that thousands of angels will descend upon that gathering with every letter that is read. There is a Prophetic tradition that says that if a person is fearful and agitated, reading the *Qur'an* will calm them, and ease will descend upon them. Another tradition states that if one who is in need reads the *Qur'an* he or she will feel content and satisfied.

This chapter contains the crux of the issue of life: we are here as passers-by and there is a purpose to this journey. Allah in His Infinite Mercy has, over thousands of years, given us different maps and directions to traverse this life. Thousands of messengers, apostles and others have come to guide us, and we are fortunate to have been born towards the latter part of this history because there is greater clarity in the message.

Sūrat al-Yā Sīn is considered to have come after *Sūrat al-Fath* (chapter 48). In the last few verses of *Sūrat al-Fath* Allah says, 'and whenever We send a messenger to warn them, they became more arrogant and despising of this message, and they turn away from it.' *Sūrat al-Yā Sīn* continues to elaborate on that. What is the story? What is the message? Why do we turn away?

There are a dozen verses from among *Sūrat al-Yā Sīn's* 83 verses that are immensely potent and which emphasise that there is nothing other than The One Power that Controls all. It highlights The Creator and The Maintainer of all and that everything emanates from Him and returns to Him.

Qur'anic Verses

The Arabic text and the English translation of the entire *Sūrat al-Yā Sīn* follow immediately below. Thereafter, I will focus my commentary on selected verses and words.

بِسْمِ ٱللَّهِ ٱلرَّحْمَٰنِ ٱلرَّحِيمِ

In the name of Allah, the Merciful to all, the Compassionate to each!

يسٓ ١

1. Yā Sīn

وَٱلْقُرْءَانِ ٱلْحَكِيمِ ٢

2. By the wise Qur'an.

إِنَّكَ لَمِنَ ٱلْمُرْسَلِينَ ٣

3. You are indeed one of the messengers

عَلَىٰ صِرَٰطٍ مُّسْتَقِيمٍ ﴿٤﴾

4. upon a straight path.

تَنزِيلَ ٱلْعَزِيزِ ٱلرَّحِيمِ ﴿٥﴾

5. This is the Revelation of the Almighty, Compassionate to
each,

لِتُنذِرَ قَوْمًا مَّآ أُنذِرَ ءَابَآؤُهُمْ فَهُمْ غَٰفِلُونَ ﴿٦﴾

6. in order that you warn a people whose ancestors were not
warned, and thus are heedless.

لَقَدْ حَقَّ ٱلْقَوْلُ عَلَىٰٓ أَكْثَرِهِمْ فَهُمْ لَا يُؤْمِنُونَ ﴿٧﴾

7. Upon most of them the Word has come true, and they do not
believe.

إِنَّا جَعَلْنَا فِىٓ أَعْنَٰقِهِمْ أَغْلَٰلًا فَهِىَ إِلَى ٱلْأَذْقَانِ فَهُم مُّقْمَحُونَ ﴿٨﴾

8. We have placed collars on their necks, reaching to their chins,
so their heads are upraised,

وَجَعَلْنَا مِنۢ بَيْنِ أَيْدِيهِمْ سَدًّا وَمِنْ خَلْفِهِمْ سَدًّا فَأَغْشَيْنَٰهُمْ فَهُمْ لَا يُبْصِرُونَ ﴿٩﴾

9. and We have set a barrier before them and a barrier behind them,
and We have enshrouded them in veils so that they cannot see.

وَسَوَآءٌ عَلَيْهِمْ ءَأَنذَرْتَهُمْ أَمْ لَمْ تُنذِرْهُمْ لَا يُؤْمِنُونَ ﴿١٠﴾

10. It is all the same to them whether you warn or do not warn
them – they have no faith.

إِنَّمَا تُنذِرُ مَنِ ٱتَّبَعَ ٱلذِّكْرَ وَخَشِيَ ٱلرَّحْمَٰنَ بِٱلْغَيْبِ فَبَشِّرْهُ بِمَغْفِرَةٍ وَأَجْرٍ
كَرِيمٍ ﴿١١﴾

11. You only warn him who follows the Remembrance and fears
the All-Merciful in the Unseen. To him give glad tidings of
forgiveness and a noble wage.

إِنَّا نَحْنُ نُحْيِ ٱلْمَوْتَىٰ وَنَكْتُبُ مَا قَدَّمُوا۟ وَءَاثَٰرَهُمْ وَكُلَّ شَىْءٍ أَحْصَيْنَٰهُ فِىٓ إِمَامٍ
مُّبِينٍ ﴿١٢﴾

12. It is We Who revive the dead, We Who register what deeds
they committed, what traces they left behind. All things have
We tallied in a Manifest Record.

وَٱضْرِبْ لَهُم مَّثَلًا أَصْحَٰبَ ٱلْقَرْيَةِ إِذْ جَآءَهَا ٱلْمُرْسَلُونَ ﴿١٣﴾

13. And strike for them the parable of the people of the town,
when messengers arrived.

إِذْ أَرْسَلْنَآ إِلَيْهِمُ اثْنَيْنِ فَكَذَّبُوهُمَا فَعَزَّزْنَا بِثَالِثٍ فَقَالُوٓاْ إِنَّآ إِلَيْكُم مُّرْسَلُونَ ﴿١٤﴾

14. We had sent them two but they called them liars, so We backed them with a third, and they said: 'We are messengers to you.'

قَالُواْ مَآ أَنتُمْ إِلَّا بَشَرٌ مِّثْلُنَا وَمَآ أَنزَلَ ٱلرَّحْمَٰنُ مِن شَىْءٍ إِنْ أَنتُمْ إِلَّا تَكْذِبُونَ ﴿١٥﴾

15. They said: 'You are merely human beings like us. The All-Merciful has revealed nothing. You are nothing but liars.'

قَالُواْ رَبُّنَا يَعْلَمُ إِنَّآ إِلَيْكُمْ لَمُرْسَلُونَ ﴿١٦﴾

16. They said: 'Our Lord knows that we are sent as messengers to you,

وَمَا عَلَيْنَآ إِلَّا ٱلْبَلَٰغُ ٱلْمُبِينُ ﴿١٧﴾

17. is only to convey a manifest declaration.'

قَالُوٓاْ إِنَّا تَطَيَّرْنَا بِكُمْ لَئِن لَّمْ تَنتَهُواْ لَنَرْجُمَنَّكُمْ وَلَيَمَسَّنَّكُم مِّنَّا عَذَابٌ أَلِيمٌ ﴿١٨﴾

18. They said: 'We hold you to be an evil omen. If you do not desist, we will stone you and a most painful torment will touch you from us.'

قَالُوٓا۟ طَـٰٓئِرُكُم مَّعَكُمْ أَئِن ذُكِّرْتُم بَلْ أَنتُمْ قَوْمٌ مُّسْرِفُونَ ﴿١٩﴾

19. They said: 'Your evil omen is upon you. Is it because you have been reminded of Allah? You are indeed a people far gone in transgression.'

وَجَآءَ مِنْ أَقْصَا ٱلْمَدِينَةِ رَجُلٌ يَسْعَىٰ قَالَ يَـٰقَوْمِ ٱتَّبِعُوا۟ ٱلْمُرْسَلِينَ ﴿٢٠﴾

20. Then, from the furthest part of the city, a man came running. He said, 'My people, follow the messengers.

ٱتَّبِعُوا۟ مَن لَّا يَسْـَٔلُكُمْ أَجْرًا وَهُم مُّهْتَدُونَ ﴿٢١﴾

21. Follow him who asks you no wage. These men are guided aright.

وَمَا لِىَ لَآ أَعْبُدُ ٱلَّذِى فَطَرَنِى وَإِلَيْهِ تُرْجَعُونَ ﴿٢٢﴾

22. And why should I not serve Him who originated me, and unto whom you shall be returned?

ءَأَتَّخِذُ مِن دُونِهِۦٓ ءَالِهَةً إِن يُرِدْنِ ٱلرَّحْمَـٰنُ بِضُرٍّ لَّا تُغْنِ عَنِّى شَفَـٰعَتُهُمْ شَيْـًٔا وَلَا يُنقِذُونِ ﴿٢٣﴾

23. Am I to take other gods instead of Him? If the All-Merciful wishes me ill, their intercession will not benefit me in the least, nor will they be able to save me.

إِنِّىٓ إِذًا لَّفِى ضَلَلٍ مُّبِينٍ ﴿٢٤﴾

24. *I would then be in manifest error.*

إِنِّىٓ ءَامَنتُ بِرَبِّكُمْ فَٱسْمَعُونِ ﴿٢٥﴾

25. *I believe in your Lord, so listen to me.'*

قِيلَ ٱدْخُلِ ٱلْجَنَّةَ قَالَ يَلَيْتَ قَوْمِى يَعْلَمُونَ ﴿٢٦﴾

26. *It was said to him: 'Enter the Garden.' He said: 'If only my people knew.*

بِمَا غَفَرَ لِى رَبِّى وَجَعَلَنِى مِنَ ٱلْمُكْرَمِينَ ﴿٢٧﴾

27. *that my Lord has forgiven me and that He has placed me among the honoured.'*

۞ وَمَآ أَنزَلْنَا عَلَىٰ قَوْمِهِۦ مِنۢ بَعْدِهِۦ مِن جُندٍ مِّنَ ٱلسَّمَآءِ وَمَا كُنَّا مُنزِلِينَ ﴿٢٨﴾

28. *After him, We sent no troops from heaven against his people, nor did We intend to do so.*

إِن كَانَتْ إِلَّا صَيْحَةً وَٰحِدَةً فَإِذَا هُمْ خَٰمِدُونَ ﴿٢٩﴾

29. *It was but a single Scream and, behold, they were lifeless.*

$$\text{يَـٰحَسْرَةً عَلَى ٱلْعِبَادِ مَا يَأْتِيهِم مِّن رَّسُولٍ إِلَّا كَانُواْ بِهِ يَسْتَهْزِءُونَ ﴿٣٠﴾}$$

30. *Alas for the slaves! Never does a messenger come to them but*
they mock him.

$$\text{أَلَمْ يَرَوْاْ كَمْ أَهْلَكْنَا قَبْلَهُم مِّنَ ٱلْقُرُونِ أَنَّهُمْ إِلَيْهِمْ لَا يَرْجِعُونَ ﴿٣١﴾}$$

31. *Have they not observed how many generations We destroyed*
before them, and that they do not return to them?

$$\text{وَإِن كُلٌّ لَّمَّا جَمِيعٌ لَّدَيْنَا مُحْضَرُونَ ﴿٣٢﴾}$$

32. *But all of them shall certainly be brought before Us.*

$$\text{وَءَايَةٌ لَّهُمُ ٱلْأَرْضُ ٱلْمَيْتَةُ أَحْيَيْنَـٰهَا وَأَخْرَجْنَا مِنْهَا حَبًّا فَمِنْهُ يَأْكُلُونَ ﴿٣٣﴾}$$

33. *Here is a sign for them: a dead land which We revive, and*
from which We sprout grains for them to eat.

$$\text{وَجَعَلْنَا فِيهَا جَنَّـٰتٍ مِّن نَّخِيلٍ وَأَعْنَـٰبٍ وَفَجَّرْنَا فِيهَا مِنَ ٱلْعُيُونِ ﴿٣٤﴾}$$

34. *In it We planted gardens of palms and vines, and caused*
fountains to burst forth,

$$\text{لِيَأْكُلُواْ مِن ثَمَرِهِ وَمَا عَمِلَتْهُ أَيْدِيهِمْ أَفَلَا يَشْكُرُونَ ﴿٣٥﴾}$$

35. *that they may eat of its fruits and the work of their hands –*
will they not render thanks?

سُبْحَنَ ٱلَّذِى خَلَقَ ٱلْأَزْوَجَ كُلَّهَا مِمَّا تُنۢبِتُ ٱلْأَرْضُ وَمِنْ أَنفُسِهِمْ وَمِمَّا لَا يَعْلَمُونَ ﴿٣٦﴾

36. *Glory be to Him, who created all the pairs of what the earth produces, and of themselves, and of what they know not.*

وَءَايَةٌ لَّهُمُ ٱلَّيْلُ نَسْلَخُ مِنْهُ ٱلنَّهَارَ فَإِذَا هُم مُّظْلِمُونَ ﴿٣٧﴾

37. *And a sign to them is the night. We strip from it the day, then they are in darkness.*

وَٱلشَّمْسُ تَجْرِى لِمُسْتَقَرٍّ لَّهَا ذَٰلِكَ تَقْدِيرُ ٱلْعَزِيزِ ٱلْعَلِيمِ ﴿٣٨﴾

38. *And the sun runs its own course, unchanging, such is the disposition of the Almighty, the All-Knowing.*

وَٱلْقَمَرَ قَدَّرْنَهُ مَنَازِلَ حَتَّىٰ عَادَ كَٱلْعُرْجُونِ ٱلْقَدِيمِ ﴿٣٩﴾

39. *And the moon, We disposed in phases until it comes back like a withered stalk of palm.*

لَا ٱلشَّمْسُ يَنۢبَغِى لَهَا أَن تُدْرِكَ ٱلْقَمَرَ وَلَا ٱلَّيْلُ سَابِقُ ٱلنَّهَارِ وَكُلٌّ فِى فَلَكٍ يَسْبَحُونَ ﴿٤٠﴾

40. *Neither the sun may outstrip the moon nor the night the day: each plies its own orbit.*

وَءَايَةٌ لَّهُمْ أَنَّا حَمَلْنَا ذُرِّيَّتَهُمْ فِى ٱلْفُلْكِ ٱلْمَشْحُونِ ﴿٤١﴾

41. *And a sign for them is that We carried their seed in the laden ship,*

وَخَلَقْنَا لَهُم مِّن مِّثْلِهِۦ مَا يَرْكَبُونَ ﴿٤٢﴾

42. *and We have created for them the like of it whereon they ride;*

وَإِن نَّشَأْ نُغْرِقْهُمْ فَلَا صَرِيخَ لَهُمْ وَلَا هُمْ يُنقَذُونَ ﴿٤٣﴾

43. *and if We wish We can drown them – no screaming to be heard from them, nor can they be saved,*

إِلَّا رَحْمَةً مِّنَّا وَمَتَـٰعًا إِلَىٰ حِينٍ ﴿٤٤﴾

44. *unless it be a mercy from Us and a brief enjoyment of life.*

وَإِذَا قِيلَ لَهُمُ ٱتَّقُوا۟ مَا بَيْنَ أَيْدِيكُمْ وَمَا خَلْفَكُمْ لَعَلَّكُمْ تُرْحَمُونَ ﴿٤٥﴾

45. *And when it is said to them: 'Beware of the present and the future that you may obtain mercy,'*

وَمَا تَأْتِيهِم مِّنْ ءَايَةٍ مِّنْ ءَايَـٰتِ رَبِّهِمْ إِلَّا كَانُوا۟ عَنْهَا مُعْرِضِينَ ﴿٤٦﴾

46. *and there comes to them no sign from the signs of their Lord but they turn their back upon it.*

وَإِذَا قِيلَ لَهُمْ أَنفِقُوا مِمَّا رَزَقَكُمُ اللَّهُ قَالَ الَّذِينَ كَفَرُوا لِلَّذِينَ ءَامَنُوٓا أَنُطْعِمُ مَن لَّوْ يَشَآءُ اللَّهُ أَطْعَمَهُۥٓ إِنْ أَنتُمْ إِلَّا فِى ضَلَـٰلٍ مُّبِينٍ ۝

47. *And when it is said to them: 'Expend from what Allah in His bounty has provided you,' the unbelievers say to the believers: 'Are we to feed one whom Allah can feed if He so wishes?' In truth you have strayed far in error.*

وَيَقُولُونَ مَتَىٰ هَـٰذَا الْوَعْدُ إِن كُنتُمْ صَـٰدِقِينَ ۝

48. *And they say: 'When will this promise be fulfilled if you speak the truth?'*

مَا يَنظُرُونَ إِلَّا صَيْحَةً وَٰحِدَةً تَأْخُذُهُمْ وَهُمْ يَخِصِّمُونَ ۝

49. *All they can expect is a single Scream, which shall seize them while they dispute,*

فَلَا يَسْتَطِيعُونَ تَوْصِيَةً وَلَآ إِلَىٰٓ أَهْلِهِمْ يَرْجِعُونَ ۝

50. *so that they have no time to make a bequest, nor return home to their families.*

وَنُفِخَ فِى الصُّورِ فَإِذَا هُم مِّنَ الْأَجْدَاثِ إِلَىٰ رَبِّهِمْ يَنسِلُونَ ۝

51. *And the Trumpet shall be sounded and, behold, from their graves and to their Lord they shall hurry.*

قَالُوا۟ يَـٰوَيْلَنَا مَنۢ بَعَثَنَا مِن مَّرْقَدِنَا ۗ هَـٰذَا مَا وَعَدَ ٱلرَّحْمَـٰنُ وَصَدَقَ ٱلْمُرْسَلُونَ ۝

52. *They shall say: 'Alas for us! Who resurrected us from our resting place?' This is what the All-Merciful promised, and the messengers spoke the truth.*

إِن كَانَتْ إِلَّا صَيْحَةً وَٰحِدَةً فَإِذَا هُمْ جَمِيعٌ لَّدَيْنَا مُحْضَرُونَ ۝

53. *It shall be but a single Scream and, behold, they will all be conducted before Us.*

فَٱلْيَوْمَ لَا تُظْلَمُ نَفْسٌ شَيْـًٔا وَلَا تُجْزَوْنَ إِلَّا مَا كُنتُمْ تَعْمَلُونَ ۝

54. *Today no soul shall be wronged one jot, and you will be recompensed only for the deeds you committed.*

إِنَّ أَصْحَـٰبَ ٱلْجَنَّةِ ٱلْيَوْمَ فِى شُغُلٍ فَـٰكِهُونَ ۝

55. *Today the denizens of the Garden are preoccupied with joy,*

هُمْ وَأَزْوَٰجُهُمْ فِى ظِلَـٰلٍ عَلَى ٱلْأَرَآئِكِ مُتَّكِـُٔونَ ۝

56. *they and their spouses, reclining on cushions under the shade.*

لَهُمْ فِيهَا فَـٰكِهَةٌ وَلَهُم مَّا يَدَّعُونَ ۝

57. *therein they have fruits, and they have all that they call for.*

$$\text{سَلَٰمٌ قَوْلًا مِّن رَّبٍّ رَّحِيمٍ} \quad \textcircled{٥٨}$$

58. 'Peace' shall be the word from a Compassionate Lord.

$$\text{وَٱمْتَٰزُوا۟ ٱلْيَوْمَ أَيُّهَا ٱلْمُجْرِمُونَ} \quad \textcircled{٥٩}$$

59. Today, O guilty, keep yourselves apart!

$$\text{۞ أَلَمْ أَعْهَدْ إِلَيْكُمْ يَٰبَنِىٓ ءَادَمَ أَن لَّا تَعْبُدُوا۟ ٱلشَّيْطَٰنَ إِنَّهُۥ لَكُمْ عَدُوٌّ مُّبِينٌ} \quad \textcircled{٦٠}$$

60. Did I not charge you, O children of Adam, not to worship the Shaytan? Surely he is your open enemy!

$$\text{وَأَنِ ٱعْبُدُونِى هَٰذَا صِرَٰطٌ مُّسْتَقِيمٌ} \quad \textcircled{٦١}$$

61. And that you should worship Me. This is the straight path.

$$\text{وَلَقَدْ أَضَلَّ مِنكُمْ جِبِلًّا كَثِيرًا أَفَلَمْ تَكُونُوا۟ تَعْقِلُونَ} \quad \textcircled{٦٢}$$

62. And certainly he led astray a great multitude of you. Were you not able to understand?

$$\text{هَٰذِهِۦ جَهَنَّمُ ٱلَّتِى كُنتُمْ تُوعَدُونَ} \quad \textcircled{٦٣}$$

63. This is the Hell you were promised [if you followed him].

اَصْلَوْهَا الْيَوْمَ بِمَا كُنتُمْ تَكْفُرُونَ ۝٦٤

64. Endure it today as an outcome of your persistent denial of the truth!

الْيَوْمَ نَخْتِمُ عَلَى أَفْوَاهِهِمْ وَتُكَلِّمُنَا أَيْدِيهِمْ وَتَشْهَدُ أَرْجُلُهُم بِمَا كَانُوا يَكْسِبُونَ ۝٦٥

65. Today We shall seal their mouths and it will be their hands that shall speak to Us and their feet that shall testify as to what they earned.

وَلَوْ نَشَاءُ لَطَمَسْنَا عَلَى أَعْيُنِهِمْ فَاسْتَبَقُوا الصِّرَاطَ فَأَنَّى يُبْصِرُونَ ۝٦٦

66. And if We wished, We could certainly put out their eyes, then they would run about groping for the way, but how could they see?

وَلَوْ نَشَاءُ لَمَسَخْنَاهُمْ عَلَى مَكَانَتِهِمْ فَمَا اسْتَطَاعُوا مُضِيًّا وَلَا يَرْجِعُونَ ۝٦٧

67. And if We wished, We could surely transform them in their place. Then they would not be able to advance or turn back.

وَمَن نُّعَمِّرْهُ نُنَكِّسْهُ فِي الْخَلْقِ أَفَلَا يَعْقِلُونَ ۝٦٨

68. Whomever We grant old age, We cause to droop in figure: will they not be reasonable?

وَمَا عَلَّمْنَـٰهُ ٱلشِّعْرَ وَمَا يَنۢبَغِى لَهُۥٓ ۚ إِنْ هُوَ إِلَّا ذِكْرٌ وَقُرْءَانٌ مُّبِينٌ ﴿٦٩﴾

69. *And, we did not teach him poetry, nor does this befit him. It is nothing but a Remembrance, and a Manifest Qur'an.*

لِّيُنذِرَ مَن كَانَ حَيًّا وَيَحِقَّ ٱلْقَوْلُ عَلَى ٱلْكَـٰفِرِينَ ﴿٧٠﴾

70. *Therewith to warn him who is living, and to fulfil the Word against the unbelievers.*

أَوَلَمْ يَرَوْا۟ أَنَّا خَلَقْنَا لَهُم مِّمَّا عَمِلَتْ أَيْدِينَآ أَنْعَـٰمًا فَهُمْ لَهَا مَـٰلِكُونَ ﴿٧١﴾

71. *Have they not observed that We created for them, from Our handiwork, cattle which they come to possess?*

وَذَلَّلْنَـٰهَا لَهُمْ فَمِنْهَا رَكُوبُهُمْ وَمِنْهَا يَأْكُلُونَ ﴿٧٢﴾

72. *And We have subjected these animals to them, so some of them they ride and some they eat.*

وَلَهُمْ فِيهَا مَنَـٰفِعُ وَمَشَارِبُ ۖ أَفَلَا يَشْكُرُونَ ﴿٧٣﴾

73. *And from them they have [other] benefits [besides], and yet they get [milk] to drink. Will they not then be grateful?*

وَٱتَّخَذُوا۟ مِن دُونِ ٱللَّهِ ءَالِهَةً لَّعَلَّهُمْ يُنصَرُونَ ﴿٧٤﴾

74. *And yet, instead of Allah, they take to themselves gods, hoping for success.*

لَا يَسْتَطِيعُونَ نَصْرَهُمْ وَهُمْ لَهُمْ جُندٌ مُّحْضَرُونَ ﴿٧٥﴾

75. *These cannot grant them success, though they possess troops massed in their service.*

فَلَا يَحْزُنكَ قَوْلُهُمْ إِنَّا نَعْلَمُ مَا يُسِرُّونَ وَمَا يُعْلِنُونَ ﴿٧٦﴾

76. *Therefore, let not their speech sadden you: We know what they conceal and what declare.*

أَوَلَمْ يَرَ ٱلْإِنسَـٰنُ أَنَّا خَلَقْنَـٰهُ مِن نُّطْفَةٍ فَإِذَا هُوَ خَصِيمٌ مُّبِينٌ ﴿٧٧﴾

77. *Has not man observed that We created him from a sperm drop but, behold, he becomes a determined adversary?*

وَضَرَبَ لَنَا مَثَلًا وَنَسِىَ خَلْقَهُۥ قَالَ مَن يُحْىِ ٱلْعِظَـٰمَ وَهِىَ رَمِيمٌ ﴿٧٨﴾

78. *And he has struck for Us a similitude and forgotten his creation; he says, 'Who shall quicken the bones when they are decayed?'*

قُل يُحْيِيهَا ٱلَّذِىٓ أَنشَأَهَآ أَوَّلَ مَرَّةٍ وَهُوَ بِكُلِّ خَلْقٍ عَلِيمٌ ﴿٧٩﴾

79. *Say: 'He will give life to them Who brought them into
existence at first, and He is cognizant of all creation,*

ٱلَّذِى جَعَلَ لَكُم مِّنَ ٱلشَّجَرِ ٱلۡأَخۡضَرِ نَارًا فَإِذَآ أَنتُم مِّنۡهُ تُوقِدُونَ ﴿٨٠﴾

80. *who has made for you out of the green tree fire and lo, from it
you kindle.*

أَوَلَيۡسَ ٱلَّذِى خَلَقَ ٱلسَّمَٰوَٰتِ وَٱلۡأَرۡضَ بِقَٰدِرٍ عَلَىٰٓ أَن يَخۡلُقَ مِثۡلَهُم بَلَىٰ وَهُوَ ٱلۡخَلَّٰقُ
ٱلۡعَلِيمُ ﴿٨١﴾

81. *Is not He, who created the heavens and earth, able to create
the like of them? Yes indeed; He is the All-Creator, the All-
Knowing.*

إِنَّمَآ أَمۡرُهُۥٓ إِذَآ أَرَادَ شَيۡـًٔا أَن يَقُولَ لَهُۥ كُن فَيَكُونُ ﴿٨٢﴾

82. *His command, when He desires a thing, is to say to it "Be,"
and it is.*

فَسُبۡحَٰنَ ٱلَّذِى بِيَدِهِۦ مَلَكُوتُ كُلِّ شَيۡءٍ وَإِلَيۡهِ تُرۡجَعُونَ ﴿٨٣﴾

83. *So, glory be to Him, in whose hand is the dominion of
everything, and unto whom you shall be returned.'*

Commentary on selected verses

Scholars and commentators of the past have divided *Sūrat al-Yā Sīn* into five sections, and each section has a fairly self-contained package of the Message.

The first section, verses 1 to 12, addresses the warning: 'Oh Prophet, there were many people before you, and people do not like to listen because they are used to their habits. They don't want to change; they don't want to suddenly turn and modify and be transformed.'

The second section, verses 13 to 32, provides a historical *mithāl* (similitude). We look back at our history to understand our present day.

Section One: Verses 1 to 12

يسٓ ①

Yā Sīn (36:1)

وَٱلْقُرْءَانِ ٱلْحَكِيمِ ②

By the wise *Qur'an*. (36:2)

إِنَّكَ لَمِنَ ٱلْمُرْسَلِينَ ③

You are indeed one of the messengers (36:3)

عَلَىٰ صِرَٰطٍ مُّسْتَقِيمٍ ④

upon a straight path. (36:4)

There are a number of commentaries that deal with the meaning of *Yā Sīn*, one of which is *Yā Insān*, which means 'oh human being'.

However, *Yā Sīn* was one of the Prophet's names. It is narrated that the Prophet (S) said there are seven different names ascribed to him in the *Qur'an*, such as Ahmed and Muhammad. Some of these names are included in this chapter. The chapter begins with an address to the Prophet (S) as well as to us as the followers of the Prophet (S). In these verses, Allah is saying: *Yā Sīn*, Oh man of *Haqq* (truth), oh man of Allah, oh true Messenger of Allah, surely you are one of the messengers and you are from amongst the great beings who carry the sacred divine message.

Sirāt is considered to be that subtle line or the interspace between *haqq* and *bātil*, between good and bad, between this life and the next life. Adam (AS) descended to this earth from another realm and thereafter ascended. We, as the children of Adam (AS), descended from the heavens into this realm, which contains within it both *Janna* (paradise) and Jahannam (the fire), the good and the bad, the up and the down, so that we may ascend back. In other words, the message has been sent to us to enable us to climb back up the rope.

تَنزِيلَ ٱلْعَزِيزِ ٱلرَّحِيمِ ﴿٥﴾

This is the Revelation of the Almighty, Compassionate to each, (36:5)

لِتُنذِرَ قَوْمًا مَّآ أُنذِرَ ءَابَآؤُهُمْ فَهُمْ غَـٰفِلُونَ ﴿٦﴾

in order that you warn a people whose ancestors were not warned, and thus are heedless. (36:6)

لَقَدْ حَقَّ ٱلْقَوْلُ عَلَىٰٓ أَكْثَرِهِمْ فَهُمْ لَا يُؤْمِنُونَ ﴿٧﴾

Upon most of them the Word has come true, and they do not believe. (36:7)

إِنَّا جَعَلْنَا فِىٓ أَعْنَـٰقِهِمْ أَغْلَـٰلًا فَهِىَ إِلَى ٱلْأَذْقَانِ فَهُم مُّقْمَحُونَ ﴿٨﴾

We have placed collars on their necks, reaching to their chins, so their heads are upraised, (36:8)

وَجَعَلْنَا مِنْ بَيْنِ أَيْدِيهِمْ سَدًّا وَمِنْ خَلْفِهِمْ سَدًّا فَأَغْشَيْنَاهُمْ فَهُمْ لَا يُبْصِرُونَ ﴿٩﴾

and We have set a barrier before them and a barrier behind them,
and We have enshrouded them in veils so that they cannot see. (36:9)

وَسَوَاءٌ عَلَيْهِمْ ءَأَنذَرْتَهُمْ أَمْ لَمْ تُنذِرْهُمْ لَا يُؤْمِنُونَ ﴿١٠﴾

It is all the same to them whether you warn or do not warn them
– they have no faith. (36:10)

This message is a wonderful map to eternal life. It is for us to follow and live according to its outer and inner revelations. Verse 8 is a reference to people who are in *ghafla* (heedlessness, carelessness, negligence, foolishness, stupidity). *Ghāfilun* means distracted. Our world is a world of distractions, and distraction often leads to destruction. Accidents happen because we are not focused and present, meaning we are not referring to our guiding faculties, senses, and hearts.

We have so many reminders from great beings. What if you were to die performing whatever action you're undertaking? Why are you here? Why are you rushing? The *tanzīl* (this gift, this revelation) has come down to remind us that we are here in a passage back into the unseen.

In these verses, we are presented with a grave description of the people who cannot hear, who will not listen, reflect or change according to what they read and learn. These are people who have not internalised the meaning, and so the message does not impact them. The *mithāl* (similitude) that is presented here is very descriptive: like those who have chains hanging on their necks, in such a way that their head had to be lifted so high that they don't see what's in front of them. It is like they are in a box, and they don't see around them, so they are cut off.

Verses 8 to 10 imply that we need references, and we need to understand our context to ensure that our actions are appropriate. Is it the right place? Is it the right time? Is it the right intention? What about the outer environment? Who are you? What are you doing? We apply these references to assist us in identifying what is appropriate. There is only goodness and success in every appropriate situation.

Those who do not absorb this message resemble beings whose necks are fettered down to earth, but they have to lift their heads for them to be balanced, for they only see the infinite vastness without seeing direction.

$$ إِنَّمَا تُنذِرُ مَنِ ٱتَّبَعَ ٱلذِّكْرَ وَخَشِيَ ٱلرَّحْمَٰنَ بِٱلْغَيْبِ فَبَشِّرْهُ بِمَغْفِرَةٍ وَأَجْرٍ كَرِيمٍ ۝ $$

You only warn him who follows the Remembrance and fears the All-Merciful in the Unseen. To him give glad tidings of forgiveness and a noble wage. (36:11)

This message, this warning, this map can only help those who trust in the unseen and who trust that Allah is in charge. We cannot see or measure Allah. Everything is within His power and His *rahma* (mercy) overflows from it. To those people who trust in the unseen, give them the good news that their struggle in the seen world will connect with the unseen because they are connecting *'Ālam al-Ghayb* (the Dominion of the unseen) with *'Ālam ash shahadat* (the Dominion of Witnessing). We are responsible for what we do. If our actions always begin with *bismillah*, with the best intentions and if we are willing to be accountable and correct our actions, then we are connecting with the vast unseen.

إِنَّا نَحْنُ نُحْيِ ٱلْمَوْتَىٰ وَنَكْتُبُ مَا قَدَّمُوا وَءَاثَٰرَهُمْ وَكُلَّ شَىْءٍ أَحْصَيْنَٰهُ فِىٓ إِمَامٍ مُّبِينٍ ۝

It is We Who revive the dead, We Who register what deeds they committed, what traces they left behind. All things have We tallied in a Manifest Record. (36:12)

There is nothing in existence unless it is according to a measure and whatever is alive will also experience death. It is a very important reminder that our life on this earth is in-between, meaning we are born and one second after we are born, we are one second closer to our departure from the seen to the unseen by the mercy of some semblance of awareness in this world of transition.

Section Two: Verses 13 to 32

وَاَضْرِبْ لَهُم مَّثَلًا أَصْحَبَ الْقَرْيَةِ إِذْ جَاءَهَا الْمُرْسَلُونَ ۞ ١٣

And strike for them the parable of the people of the town, when messengers arrived. (36:13)

إِذْ أَرْسَلْنَا إِلَيْهِمُ اثْنَيْنِ فَكَذَّبُوهُمَا فَعَزَّزْنَا بِثَالِثٍ فَقَالُوٓا إِنَّا إِلَيْكُم مُّرْسَلُونَ ۞ ١٤

We had sent them two but they called them liars, so We backed them with a third, and they said: 'We are messengers to you.' (36:14)

قَالُوا مَا أَنتُمْ إِلَّا بَشَرٌ مِّثْلُنَا وَمَا أَنزَلَ الرَّحْمَٰنُ مِن شَىْءٍ إِنْ أَنتُمْ إِلَّا تَكْذِبُونَ ۞ ١٥

They said: 'You are merely human beings like us. The All-Merciful has revealed nothing. You are nothing but liars.' (36:15)

The second section of *Sūrat Yā Sīn* narrates a historical incident about Prophet Isa (AS) when he sent two people who were close to him to the city of Antakya, in the northwest of present-day Syria (note that this story is also narrated in the Bible).

The *Qur'an* does not name the people. However, it says that when they arrived at the outskirts of the city the people asked them, 'What are you doing? What do you want? Why are you here?'

They said: 'We have come from a great being, Isa (A.S), and we have come to remind you that you have a purpose in this life.' The people then asked them, 'What can you do?'

The two men then met an old man named Habib Al-Najjar who said to them, 'I have a son who is very sick. He has been on his deathbed for a long time. If you can heal him, perhaps these people will take note of the miraculous event.'

So the son was healed, and the news spread through the city. Upon hearing of it, the governor was not happy because he perceived it as a threat to his power. A loss of power to another often results in jealousy and hatred. The governor rejected the news and he tried to oppress those who accepted this message.

قَالُوا۟ رَبُّنَا يَعْلَمُ إِنَّآ إِلَيْكُمْ لَمُرْسَلُونَ ﴿١٦﴾

They said: 'Our Lord knows that we are sent as messengers to you, (36:16)

وَمَا عَلَيْنَآ إِلَّا ٱلْبَلَٰغُ ٱلْمُبِينُ ﴿١٧﴾

is only to convey a manifest declaration.' (36:17)

These two Messengers who were sent by Allah's command said, 'All that we can do is to give you the news and the warning.'

قَالُوٓا۟ إِنَّا تَطَيَّرْنَا بِكُمْ لَئِن لَّمْ تَنتَهُوا۟ لَنَرْجُمَنَّكُمْ وَلَيَمَسَّنَّكُم مِّنَّا عَذَابٌ أَلِيمٌ ﴿١٨﴾

They said: 'We hold you to be an evil omen. If you do not desist, we will stone you and a most painful torment will touch you from us.' (36:18)

قَالُوا۟ طَـٰٓئِرُكُم مَّعَكُمْ أَئِن ذُكِّرْتُم بَلْ أَنتُمْ قَوْمٌ مُّسْرِفُونَ ﴿١٩﴾

*They said: 'Your evil omen is upon you. Is it because you have
been reminded of Allah? You are indeed a people far gone in
transgression.' (36:19)*

At this point, there is a discussion between the two messengers
and the people. The people said: 'We are depressed, we do not like
this news.' The word *ta'ir* is among various terms in the *Qur'an* that
require you to consider the cultural context at the time to understand
what was meant. It means 'a bird'. What does a bird have to do
with this incident? The word, *tatayarnabikum* means 'to receive bad
news or a bad omen'. The cultural reference is that during that time
when people exited their homes and saw birds flying overhead,
they regarded this as a bad omen due to their superstitions. So, the
word *taairukum* or *ta'ir* meant 'what are you superstitious about?'
The people around the governor said to the messengers, 'you are
bringing us bad superstitions, please leave us.' The messengers
said 'no, your bad superstition is with you,' meaning that your bad
thoughts, intentions, or wrong actions will damage you.

As Allah reminds us in the *Qur'an* in *Sūrat Hud* 11:101: 'Allah does
not wrong us, we do it to ourselves through our ignorance and our
stubbornness in not following a clear direction.'

وَجَآءَ مِنْ أَقْصَا ٱلْمَدِينَةِ رَجُلٌ يَسْعَىٰ قَالَ يَـٰقَوْمِ ٱتَّبِعُوا۟ ٱلْمُرْسَلِينَ ﴿٢٠﴾

*Then, from the furthest part of the city, a man came running. He
said, 'My people, follow the messengers. (36:20)*

$$\text{اتَّبِعُوا۟ مَن لَّا يَسْـَٔلُكُمْ أَجْرًا وَهُم مُّهْتَدُونَ ﴿٢١﴾}$$

Follow him who asks you no wage. These men are guided aright.
(36:21)

Then the *Qur'an* tells us a third messenger was sent and according to both the prophetic and biblical traditions, the third messenger was the head of the followers of Prophet Isa (AS). In Arabic, his name is Sham'un as-Safa and in English or Hebrew, it is Shymuon. *As-Safi* means 'the pure'. He was the head of the Hawari. Our Prophet Muhammad (S) and commentators referred to him as *Sahed yā-sin*, referring to the fellow in *Sūrat al-Yā Sīn*.

Sham'un as-Safa approached the situation differently from the first two messengers. He had initially ingratiated himself with the governor and was not viewed as an enemy because the governor and his people considered him a most unusual person. He said to the people: 'Look here, oh, people, follow those who are guided and who are not asking you for payment. They are here only to give you a message that improves your lot on this earth and the Hereafter.'

One of the conditions of true guidance is that it is not offered for money and that is why it is considered unacceptable to take money for teaching the *dīn* or teaching the *Qur'an*. Equally, it is also not permitted to charge money for washing the dead, because it is a gift to see yourself as a dead body and to recognise that you too will reach that point.

$$\text{وَمَا لِىَ لَآ أَعْبُدُ ٱلَّذِى فَطَرَنِى وَإِلَيْهِ تُرْجَعُونَ ﴿٢٢﴾}$$

And why should I not serve Him who originated me, and unto
whom you shall be returned? (36:22)

ءَأَتَّخِذُ مِن دُونِهِۦٓ ءَالِهَةً إِن يُرِدۡنِ ٱلرَّحۡمَـٰنُ بِضُرٍّ لَّا تُغۡنِ عَنِّي شَفَـٰعَتُهُمۡ شَيۡـًٔا وَلَا يُنقِذُونِ ﴿٢٣﴾

*Am I to take other gods instead of Him? If the All-Merciful
wishes me ill, their intercession will not benefit me in the least,
nor will they be able to save me. (36:23)*

At this point, he imparts good reasoning by saying, 'and what is
wrong with worshipping One Creator Who has saved us from the
afflictions we have? Is this not a good thing?'

Here we have a historical example of the fact that there is no
place on earth which has not received the message. 'Oh human
beings, you are here by virtue of and by the grace of *Allah Azza wa
Jal* to know more about Allah's Ways so that you can adopt them,
live by them, and be transformed by them.'

إِنِّىٓ إِذًا لَّفِى ضَلَـٰلٍ مُّبِينٍ ﴿٢٤﴾

I would then be in manifest error. (36:24)

إِنِّىٓ ءَامَنتُ بِرَبِّكُمۡ فَٱسۡمَعُونِ ﴿٢٥﴾

I believe in your Lord, so listen to me.' (36:25)

Here it says: 'If I do not do that then I will be in great darkness,
which means I will not hear what comes from the unseen or the
unheard and I will miss the opportunity of making my life worthy
of the *khalīfat* (leadership) of Adam (AS).'

$$\text{قِيلَ ٱدْخُلِ ٱلْجَنَّةَ قَالَ يَٰلَيْتَ قَوْمِى يَعْلَمُونَ ﴿٢٦﴾}$$

It was said to him: 'Enter the Garden.' He said: 'If only my people knew. (36:26)

$$\text{بِمَا غَفَرَ لِى رَبِّى وَجَعَلَنِى مِنَ ٱلْمُكْرَمِينَ ﴿٢٧﴾}$$

that my Lord has forgiven me and that He has placed me among the honoured.' (36:27)

This is an immense outcome of the acceptance of *Islām*, *Imān* and *Ihsān*. He says the voice comes to him and says: 'Enter the Garden; realise the perfection of the *nūr* (light) that is also in your heart. Realise that the garden state is already here.'

He says in verse 26: 'I wish my people know what has been gifted to me. I wish to *share* this ultimate gift with other human beings.'

And this is the lesson we can take the people of that time. Whenever we have something uplifting, durable, or sustainable goodness, we want to share it, meaning there is an overflow. Each of us has a conscience and the more we use that conscience the more we will be *'Abd Allah* (a servant of Allah, complete). Those who are completely closed are considered to be in utter darkness and cannot tap into that conscience. Such people are considered in the *Qur'an* to be unreachable.

$$\text{وَمَا أَنزَلْنَا عَلَىٰ قَوْمِهِۦ مِنۢ بَعْدِهِۦ مِن جُندٍ مِّنَ ٱلسَّمَاءِ وَمَا كُنَّا مُنزِلِينَ ﴿٢٨﴾}$$

After him, We sent no troops from heaven against his people, nor did We intend to do so. (36:28)

Allah says in this verse that it is not a case of thunderbolts and *malā'ika* (angels) suddenly descending upon people. Many communities and people condemn themselves for their actions and it is not always the case that negative consequences are directly from the Heavens. Allah's Ways penetrate every imaginable situation. Where is it that His Power is not?

$$إِن كَانَتْ إِلَّا صَيْحَةً وَٰحِدَةً فَإِذَا هُمْ خَٰمِدُونَ ﴿٢٩﴾$$

It was but a single Scream and, behold, they were lifeless. (36:29)

$$يَٰحَسْرَةً عَلَى ٱلْعِبَادِ مَا يَأْتِيهِم مِّن رَّسُولٍ إِلَّا كَانُوا۟ بِهِۦ يَسْتَهْزِءُونَ ﴿٣٠﴾$$

*Alas for the slaves! Never does a messenger come to them but they
mock him. (36:30)*

There will come a time when the ultimate finality occurs as a big collapse. What a pity for all of these millions of people who made fun of these messages instead of internalising or living them. They were not moved into basking in the security of *Imān* and translating it into the action of *Ihsān* and doing it with no expectation, with the knowledge that they were Allah's guests for this short duration.

$$أَلَمْ يَرَوْا۟ كَمْ أَهْلَكْنَا قَبْلَهُم مِّنَ ٱلْقُرُونِ أَنَّهُمْ إِلَيْهِمْ لَا يَرْجِعُونَ ﴿٣١﴾$$

*Have they not observed how many generations We destroyed
before them, and that they do not return to them? (36:31)*

$$وَإِن كُلٌّ لَّمَّا جَمِيعٌ لَّدَيْنَا مُحْضَرُونَ ﴿٣٢﴾$$

But all of them shall certainly be brought before Us. (36:32)

Do you not see that this situation applies to all of creation and that everything will come to an end when humans come into Our

Presence? Everybody will know after death. Will know what? That whatever power you have is by proxy and was loaned to you. Whatever knowledge you have is a minuscule part of *al-'Alim*, The Knower of it All. Do not forget that your body and faculties are all on loan to you for a while for you to use to unify the 'seen' (through your senses and mind) and the unseen, which is vast and all-encompassing.

Sections Three to Five

In the paragraphs which follow, we continue to share the outer, inner, higher, lower, and in-between messages of the *Qur'an* as revealed in *Sūrat Yā Sīn*. We have covered two out of five sections of this chapter. The first section addresses the 'Warning'. It says: 'Oh Prophet, people do not like to listen because they are used to their habits. They don't want to change.' The second section is a historical account of how the people of Antakyah had messengers sent to them by the Prophet Isa (AS), and they denied the message. Later, a third man told the rulers and their people to 'listen and follow those who are not asking for any worldly gains as they are guided.' Similarly, and oftentimes, you may be guided by a subtle voice from your conscience or heart which says, 'Wait, be a bit more generous, be patient.' These are messages for you to follow.

Many of the verses of the *Qur'an* were revealed in relation to specific historical events, but those events are often repeated in human history. The events are often an anchor for the verse.

Section Three: Verses 33 to 50

وَءَايَةٌ لَّهُمُ ٱلْأَرْضُ ٱلْمَيْتَةُ أَحْيَيْنَٰهَا وَأَخْرَجْنَا مِنْهَا حَبًّا فَمِنْهُ يَأْكُلُونَ ﴿٣٣﴾

Here is a sign for them: a dead land which We revive, and from which We sprout grains for them to eat. (36:33)

Allah says, 'Look at how from the dead earth, water emerges.' Water was poured onto it and from that life began. Contemplate how life emerges from the dead and how these amazing events occurred.

We are humbled by the need to eat and sustain ourselves, but Allah is *Al-Samad*, the Self-Sufficient. He has no needs, while we have constant needs; if it is not the body, it is the mind and if it is not the mind then it is the heart, that needs to be purified.

وَجَعَلْنَا فِيهَا جَنَّٰتٍ مِّن نَّخِيلٍ وَأَعْنَٰبٍ وَفَجَّرْنَا فِيهَا مِنَ ٱلْعُيُونِ ﴿٣٤﴾

In it We planted gardens of palms and vines, and caused fountains to burst forth, (36:34)

لِيَأْكُلُوا۟ مِن ثَمَرِهِۦ وَمَا عَمِلَتْهُ أَيْدِيهِمْ ۖ أَفَلَا يَشْكُرُونَ ﴿٣٥﴾

that they may eat of its fruits and the work of their hands – will they not render thanks? (36:35)

Are we not able to be grateful for wonderful gardens and herbage? Do we not see the gardens of this earth? Every human being loves to have a little garden because the gardenic state is implanted in our *rūh* (soul), so we try to replicate it here. Our world is a sample of what we will experience after death.

The Prophet (S) says you die according to the state in which you lived, and you will be resurrected according to that. That is why we always have to be prepared to declare *Allahu Akbar*. We must be accountable to friends and others who remind us that this short stay will lead to another state, that is not subject to the same space and time continuum that we are in.

$$\text{سُبْحَنَ ٱلَّذِى خَلَقَ ٱلْأَزْوَجَ كُلَّهَا مِمَّا تُنۢبِتُ ٱلْأَرْضُ وَمِنْ أَنفُسِهِمْ وَمِمَّا لَا يَعْلَمُونَ ۝}$$

Glory be to Him, who created all the pairs of what the earth produces, and of themselves, and of what they know not. (36:36)

Verse 36 reminds us that everything we see, touch, and discern on earth is one of two, yet another reference to the duality. Often, these two are complementary, but sometimes they appear as though they are opposing.

Glory be to He, the Source of Oneness, the One and Only Reality, The One and Only Original Light, who has created pairs. All that we experience through our five senses is a perspective of duality, but we judge the experience according to the oneness within our self, the *nūr* (light) in our hearts. All of our senses combine what we see and hear, to create a connected and integrated experience.

Islamic philosophers describe different faculties: the connecting faculty (*mushtarak*), the imaginal (*khayāl*) and the illusion or private imagination (*wahm*). This is our make-up and the ultimate purpose of it all, is as a sample of what comes later.

$$\text{وَءَايَةٌ لَّهُمُ ٱلَّيْلُ نَسْلَخُ مِنْهُ ٱلنَّهَارَ فَإِذَا هُم مُّظْلِمُونَ ۝}$$

And a sign to them is the night. We strip from it the day then they are in darkness. (36:37)

وَٱلشَّمْسُ تَجْرِى لِمُسْتَقَرٍّ لَّهَا ذَٰلِكَ تَقْدِيرُ ٱلْعَزِيزِ ٱلْعَلِيمِ ﴿٣٨﴾

And the sun runs its own course, unchanging, such is the disposition of the Almighty, the All-Knowing. (36:38)

وَٱلْقَمَرَ قَدَّرْنَٰهُ مَنَازِلَ حَتَّىٰ عَادَ كَٱلْعُرْجُونِ ٱلْقَدِيمِ ﴿٣٩﴾

And the moon, We disposed in phases until it comes back like a withered stalk of palm. (36:39)

لَا ٱلشَّمْسُ يَنۢبَغِى لَهَآ أَن تُدْرِكَ ٱلْقَمَرَ وَلَا ٱلَّيْلُ سَابِقُ ٱلنَّهَارِ وَكُلٌّ فِى فَلَكٍ يَسْبَحُونَ ﴿٤٠﴾

Neither the sun may outstrip the moon nor the night the day: each plies its own orbit. (36:40)

The Prophet (S) was often asked which was first, day or night. His response was that 'day' came first and was followed by shadows and darkness. If there was no light to begin with, we would not know darkness.

In these verses, Allah refers to the signs, the light and the day; the sun and how it moves on; and the moon and how it also has its own circuit. All of the planetary systems follow their destiny in the most perfect, dynamic, and stable way. However, there also appears to be substantial instability which manifests as colliding asteroids or falling stars, yet the entire system is stable.

وَءَايَةٌ لَّهُمْ أَنَّا حَمَلْنَا ذُرِّيَّتَهُمْ فِى ٱلْفُلْكِ ٱلْمَشْحُونِ ﴿٤١﴾

And a sign for them is that We carried their seed in the laden ship,
(36:41)

وَخَلَقْنَا لَهُم مِّن مِّثْلِهِۦ مَا يَرْكَبُونَ ﴿٤٢﴾

and We have created for them the like of it whereon they ride;
(36:42)

وَإِن نَّشَأْ نُغْرِقْهُمْ فَلَا صَرِيخَ لَهُمْ وَلَا هُمْ يُنقَذُونَ ﴿٤٣﴾

Aand if We wish We can drown them – no screaming to be heard
from them, nor can they be saved, (36:43)

إِلَّا رَحْمَةً مِّنَّا وَمَتَٰعًا إِلَىٰ حِينٍ ﴿٤٤﴾

unless it be a mercy from Us and a brief enjoyment of life. (36:44)

In these verses, Allah describes the amazing physical phenomena of heavy objects floating on water and of three-quarters of this earth being covered with water.

We have been given the faculty of 'aql, of reason, of reflection, of cause and effect. If we apply 'aql, we will recognise that these gifts have given us the ability to connect with other people and cultures, to enable us to discover that all human beings desire the same thing. We all want to know the origin of it all, how it will end, and what we can do so that we are least upset, saddened, or frightened by the end. Allah reminds us in verse 43 that all of it can be wiped out at any moment.

وَإِذَا قِيلَ لَهُمُ ٱتَّقُوا۟ مَا بَيْنَ أَيْدِيكُمْ وَمَا خَلْفَكُمْ لَعَلَّكُمْ تُرْحَمُونَ ﴿٤٥﴾

And when it is said to them: 'Beware of the present and the future that you may obtain mercy,' (36:45)

وَمَا تَأْتِيهِم مِّنْ ءَايَةٍ مِّنْ ءَايَٰتِ رَبِّهِمْ إِلَّا كَانُوا۟ عَنْهَا مُعْرِضِينَ ﴿٤٦﴾

and there comes to them no sign from the signs of their Lord but they turn their back upon it. (36:46)

These verses reference the previous section. Allah says in these verses that human beings are in denial. It is difficult to say, 'I was wrong, and I am willing to correct my attitude, my action, or my intention.' We resist because of the ego.

وَإِذَا قِيلَ لَهُمْ أَنفِقُوا۟ مِمَّا رَزَقَكُمُ ٱللَّهُ قَالَ ٱلَّذِينَ كَفَرُوا۟ لِلَّذِينَ ءَامَنُوٓا۟ أَنُطْعِمُ مَن لَّوْ يَشَآءُ ٱللَّهُ أَطْعَمَهُۥٓ إِنْ أَنتُمْ إِلَّا فِى ضَلَٰلٍ مُّبِينٍ ﴿٤٧﴾

And when it is said to them: 'Expend from what Allah in His bounty has provided you,' the unbelievers say to the believers: 'Are we to feed one whom Allah can feed if He so wishes?' In truth you have strayed far in error. (36:47)

وَيَقُولُونَ مَتَىٰ هَٰذَا ٱلْوَعْدُ إِن كُنتُمْ صَٰدِقِينَ ﴿٤٨﴾

And they say: 'When will this promise be fulfilled if you speak the truth?' (36:48)

These verses refer to a historical event. At that time, the people of Makkah had been subjected to a period of immense poverty and this verse was revealed during that period. In response to poverty, many people began questioning the nature of God. Could He not feed these poor miserable people? Why should we be giving them alms? Why should we share the little that we have during these difficult times?

This is a key verse which addresses decree and destiny. Is there free will or is it all pre-destined? Is it all completely Allah's Way and Allah's Power, or do I have a hand in it? Though I am limited in my ability to act, I also have a certain measure of freedom to act. I am free to lift my hand, but the power I have been given to lift my hand is from Allah; the will to lift my hand is also from Allah. Therefore, I am a proxy. I am a *khalīfa* (vicegerent or steward).

The same applies to my knowledge of divine attributes. We all love generosity; Allah is the Generous. We all love *qadr* and Allah is *Al-Qadr* (Most Powerful). He is the Ultimate Source of all wills. And He is *al-'Alīm*. He Knows it all and we are given a little bit of that knowledge.

Why does Allah do that? Allah does this to soften your heart so that you become more connected. This is Allah's Way, and He contains it all. The last verse of this chapter sums it all up: 'all of it is in His Hands.'

$$مَا يَنظُرُونَ إِلَّا صَيْحَةً وَاحِدَةً تَأْخُذُهُمْ وَهُمْ يَخِصِّمُونَ ﴿٤٩﴾$$

All they can expect is a single Scream, which shall seize them
while they dispute, (36:49)

$$فَلَا يَسْتَطِيعُونَ تَوْصِيَةً وَلَا إِلَىٰ أَهْلِهِمْ يَرْجِعُونَ ﴿٥٠﴾$$

so that they have no time to make a bequest, nor return home to
their families. (36:50)

Section Four: Verses 51 to 67

This section deals primarily with the *ākhira* (the Next Life).

وَنُفِخَ فِى ٱلصُّورِ فَإِذَا هُم مِّنَ ٱلْأَجْدَاثِ إِلَىٰ رَبِّهِمْ يَنسِلُونَ ﴿٥١﴾

And the Trumpet shall be sounded and, behold, from their graves and to their Lord they shall hurry. (36:51)

قَالُوا۟ يَٰوَيْلَنَا مَنۢ بَعَثَنَا مِن مَّرْقَدِنَا ۗ هَٰذَا مَا وَعَدَ ٱلرَّحْمَٰنُ وَصَدَقَ ٱلْمُرْسَلُونَ ﴿٥٢﴾

They shall say: 'Alas for us! Who resurrected us from our resting place?' This is what the All-Merciful promised, and the messengers spoke the truth. (36:52)

إِن كَانَتْ إِلَّا صَيْحَةً وَٰحِدَةً فَإِذَا هُمْ جَمِيعٌ لَّدَيْنَا مُحْضَرُونَ ﴿٥٣﴾

It shall be but a single Scream and, behold, they will all be conducted before Us. (36:53)

There are numerous descriptions in the *Qur'an* that reiterate the same message about what happens after death and when the entire celestial system will collapse at the end of the Universe. There are no less than nine different occasions which describe the stages of this collapse as follows:

First stage: Everything that is alive on this earth including *jinn* (invisible beings) will die.

Second stage: The trumpet will sound (this is a symbolic reference).

Third stage: Everything will come back to life without its shadow. In our current existence, we are made up of body and mind, which includes shadows. However, at this stage, there are no shadows, only the inner-inner-most. After the destruction of everything, there is only intention in this next phase. You can only see people in terms of what they meant in their hearts, and the more we practice transparency, the easier the passage will be for us from this world to the Hereafter.

Verse 53 reminds us that there is one major cry, sound, or bang (*Sūr* also means 'horn') followed by the second sound where everything comes alive.

فَٱلْيَوْمَ لَا تُظْلَمُ نَفْسٌ شَيْئًا وَلَا تُجْزَوْنَ إِلَّا مَا كُنتُمْ تَعْمَلُونَ ﴿٥٤﴾

Today no soul shall be wronged one jot, and you will be
recompensed only for the deeds you committed. (36:54)

On that day, everybody will see who they are and what they have done in this world. How much we have given, served, revealed of our innermost and how much we have acknowledged that we are here by Allah's *rahma* (mercy).

The more aware we are of that, the more we can render our accounts now and this means we are less likely to go through a heavy interrogation. *Yawm* means 'of that period' or 'in that state'. Allah says, 'On that occasion, everybody will know what they have done, what they have hidden, and what love they have had.

Allah says, 'Is there love in your heart other than for Me?' We know everything is being recorded in us by the mysterious amazing Power of Allah. For this reason, we practice having fewer agendas and we strive instead for transparency. We know that we are here as guests in this short-lived life and that we will return to the Essence of it, without any ability to act or hide.

إِنَّ أَصْحَٰبَ ٱلْجَنَّةِ ٱلْيَوْمَ فِى شُغُلٍ فَٰكِهُونَ ﴿٥٥﴾

Today the denizens of the Garden are preoccupied with joy,
(36:55)

$$\text{هُمْ وَأَزْوَٰجُهُمْ فِى ظِلَٰلٍ عَلَى ٱلْأَرَآئِكِ مُتَّكِـُٔونَ ﴿٥٦﴾}$$

they and their spouses, reclining on cushions under the shade.
(36:56)

$$\text{لَهُمْ فِيهَا فَٰكِهَةٌ وَلَهُم مَّا يَدَّعُونَ ﴿٥٧﴾}$$

therein they have fruits, and they have all that they call for. (36:57)

$$\text{سَلَٰمٌ قَوْلًا مِّن رَّبٍّ رَّحِيمٍ ﴿٥٨﴾}$$

'Peace' shall be the word from a Compassionate Lord. (36:58)

These verses describe the state of those who have been liberated, saved, and have gone through the process of transformation through *Imān* (certainty and security that Allah knows and Allah sees), *Islām* (submission) and *Ihsān* (inner and outer excellence in thought and conduct). It says these people are in paradise, where there are no more dualities and they have been joined and are in a state of ecstasy, where there are no desires or needs and all of it is fulfilled.

$$\text{وَٱمْتَٰزُوا۟ ٱلْيَوْمَ أَيُّهَا ٱلْمُجْرِمُونَ ﴿٥٩﴾}$$

Today, O guilty, keep yourselves apart! (36:59)

$$\text{أَلَمْ أَعْهَدْ إِلَيْكُمْ يَٰبَنِىٓ ءَادَمَ أَن لَّا تَعْبُدُوا۟ ٱلشَّيْطَٰنَ إِنَّهُۥ لَكُمْ عَدُوٌّ مُّبِينٌ ﴿٦٠﴾}$$

Did I not charge you, O children of Adam, not to worship the Shaytan? Surely he is your open enemy! (36:60)

وَأَنِ اعْبُدُونِي هَذَا صِرَاطٌ مُّسْتَقِيمٌ ﴿٦١﴾

And that you should worship Me. This is the straight path. (36:61)

وَلَقَدْ أَضَلَّ مِنكُمْ جِبِلًّا كَثِيرًا أَفَلَمْ تَكُونُوا تَعْقِلُونَ ﴿٦٢﴾

And certainly, he led astray a great multitude of you. Were you not able to understand? (36:62)

هَذِهِ جَهَنَّمُ الَّتِي كُنتُمْ تُوعَدُونَ ﴿٦٣﴾

This is the Hell you were promised [if you followed him]. (36:63)

اصْلَوْهَا الْيَوْمَ بِمَا كُنتُمْ تَكْفُرُونَ ﴿٦٤﴾

Endure it today as an outcome of your persistent denial of the truth! (36:64)

These verses address the contrasting position of human beings who have not risen to their potential, who have not discovered the purpose of this life, or lived according to the light that guides them and enables them to walk on this earth. The life you have is loaned to you. How are you repaying it? You repay it by not doing anything unless it is liberating you from your body, according to Allah's mercy. Otherwise, we will end up in *Jahannam* (the fire), as followers of *shaytān* (satan; ego-self).

The word *shaytān* is from the verb *shatana*, which means to rebel or to be far away. It means being far away from the zone of tranquillity, bliss, and ease. Whenever we make a mistake, it is because of *ghafla* (heedlessness, carelessness, negligence, foolishness, stupidity) and these are also different attributes of satanic tendencies.

ٱلۡيَوۡمَ نَخۡتِمُ عَلَىٰٓ أَفۡوَٰهِهِمۡ وَتُكَلِّمُنَآ أَيۡدِيهِمۡ وَتَشۡهَدُ أَرۡجُلُهُم بِمَا كَانُوا۟ يَكۡسِبُونَ ۝٦٥

Today We shall seal their mouths and it will be their hands that shall speak to Us and their feet that shall testify as to what they earned. (36:65)

وَلَوۡ نَشَآءُ لَطَمَسۡنَا عَلَىٰٓ أَعۡيُنِهِمۡ فَٱسۡتَبَقُوا۟ ٱلصِّرَٰطَ فَأَنَّىٰ يُبۡصِرُونَ ۝٦٦

And if We wished, We could certainly put out their eyes, then they would run about groping for the way, but how could they see? (36:66)

وَلَوۡ نَشَآءُ لَمَسَخۡنَٰهُمۡ عَلَىٰ مَكَانَتِهِمۡ فَمَا ٱسۡتَطَٰعُوا۟ مُضِيًّا وَلَا يَرۡجِعُونَ ۝٦٧

And if We wished, We could surely transform them in their place. Then they would not be able to advance or turn back. (36:67)

These verses complete this section which focuses on the *ākhira* (the Next Life). We should constantly bear in mind that our actions, intentions, and attention will change. We will begin to be transformed. We are creatures on earth, but not of the earth. We have descended from heaven and will return to heaven. So, these verses warn us to be constantly vigilant about what comes next.

In this earthly existence, we experience a bit of pain which lasts for a few days, a few months, or a few years, but the state of agitation of not being in the garden is beyond the earthly measure of years. On the contrary, it is infinite and that is why it is severe!

351

Section Five: Verses 68 to 83

The last section is the summary of everything: a summary of *Sūrat al-Yā Sīn*, a summary of the *Qur'an*, and even a summary of who we are, what we are, and what we should do.

وَمَن نُّعَمِّرْهُ نُنَكِّسْهُ فِى ٱلْخَلْقِ أَفَلَا يَعْقِلُونَ ﴿٦٨﴾

Whomever We grant old age, We cause to droop in figure: will they not be reasonable? (36:68)

وَمَا عَلَّمْنَـٰهُ ٱلشِّعْرَ وَمَا يَنۢبَغِى لَهُۥٓ إِنْ هُوَ إِلَّا ذِكْرٌ وَقُرْءَانٌ مُّبِينٌ ﴿٦٩﴾

And, we did not teach him poetry, nor does this befit him. It is nothing but a Remembrance, and a Manifest Qur'an. (36:69)

In these verses, Allah reminds us of an immense message: Don't you see? As you grow, you become strong (your mind develops, and your physical body grows) but you also revert to being feeble, weak and sometimes even unable to think. It says: 'Don't you see the cycle?' Everything in existence is cyclical, whether it is the human or the planetary system of relationships. You are born weak and the first thing you do when you are born is to cry, to inhale air after having been in a protective aqueous solution for nine months. Suddenly, you begin to use your senses and your mind, until you mature by the age of 40. By the age of maturity, you must realise that you are on your way back and that you were one day closer to departure, from the moment you were born. Are you ready? Have you packed your bags for the next station, for the next city, for after death? When you are moving from one place to another, you prefer to have a map and to understand the culture so that you are prepared. Are you ready to leave now?

You have to be inwardly ready. That is what will give you freshness in everything, so that it does not become either attraction or repulsion. You are like a swing, good and bad, up, and down, and then you see things as they are. See verse 48:8, 'We have sent thee as a witness [to the truth], and as a herald of glad tidings and a warner.' If you do not do it now, it will be too late and you will have lost one more day, until you are on the edge between this world and the next.

$$ لِّيُنذِرَ مَن كَانَ حَيًّا وَيَحِقَّ ٱلْقَوْلُ عَلَى ٱلْكَٰفِرِينَ ۝ $$

Therewith to warn him who is living, and to fulfil the Word against the unbelievers. (36:70)

This is a wonderful verse. The word *hayy* (living or alive) in the *Qur'an* is used in two ways: one is biological, as we all are, and the other is awakened to the Truth that *Lā ilāha illā Allāh*.

So many of these verses are a warning to all, but only those who have accepted *Imān*, who have trusted, who have taken the message as *'ilm al-yaqīn* will have heard the news. This is *'ilm* and it is the first phase. The next phase is *'ayn al-yaqīn* that you are leaving this world, and the third phase is *haqq al-yaqīn*, meaning you no longer see time and you are already looking at the timeless zone in you. These are different phases that a mature person will go through.

The true awakening will come to those who have accepted *Imān*, who are doing their utmost in *Ihsān*, acting as a conduit from the highest of goodness which can be rendered to anyone at any time.

$$ أَوَلَمْ يَرَوْاْ أَنَّا خَلَقْنَا لَهُم مِّمَّا عَمِلَتْ أَيْدِينَآ أَنْعَٰمًا فَهُمْ لَهَا مَٰلِكُونَ ۝ $$

Have they not observed that We created for them, from Our handiwork, cattle which they come to possess? (36:71)

$$وَذَلَّلْنَـٰهَا لَهُمْ فَمِنْهَا رَكُوبُهُمْ وَمِنْهَا يَأْكُلُونَ ﴿٧٢﴾$$

And We have subjected these animals to them, so some of them
they ride and some they eat. (36:72)

$$وَلَهُمْ فِيهَا مَنَـٰفِعُ وَمَشَارِبُ أَفَلَا يَشْكُرُونَ ﴿٧٣﴾$$

And from them they have [other] benefits [besides], and yet they
get [milk] to drink. Will they not then be grateful? (36:73)

Look at all the ease and benefits you have on this earth. Look at
the animal kingdom. How can you not be in utter gratitude?

Earlier on, in the same chapter, the verse reminds us that you
may plant the tree, but you have not programmed the fruiting or
the way it will grow.

These verses confirm the message that Allah says, 'My Hands
did it, you did not do it. You were just there to take the seed and
to put it in the ground.' Accordingly, we participate in a small way
in this amazing act of creation, growth, consumption and return.
This earth is Allah's kindergarten. Everything is already in it, but
we have to observe the right courtesy, apply some outer action, and
participate in it with generosity, goodness, and care.

$$وَٱتَّخَذُوا مِن دُونِ ٱللَّهِ ءَالِهَةً لَّعَلَّهُمْ يُنصَرُونَ ﴿٧٤﴾$$

And yet, instead of Allah, they take to themselves gods, hoping
for success. (36:74)

$$\text{لَا يَسْتَطِيعُونَ نَصْرَهُمْ وَهُمْ لَهُمْ جُندٌ مُّحْضَرُونَ} \textcircled{٧٥}$$

These cannot grant them success, though they possess troops massed in their service. (36:75)

Those who are in denial of the purpose of life and the message, will regret it and they will have no success. We are reminded in the *Qur'an*: 'Don't look at them for having wealth and power or strong looking bodies and so on. These are fads, they will pass.'

$$\text{فَلَا يَحْزُنكَ قَوْلُهُمْ إِنَّا نَعْلَمُ مَا يُسِرُّونَ وَمَا يُعْلِنُونَ} \textcircled{٧٦}$$

Therefore, let not their speech sadden you: We know what they conceal and what declare. (36:76)

Do not ever be saddened by what they, who do not believe, say. Do not be concerned by denial and by all the other mischief that human beings have conducted throughout the ages. Look at the horrendous killings that went on for almost 4,000 years in the Middle East. Five thousand years ago, the pharaohs of Egypt conquered other lands and constructed tablets that said, 'this is the border of our land.' Some years later, those same tablets were thrown down and yet another tribe emerged to conquer. Today we do similar things in an apparently more civilised way, and we call it a competition. All it reflects is a love for control, and it is the reason for the mess we find ourselves in.

Why do we love to control? It is because we are controlled by our souls.

أَوَلَمْ يَرَ ٱلْإِنسَٰنُ أَنَّا خَلَقْنَٰهُ مِن نُّطْفَةٍ فَإِذَا هُوَ خَصِيمٌ مُّبِينٌ ۝

Has not man observed that We created him from a sperm drop but, behold, he becomes a determined adversary? (36:77)

وَضَرَبَ لَنَا مَثَلًا وَنَسِيَ خَلْقَهُۥ قَالَ مَن يُحْىِ ٱلْعِظَٰمَ وَهِىَ رَمِيمٌ ۝

And he has struck for Us a similitude and forgotten his creation; he says, 'Who shall quicken the bones when they are decayed?' (36:78)

قُلْ يُحْيِيهَا ٱلَّذِىٓ أَنشَأَهَآ أَوَّلَ مَرَّةٍ وَهُوَ بِكُلِّ خَلْقٍ عَلِيمٌ ۝

Say: 'He will give life to them Who brought them into existence at first, and He is cognizant of all creation, (36:79)

Do you reflect upon the very beginning of your earthly manifestation as a tiny clot in the womb? Do you give thought to how and where this clot came from? Do you remember the time when you were in the womb? Do you know how you were born? The *Qur'an* says, 'But we forget, we don't remember, and we start arguing. Who is going to create?' There is a historical context to this verse. During the time of the Prophet (S), one of the argumentative people brought some bones before the Prophet (S) and said: 'Is he going to make a human being out of this dust?'

So the Prophet (S) replied: 'Who can create this? Who can make this dust into a human being with willpower and consciousness? He who brought it in the first place, He will do that.'

Then this magical verse is revealed:

$$\text{ٱلَّذِى جَعَلَ لَكُم مِّنَ ٱلشَّجَرِ ٱلْأَخْضَرِ نَارًا فَإِذَآ أَنتُم مِّنْهُ تُوقِدُونَ ﴿٨٠﴾}$$

who has made for you out of the green tree fire and lo, from it you kindle. (36:80)

It was well known at that time that in the desert there were two types of trees: those that were wet and others that when rubbed together would create a spark to make a fire. Making a fire sometimes involves taking pieces of hardwood and rubbing them against each other and adding tinder around the pieces until flames emerge. The discovery and control of fire was a significant event in the history of civilisation as was the invention of the needle. These two big events enabled human beings to migrate. So, He says: 'Look at how from green wood you can make fire.'

$$\text{أَوَلَيْسَ ٱلَّذِى خَلَقَ ٱلسَّمَٰوَٰتِ وَٱلْأَرْضَ بِقَٰدِرٍ عَلَىٰٓ أَن يَخْلُقَ مِثْلَهُم بَلَىٰ وَهُوَ ٱلْخَلَّٰقُ ٱلْعَلِيمُ ﴿٨١﴾}$$

Is not He, who created the heavens and earth, able to create the like of them? Yes indeed; He is the All-Creator, the All-Knowing. (36:81)

$$\text{إِنَّمَآ أَمْرُهُۥٓ إِذَآ أَرَادَ شَيْـًٔا أَن يَقُولَ لَهُۥ كُن فَيَكُونُ ﴿٨٢﴾}$$

His command, when He desires a thing, is to say to it "Be," and it is. (36:82)

Is it hard to contemplate that He Who has created the heavens and the earth, the millions of stars and the galaxies can re-create you again? It is that Power, that by the slightest Will, *kun*, everything will be.

The *Qur'an* is full of stories of when others asked the Prophet (S) for a miracle. We want a miracle to believe in the unseen and we all look for miracles, but what about the miracle that is you? It is a miracle that when you sleep you disappear, and when you awaken you re-appear. Is it not a miracle that you breathe in and out without effort? Miracle upon miracle! Yet we take the miracles for granted.

And the chapter concludes with this magnificent verse:

$$\text{فَسُبْحَٰنَ ٱلَّذِى بِيَدِهِۦ مَلَكُوتُ كُلِّ شَىْءٍ وَإِلَيْهِ تُرْجَعُونَ ﴿٨٣﴾}$$

So, glory be to Him, in whose hand is the dominion of everything, and unto whom you shall be returned.' (36:83)

Metaphorically, it says whatever you can imagine in existence in the cosmos, is in His Hands and everything returns to Him. What an amazing, incredible revelation and story. Everything emanated from that mysterious, ever-present, ever-engulfing Universal Power and to It everything returns.

This is the good news! The more important news is that we have to participate in living that message, so that we are accountable as we progress towards agelessness and after we return the body to the earth where it belongs.

CONCLUSION

We believe, trust and know that the *Qur'an* is the foundation of the perfect way of living, surviving, growing and awakening. We believe that Allah revealed the truth through His great beings, from the Prophet Ibrahim (A.S) and culminating with the Prophet Muhammad (S). This knowledge was revealed by connecting the unseen (which is the infinite, the truth, the absolute) with the seen. The *Qur'an* is the book of signs, symbols, knowledge, and wisdom and relates what is in the heavens, to that which is earthly, so that we may find a path. I have commented on selected verses with the hope that it will enable you to explore similar commentaries on other verses.

Dīn means a way of living. It is a debt to be paid upon ourselves for our own emancipation, salvation, freedom and arrival to that which is always there, which is the original *nūr* of Allah. The Qur'anic phrase *nūrun 'ala nūr* (24:35) refers to infinite levels of light and, infinite levels of consciousness, and the infinite means of manifesting that light through creation. Since we believe and accept that the *Qur'an* is the foundation, we need to not only read, recite and remember it by heart, but also to live by it.

Most of the practices in our life transactions are to remind us to turn away from the destructiveness and distraction of the senses and of the world. It is not to denounce the senses or the mind. The mind is the means through which the *rūh* (soul) connects with the lower self. This refers to the physical body, which is like a prison but also houses the ever-present light of *Allah Azza wa Jal*, which allows us to discriminate, discern and go beyond it.

During the month of fasting, you are sharpened by abstention from outer excess and restrictions, and by curbing thoughtless ways of eating and drinking. What about the rest of the time? Our practices are there to heighten our awareness of what we do and say. Provision is not only food for the belly. What about the mind? What about the heart, which is the soul? These are levels through which we progress by Allah's *rahma* (mercy) and this is influenced by who you are, and the extent to which you discipline yourself in your life transaction. Ideally, you should reach a point where you know that you cannot say or do anything without being accountable for your actions and that, therefore, you should be aware of the impact of all you do or say. The stronger your awareness, the more likely you are to take permission from *Allah Azza wa Jal* by constantly saying *bismillah*. If you start with *bismillah*, then you have put your ego-self aside. *Bismillah* is not always about more action. It may mean doing nothing, being silent, or going away. Sometimes more is achieved by doing less. The Prophetic teaching is very clear: 'Do not put the gems around the neck of a swine,' meaning that we should stay away from issues that do not concern us. Allah will take care of it.

I pray to Allah that we may be guided towards experiencing the benefits of using the Qur'an as a manual for transformation.

I pray to Allah Azza wa Jal to perfect our Islām (submission), Imān (certainty and security that Allah knows, and Allah sees), and Ihsān (inner and outer excellence in thought and conduct).

I pray to Allah Azza wa Jal to always show us that outer restrictions can lead to inner expansion.

I pray to Allah Azza wa Jal to always keep us in the best of company and with companions who remind us to constantly refer to that which is within every heart but which we need to access with prayers and the best of expectations of Allah Azza wa Jal.

May Allah make us utterly dependent on Him.

May Allah make us aware of His presence.

May Allah make us accountable at all times.

May Allah make us accountable for our intentions.

May Allah make us accountable to those who are on the path of Ash-hadu allā ilāha illAllah wa ash-hadu anna Muhamadan 'abduhū wa rasulu (I testify that there is no god except (God) Allah, and I testify that Muhammad (S) is His slave and messenger).